THE
BOY'S OWN
BOOK

THE
BOY'S OWN
BOOK

A COMPLETE ENCYCLOPEDIA

OF

ALL THE DIVERSIONS,

ATHLETIC, SCIENTIFIC, AND RECREATIVE,

OF BOYHOOD AND YOUTH.

A playground is an emblem of the world;
Its gamesome boys are men in miniature:
The most important action of the man
May find its parody 'mong childhood's sports;
And life itself, when longest, happiest,—
In boyhood's brief and jocund holiday.

APPLEWOOD BOOKS
BEDFORD, MASSACHUSETTS

The Boy's Own Book was first published in 1829 by Munroe and Francis, Boston, and Charles S. Francis, New York.

ISBN 1-55709-505-1

Thank you for purchasing an Applewood Book.
Applewood reprints America's lively classics—books
from the past that are still of interest to modern readers.
For a free copy of our current catalog, write to:
Applewood Books, P.O. Box 365, Bedford, MA 01730.

10 9 8 7 6 5

Library of Congress Cataloging-in-Publication Data
Clarke, William, 1800-1838.
   The boy's own book: a complete encyclopedia of all the diver-
sions, athletic, scientific, and recreative, of boyhood and youth.
       p.   cm.
   Originally published: 1st American ed. Boston: Munroe and
Francis; New York: C.S. Francis, 1829.
   Includes index.
   Summary: Includes material for all interests and for all seasons
of the year, for the robust and the delicate, and for the contemplative as well as the ingenious.
   ISBN 1-55709-505-1
   1. Amusements—Juvenile literature.   2. Games—Juvenile literature.   3. Sports—Juvenile literature.   4. Scientific recreations—Juvenile literature.   [1. Amusements.   2. Games.
3. Sports.   4. Scientific recreations.]   I. Title.
GV1204.997.C54   1996   95-42274
796'.0194–dc20   CIP
                                                      AC

PRELUDE.

A POPULAR ENCYCLOPEDIA of the Sports and Pastimes of Youth,—
a companion for all holydays,—THE BOY'S OWN BOOK,—unmixed with
aught that was not highly interesting to himself, had long been a deside-
ratum; to supply which, he was usually led to become his own caterer,
and purchase publications of an objectionable character, merely because
their low price placed them within his reach. The present Work was an
attempt to obviate this inconvenience, by enabling those, who had the
guardianship of youth, to present their young protegés, in the form of a
Holyday or Birthday Present, with a concentration of all that usually
delights them, executed in such a manner as their own judgment would
approve, and much more amusing and instructive to the juvenile mind,
than the cheap trash on which the hoarded shilling is usually expended.
The event has fully justified the expectations of the Publishers; few works
have met with so flattering a reception, from the press and the public;
the whole of the first edition, which extended to three thousand copies,
having been sold without advertisements, in little more than two months.
The present edition contains many alterations and improvements: it is
augmented, in bulk, by an extra half sheet; and, in quantity of matter,
nearly a sheet and a half, by an increase in the size of its pages: the
articles have all been improved, and some of them re-written, and the
volume is enriched with many new engravings of superior design and
execution.

PRELUDE.

A wider field than we have taken cannot well be imagined. Our plan embraces the amusements of all minds, and of all seasons,—in winter and in summer,—at home and abroad; the robust and the delicate,—the contemplative and the ingenious,—have each their tastes provided for. The sports and exercises of out-door enjoyment,—the pastimes of a winter's fire-side,—and the recreation of science,—are copiously detailed in our pages, which have been printed in a close type, that we might be enabled to compress a whole library of sportful lore in the brief compass of one little volume. We can honestly say, that no pains have been spared to do justice to our plan. We have attempted to please Seniors and Juniors,—no easy task; but our failure can only be partial, for should we be condemned by a few, we are sure that the many will be in our favor; and that a host of advocates, appreciating our industry and our motives, would cheerfully undertake, on our behalf, the task of a pleader.

So far the London Preface. The American publishers have omitted a few articles, entirely useless on this side the Atlantic, as the extra expense would have debarred the more useful part from being in the hands of hundreds of Youths, who will find everything that will amuse them in our present volume. The articles omitted are, a long treatise on Chess, Singing Birds, Silk-Worms, &c. the insertion of which would have swelled the expense to double its present price, and given no real additional value to the BOY'S OWN BOOK.

Boston, November 1, 1829.

CONTENTS.

CONTENTS.

BOY'S OWN BOOK.

MINOR SPORTS AND PASTIMES.

> Blithe Boyhood is the holyday of life ;
> The joyous spirits then impart a zest
> To tops and marbles, which man's graver toys,
> Though bought at golden prices, ever lack.

WE heartily trust that our young readers will commence the perusal of our pages with pleasure equal to that which we feel in sitting down to write them, and that we shall go pleasantly together through our work. The description of these Minor Sports, most especially, will, we are convinced, be an agreeable pastime to us, and call up, from time to time, welcome reminiscences of those days of our boyhood, when we were a hero at " Ringtaw," and by no means a contemptible adversary even to the most accomplished youthful players at " Fives." It will remind us of our happy holydays and favourite school-fellows ;—of feats of agility performed at " Follow my Leader," and trophies borne off in triumph at " Peg in the Ring ;"—of those merry mornings, when the first glance of the sun awakened us, to snatch an additional half-hour for the play-ground, without encroaching on the allotted times for study ;—when, during " winter's surly reign," we joined the active few, who, instead of moping in great coats, or shivering round a fire, sallied forth into the clear, cold, invigorating air, and marking out goals and bounds in the crisp hoar frost that mantled the ground, sought

after, and found warmth and high spirits in a game of " Prisoner's Base,"
—or made the brows glow at lofty " Leap-frog,"—or defied the frost by
briskly plying the whip-top with eel-skin, and came in with glad hearts,
ruddy cheeks, perfect willingness, and the best of appetites, to our morning
repast and subsequent studies. It will bring to our recollection also, those
smooth and shady spots, where, when the noontide sun was midway in the
heavens, in the sultry month of August, we alternately perused pleasant
and instructive books, and played with our class-mates at " Increase-
pound," or set up a pyramid of marbles for them to shoot at, or shot at one
erected by one of them. It will carry us back in imagination to the hills
and downs, where we flew our kites,—the loftiest soarers for miles around ;
—of mishaps, through breaking of strings, and long races of rivalry after
our falling favorites ;—to that cheerful parlour, in which, during the winter vacation, when mince-pies, plum-puddings, and young parties, were
most abundant,—on Christmas-eve, or mirthful Twelfth-night, most especially,—we bore a part in the exhilarating and harmless fireside sports of
the season ;—to that dilapidated ruin,—the court of that mouldering castle,
with a tall and stately elm rising from one of its corners, and ivy, apparently
ages old, the constant home and nestling-place of innumerable birds, which
bedecked and supported the outward side of its walls,—the scene of our
chief exploits at Fives ;—to the garden walk, where our school-swing was
erected, between two gigantic sister pear-trees ;—and, in brief, to all those
places where we played the games which were the delight of our holydays ;
when a sportive bout at " Saddle my Nag," was in itself an ample recom-
pense for the past two hours of study, employed in working an intricate
question in arithmetic—composing a theme on some difficult subject—ren-
dering a portion of the Iliad into Latin hexameters, or a passage of Pope
into French prose. We conceive that we are bringing no disgrace on our
boyhood, by avowing that we deeply enjoyed the sports of the play-ground.
The line of a talented writer, " A dunce at Syntax, but a dab at taw," has,
by a thoughtless few, been converted into a proverb, and those who were
most eminent for their activity and love of the usual amusements of youth
out of school, have thus been unjustly stigmatized as inattentive students.
The reverse, we have generally found to be the fact ; for, we have often
remarked, that the lads who led the sports in the play-ground, stood high in
their classes in the school-room. " There is a time for all things," is a trite,
but, in this case, an applicable observation : the scholastic discipline wisely
allots certain hours in the day for recreation ; they should be employed in
healthful and agreeable pastime, so as to render the boy prepared to return
with mental vigour to his books ;—study should give a relish to sport, and
sport to study. But while we recommend that the school-room should be
forgotten on the play-ground, we wish to impress on our young readers the
necessity of their forgetting the play-ground in the school-room.

GAMES WITH MARBLES.

THERE were, some years ago, and we believe, there still are, three or four different sorts of marbles : the Dutch, or variegated clay marbles, were reckoned the worst ; those of yellow stone, with beautiful spots or circles of black or brown, were next in estimation ; and what were called the real taws, of pink marble, with dark red veins, " blood allies," were preferred to all others. The games with marbles are not very numerous ; the following pages contain descriptions of all that have come to our knowledge.

SPANS AND SNOPS.

This is the most simple of all games with marbles ; one player first shoots his marble, the second then endeavours to strike or *snop* it, or otherwise, to shoot his own within a span of it. If he miss, or do not fire within the span, the first player, from the spot where his marble rests, in like manner, shoots at that of the second ; and so on, until a snop or span is made, when the marble snopped or spanned is taken, and the game begun anew, by the winner.

BOST-ABOUT.

This game differs from the preceding one only in this respect, namely, that the marbles, instead of being shot with the fore-finger and thumb, are pitched, or to use the technical word, bosted, by the players.

HOLES.

Three small holes are dug, about a yard and a half asunder; a line is drawn about two yards from the first hole, from which the players begin the game. Chance decides who shall have the first shoot; the object is to drive the marble into the first hole; if this be done, the player shoots again, at the distance of a span, towards the second. If, however, he miss the hole, the other player begins, and each shoots, alternately, as the other misses. After having shot the marble into a hole, the player is allowed, if his adversary's marble be near, to drive it with his own as far as he can, and if he strike it, to shoot again. The game is won by the player who gets first into the last hole, in the following order :—first hole, second, third, —second, first,—second, third. The loser places his knuckles at the first hole, the winner shoots as near to it as he can from the line, and fires three times, from the place where his marble rests, at the loser's knuckles.

KNOCK-OUT.

Two or more may play at this game. He who begins, throws a marble gently against a wall, so that it rebounds to a distance not exceeding a yard; a second player throws another marble against the wall, endeavouring to make it rebound, so as to strike or come within a span of the first; if he can do neither, the first player takes up his own marble, and, in turn, strives to snop or span that of the second. The marble that is thus snopped or spanned, is won, and the winner begins again. Where only two play, it is best to knock out two or three marbles each, alternately, before they begin to use those on the ground. In this case, a player may win his own marbles, as they are common stock when down, and take up which he pleases, to play with.

THE CONQUEROR.

This is a sport, which we do not much approve of, although we must confess, that in the days of our youth, we were very fond of it. Strong stone marbles of a moderate size must be used. The game is commenced by one boy laying his taw on a piece of smooth and tolerably hard earth, (turf and pavement are both improper,) the other player throws his taw at it, as hard as he can, so as to split it if possible. If he fail to do so, his own taw is thrown at in turn, and thus each player has, alternately, a cast at the taw of the other. A strong marble will frequently break, or conquer, fifty or a hundred others; where this game is much played, a taw that has become a conqueror of a considerable number, is very much prized, and the owner will not play it against any but those which have conquered a respectable quantity. "When Greek meets Greek," or when two conquerors are engaged, the number of marbles previously broken by the vanquished is added to those of the victor; thus, if my taw having already split twenty marbles, conquers another that has split twenty, my taw then becomes a conqueror of forty-one,—that is, twenty, its previous score; twenty, the vanquished taw's score, and one for the broken taw itself. In the west of England, the game of "The Conqueror" is also played, with small, hard, variegated shells, which are found in old banks, and from which the snails, their former inhabitants, have disappeared. The shell is held in the forefinger of the right hand, and its beak pushed vigorously against that of the adversary's; the shell which breaks is, of course, conquered.

ARCH-BOARD.

This game, in some parts of England, is called "Nine-holes;" it has various names, and is sometimes played with iron bullets instead of marbles. The marbles are bowled at a board set upright, resembling a bridge, with nine small arches, all of them numbered; if the marble strike against the sides of the arches, it becomes the property of the boy to whom the board belongs; but, if it go through any one of them, the bowler claims a number equal to the number upon the arch it passed through. We have seen the boards, in this game, marked above some of the arches with nihils, in this order:—5, 0, 1, 2, 0, 3, 0, 4, 0. In some places, where there are no nihils on the board, and the numbers go beyond five, the bowler not only loses his marble, if it strike against the sides of the arches, but also gives the board-keeper a marble each time he bowls.

RING-TAW.

The rules of Ring-taw vary in different places; the following are the most general:—A circle is drawn, into which each party places as many marbles as may be agreed on. A line, called the offing, is then drawn at some distance, from which each in turn shoots at the ring. Shooting a marble out of the ring, entitles the shooter to go on again, and thus the ring may be sometimes cleared by a good player, before his companion or companions have a chance. After the first fire, the players return no more to the offing, but shoot, when their turn comes, from the place where their marbles rested on the last occasion. Every marble struck out of the ring, is won by the striking party; but if the taw at any time remain in the ring, the player is not only out, but if he have, previously, in the course of the game, struck out any marbles, he must put them in the ring again. And if one player strike with his taw the taw of another, the player whose taw is so struck, is out; and if he have, previously, shot any marbles out of the circle, he must hand them over to the party by whose taw his has been so struck.

INCREASE-POUND.

This is superior to any other game with marbles. It differs from "Ring-taw" in the following particulars:—If, previously to any marble or shot being struck out of the ring or pound, the taw of one of the players be struck by the taw of another, (except that of his partner,) or in case he shoot his taw within the pound, in either case, he puts a shot in the ring, and before either of the others play, shoots from the offing and continues in the game; but if the first of these events occur after one or more shots have been struck out of the pound, if he have previously, during that game, obtained any shots himself, he hands them over to the party who has struck him, and also puts a shot in as before, previously to his shooting from the offing; but if he have previously obtained no shots during the game, he is put out of the game entirely, or "killed," by his taw being so struck; and again, if after a shot or shots have been struck out of the pound, his taw get within it, (on the line is nothing,) he puts his shots, if he have obtained any, with an additional one, into the pound, and shoots from the offing; but if he have not obtained a shot or shots after his taw so remains within the ring, "or gets fat," as it is called, he is "killed," and stands out for the remainder of the game. When there is only one marble left in the ring, the taw may then remain inside it, without being "fat" at this game. The players seldom put more than one marble each in the ring at first.

THE PYRAMID.

A small circle is drawn on the ground, within which, one player builds a pyramid, by placing three marbles triangularly, and a fourth in the centre, on the top of them. Any other player may then shoot at the pyramid, at an agreed distance, by giving, for each time of shooting, to the one who keeps the pyramid, a marble. If the shooter strike the pyramid with his taw, as many of the marbles composing the pyramid, as may be driven out of the circle, belong to the shooter, and the pyramid is constantly to be kept up complete by its owner. This is a good in-door game; variety and additional interest may be given to it, by each player taking the office of pyramid-keeper, at stated intervals.

GAMES WITH TOPS

HUMMING-TOP.

HUMMING-TOPS, of various sizes, are to be bought at the toy-shops; very little art is necessary to use them. After the string is wound about the upright piece, one end of it is taken in one hand, and the handle of the fork-piece in the other; the string is then to be pulled off with force, and the top is set up

WHIP-TOP.

This is an excellent amusement. The top is easily set up by twirling it with both hands on a smooth surface, and applying the whip with gentleness at first, increasing the vigour of the blows, as the top gets firm on its peg.

There is a local variety of the whip-top, which is too singular for us to pass unnoticed. We allude to the Colchester top, of which an engraving is presented in the margin. Its construction is most simple, and, for spinning, it is said considerably to excel the tops made in the common form. The only games we have ever seen with whip-tops, are "races" and "encounters;" in the former, the object is to flog the top to a certain distance first; in the latter, the tops are whipped against each other until one is knocked down. The est material for a whip, at this capital sport, is an eel-skin; it far surpasses cord, or leather thongs.

PEG-TOP.

In this favorite game considerable dexterity may be acquired by practice. About London, peg-tops are, in general, only used for the purpose of being spun, and taken up to "sleep," as it is called, in wooden spoons, which are sold at the toy-shops for that purpose; but elsewhere, regular games at peg-top are played, in which the victors carry off capital steel pegs as trophies of their prowess at the sport. A circle, whose diameter is about a yard, is first drawn on a smooth piece of ground, (pavement is objectional for this game,) and several players surround it. One volunteers to commence; he throws his top inside the circle, and the others are at liberty to cast theirs at it, so long as it remains within the ring; the moment it rolls out, he may take it up, and peg at those which still remain inside. The object of each player being to split the tops of his companions, if he succeed in any case, he keeps the peg of the split top as the spoil of his victory. If either of the players do not cast his top within the ring, or if he attempt to take it out, or if he fail to set it spinning when he throws, or if it do not spin out, or after it ceases spinning, roll out of the circle, it is called "a dead top," and must be placed in the centre of the ring for the others to peg at. When it is knocked out again without being split, the player to whom it belongs, takes it up, and plays away as before. Sometimes half-a-dozen dead tops are driven out of the ring by one cast, without any of them being damaged, and indeed, if they be made of good box, it is but rarely that they split. A top with a long peg is best at this game, as it is more calculated to swerve out of the ring after it is spun; a top that sleeps after it is cast, runs the greatest danger, and those that sleep most, are heavy bodied tops with short blunt pegs. It is advisable to wind the cord round nearly three parts of the peg, as well as the top, and to use

a button at the end instead of a loop. The Spanish peg-top, of which we give a cut in the margin, is made of fine mahogany, and tapered off less abruptly toward the peg than the English tops. The peg is very short, of an uniform thickness, and rounded, not pointed, at the end. These tops spin nearly upright, and for thrice the usual time; it is unnecessary to throw them with any degree of force; in fact, they spin best when set up under-handed; so that, for playing on flooring or pavement, they are much superior to those made in the English fashion, although, for the same reason, totally unfit for "Peg in the ring." The forms of English peg-tops, as well as those of humming-tops, and the common whip-tops, are so well known, that it would be useless for us to offer engravings of them.

GAMES WITH BALLS.

THE games with Balls are numerous and excellent; Cricket is a sport of such importance, as to claim a separate place in our work, but nearly all the other games with Balls, our young readers will find under the present head.

FIVES.

Fives may be played either single-handed or with partners. A good wall must be selected, with a sound flat piece of ground in front of it; a line must be drawn, about three feet from the ground, on the wall; another on the ground, about two yards from the wall; and a third, describing three sides of a square, of which the wall itself will be a fourth, on the ground from the wall, to mark the bounds. The players toss up for innings; the winner begins by dapping his ball on the ground, and striking it against the wall, above the line, and so that it may rebound far enough to fall outside the line on the ground; the other player then strikes it, in the same manner, either before it has touched the ground, or dapped, (i. e.) hopped from the ground, more than once; the first player then prepares to receive and strike it at its rebound; and thus the game goes on, until one of the players fail to strike the ball in his turn, before it has hopped more than once, strike it below the mark, or drive it out of bounds. If the party who is in do neither of these, he loses his innings; if the other, then the in-player reckons one, on each occasion, towards the game, which is fifteen. When partners play, the rules are precisely the same; each side keeping up the ball alternately, and the partners taking turns for innings, as one of the other side gets out. After the ball is first played out, on each occasion, it is not necessary to make it rebound beyond the ground line, which is used only to make the player who is in, give out the ball fairly in the first instance: that is, when he first takes his innings, or when he plays out the ball again, after winning a point.

NINE-HOLES, OR HAT-BALL.

Near a wall where the ground is level, dig nine, or a lesser number of holes, according to the number of players, large enough for a ball to be bowled in without difficulty. Number them, and let each player be allotted a number, by chance or choice, as it may be agreed. A line is drawn about five yards from the holes, at which one of the players places himself, and bowls the ball into one of the holes. The player to whom the hole, into which the ball is bowled, belongs, picks it up as quickly as he can, and endeavours to strike one of the others with it; (the latter all run off as soon as they perceive that the ball is not for themselves;) if the thrower miss his aim, he loses a point, and is called "a fifer," and it is his turn to bowl: if, however, he strike another, he loses nothing; but the party so struck, in case he fail to hit another with the ball, becomes "a fifer," and it is his turn to bowl. Five or six may be struck in succession, and the ball may be kept up, no matter how long, until a miss be made, when the party so missing loses a point, and bowls. It is also allowed, for one player to accept the ball from another, and run the risk of striking a third: thus, if A stand close behind B, and C have the ball in front of B, A may signify by motions that he will take the ball, which is then thrown toward him by C; he catches it, and endeavours to strike B before he can run away; if he miss, he loses a point, and bowls. The second bowling is conducted precisely as the first; but he who bowls three times without passing the ball into a hole, loses a point, and if he have lost one before, becomes "a tenner;" he must still go on, until he succeed in putting the ball into a hole; it is his own fault if he bowl into that which belongs to himself. A party who misses his aim a second time becomes "a tenner;" he who loses a third point, "a fifteener;" and when four points are lost, the party stands out. The game goes on until all the players are out but one; the latter wins the game. One of the others then takes the ball in his left hand, places his face toward the wall, and throws the ball over the right shoulder as far as he can. The player who has won stands at the spot where the ball first touches the ground, or, if it be not immediately behind the party who has thrown it, a line is drawn from the place where the ball daps, to a spot behind the thrower. Thus, suppose the thrower be at *a*,

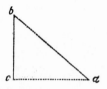

the ball falls at *b*, a line is drawn to *c*. The winner then throws the ball, from *c*, at the loser's back, three times, as hard as he pleases. The other losers throw in the same manner, one after another, and the winner has his three balls at each of their backs, from the spot where their balls respectively first touch the ground, or in a line with it, as above stated, and illustrated by the diagram in the margin.

n the vicinity of London, this game is called "Hat-ball," on account of the players using their hats, instead of digging holes, and the ball is tossed into the hats, instead of being bowled into the holes.

CATCH-BALL.

This is very similar to the preceding game. Instead of bowling the ball into holes, it is thrown in the air, and the name of the player, for whom it is intended, called out by the thrower. If it be caught, before it has twice touched the ground, by the player so called on, he loses no point, but throws it up again, and calls upon whom he pleases to catch it. If it be not caught in due time, he whose name is called must endeavour to strike one of the others with it; if he miss, he loses a point, and has his throw up. The remainder of the game, the number of points, and the losers' punishment, are all precisely as in Nine-holes; of the two, it is the better game.

FOOT-BALL.

A match is made between two sets of players of equal numbers; a large ball made of light materials,—a blown bladder, cased with leather, is the best,—is placed between them, and the object of each party is to kick the ball across the goal of the other, and to prevent it from passing their own. The party, across whose goal the ball is kicked, loses the game. The game is commenced between the two goals, which are about a hundred yards asunder.

Foot-ball was formerly much in vogue in England, though, of late years, it seems to have fallen into disrepute, and is but little practised. At what period the game of Foot-ball originated, is uncertain; it does not, however, appear among the popular exercises before the reign of Edward the Third, and then it was prohibited by a public edict; not, perhaps, from any particular objection to the sport itself, but because it co-operated, with other favorite amusements, to impede the progress of Archery.

B

The rustic boys use a blown bladder, without the covering of leather, for a foot-ball, putting peas and horse-beans inside, which occasion a rattling as it is kicked about.

GOFF, OR BANDY-BALL.

In the northen parts of the kingdom, Goff is much practised. It answers to a rustic pastime of the Romans, which they played with a ball of leather, stuffed with feathers, and the Goff-ball is composed of the same materials to this day. In the reign of Edward the Third, the Latin name "Cambuca," was applied to this pastime, and it derived the denomination, no doubt, from the crooked club, or bat, with which it was played; the bat was called a "Bandy," from its being bent, and hence is frequently called, in English, "Bandy-ball."

Goff, according to the present modification of the game, is performed with a bat, the handle of which is straight, and usually made of ash, about four feet and a half in length; the curvature is affixed to the bottom, faced with horn, and backed with lead. The ball is a little one, but exceedingly hard, being made with leather, and stuffed with feathers. There are, generally, two players, who have each of them his bat and ball. The game consists in driving the ball into certain holes made in the ground; he who achieves which the soonest, or in the fewest number of strokes, obtains the victory. The Goff-lengths, or the spaces between the first and last holes, are sometimes extended to the distance of two or three miles; the number of intervening holes is optional, but the balls must be struck into the holes and not beyond them. When four persons play, two of them are sometimes partners, and have but one ball, which they strike alternately, but every one has his own bandy. Goff was a fashionable game among the nobility at the commencement of the seventeenth century, and it was one of the exercises with which Prince Henry, eldest son to James the First, occasionally amused himself.

STOOL-BALL.

Stool-ball is frequently mentioned by the writers of the three last centuries, but without any proper definition of the game. Doctor Johnson tells us, it is a play where balls are driven from stool to stool, but does not say in what manner, or to what purpose. It consists in simply setting a stool upon the ground, and one of the players taking his place before it, while his antagonist, standing at a distance, tosses a ball with the intention of striking the stool; it is the business of the former to prevent this by beating it away with the hand, reckoning one to the game for every stroke of the ball; if, on the contrary, it should be missed by the hand, and touch the stool, the players change places; the conqueror at this game is he who strikes the ball most times before it touches the stool. In some parts of the country, a certain number of stools are set up in a circular form, at a distance from each other, and every one of them is occupied by a single player; when the ball is struck, which is done as before, with the hand, they are every one of them obliged to alter his situation, running in succession from stool to stool, and if he who threw the ball can regain it in time to strike any one of the players before he reaches the stool to which he is running, he takes his place, and the person touched must throw the ball, until he can, in like manner, return to the circle.

TRAP, BAT, AND BALL.

With the form of the trap, our young readers are, doubtless, acquainted; it will be only necessary for us to give the laws of the game. Two bounda-ries are equally placed, at a great distance from the trap, between which, it is necessary for the ball to pass, when struck by the batsman; if it fall outside either of them, he loses his innings. Innings are tossed up for, and the player who wins, places the ball in the spoon of the trap, touches the trigger with the bat, and, as the ball hops from the trap, strikes it as far as he can. One of the other players (who may be from two to half-a-dozen) endeavours to catch it. If he do so before it reaches the ground, or hops more than once, or if the striker miss the ball when he aims at it, or hits the trigger more than twice without striking the ball, he loses his innings, and the next in order, which must previously be agreed on, takes his place. Should the ball be fairly struck, and not caught, as we have stated, the out-player, into whose hands it comes, bowls it from the place where he picks it up, at the trap; which, if he hit, the striker is out. If he miss it, the striker counts one toward the game, which may be any number decided on. There is also a practice in some places, when the bowler has sent in the ball, of the striker's guessing the number of bat's lengths it is from the trap; if he guess within the real number, he reckons that number toward his game; but if he guess more than there really are, he loses his innings It is not necessary to make the game in one inning.

B 2

NORTHERN-SPELL.

Northern-spell is played with a trap, and the ball is stricken with a bat, or stout stick, at the pleasure of the players, but the latter is most commonly used. The performance of this pastime does not require the attendance of either of the parties in the field to catch or stop the ball, for the contest between them is simply, who shall strike it to the greatest distance in a given number of strokes; the length of each stroke is measured, before the ball is returned, by means of a cord made fast at one end, near the trap, the other end being stretched into the field by a person stationed there for that purpose, who adjusts it to the ball, wherever it may be; the cord is divided into yards, which are properly numbered in succession, so that the person at the bottom of the ground can easily ascertain the distance of each stroke by the number of yards, which he calls to the players, who place it to their account, and the ball is thrown back. This pastime possesses but little variety, and is by no means so amusing to the bystanders as Trap-ball.

ROUNDERS.

In the west of England this is one of the most favorite sports with the bat and ball. In the metropolis, boys play a game very similar to it, called Feeder. In rounders, the players divide into two equal parties, and chance decides which shall have first innings. Four stones or posts are placed from twelve to twenty yards asunder, as a, b, c, d, in the margin; another is put at e; one of the party which is out, who is called the pecker or feeder, places himself at e. He tosses the ball gently toward a, on the right of which one of the in-party places himself, and strikes the ball, if possible, with his bat. If he miss three times, or if the ball, when struck, fall behind a, or be caught by any of the players, who are all scattered about the field except one who stands behind a, he is out, and another takes his place. If none of these events take place, on striking the ball he drops the bat, and runs toward b, or, if he can, to c, d, or even to a again. If, however, the feeder, or any of the out-players who may happen to have the ball, strike him with it in his progress from a to b, b to c, c to d, or d to a, he is out. Supposing he can only get to b, one of his partners takes the bat, and strikes at the ball in turn; while the ball is passing from the feeder to a, if it be missed, or after it is struck, the first player gets to the next or a further goal, if possible, without being struck. If he can only get to c, or d, the second runs to b, only, or c, as the case may be, and a third player begins; as they get home, that is, to a, they play at the ball in rotation, until they all get out; then, of course, the out-players take their places.

SPORTS OF AGILITY AND SPEED.

Many of the previous sports with balls and tops, are in part games of agility and speed, and so also are several of those which will be found among the Miscellaneous Minor Sports; but the following pastimes are exclusively games either of speed or agility, for which no implements are necessary.

LEAP-FROG.

This is a most excellent pastime. It should be played in a spacious place, out of doors if possible, and the more there are engaged in it, provided they be of the same height and agility, the better is the sport. We will suppose a dozen at play :—Let eleven of them stand in a row, about six yards apart, with all their faces in one direction, arms folded, or their hands resting on their thighs, their elbows in, and their heads bent forward, so that the chin of each rests on his breast, the right foot advanced, the back a little bent, the shoulders rounded, and the body firm. The last begins the sport by taking a short run, placing his hands on the shoulders of the nearest player, and leaping with their assistance (of course, springing with his feet at the same time) over his head, as represented in the cut. Having cleared the first, he goes on to the second, third, fourth, fifth, &c. in succession, and as speedily as possible. When he has gone over the last, he goes to the proper distance, and places himself in position for all the players to leap over him in their turn. The first over whom he passed, follows him over the second, third, fourth, &c.; and when he has gone over, the one who begun the game places himself in like manner for the others to jump over him. The third follows the second, and so on until the parties are tired.

The manner of playing Leap-Frog about London is different, and as we think, much inferior in safety, appearance, and amusement :—A lad places himself with his hands on his knees, his body nearly doubled, and his side, instead of his back, turned toward the leapers, who, with a short run, take their leap at some distance from the lad who is to be vaulted over; he who takes his leap the farthest off, is reckoned the best player. This, it may be readily imagined, is by no means so lively as the real game of Leap-Frog, which we have above described. The boy, who is to be leaped over, receives the greater shock from the jumpers; and he is in more danger of being thrown down by, or having a blow on his head from, their knees.

PRISONERS' BASE.

Prisoners' Base is truly a capital game for cold weather. The best number to play at it is six or eight on each side, but there is no objection to more or fewer players. The choice of partners is decided by chance; a line, ten or twelve yards in length, is drawn about a dozen yards from a wall; other lines are drawn at each end of the first, reaching thence to the wall, and the third from the middle of the first line to the wall; one party takes possession of the bounds on one side of this middle, and the other set of players takes the bounds on the other side of it. Two prisons are also marked in a line with each other, at from one to two hundred yards (as convenience will permit) from the front of the bounds; the prison belonging to one party must be opposite the bounds of the other. The game is now commenced by a player from one side running out mid-way between the bounds and prisons; a player from the other side immediately follows, and he may be pursued by one of his adversaries, who in like manner may be followed by a player from the side which began the game, and so on; both parties being at liberty to send out as many as they think fit. The object of each player is to come up with, or intercept and touch any player of the opposite side, who has left the bounds before him; he is not at liberty to touch any that have started after him, it being their privilege, on the contrary, if they can, to touch him before he can get back within his bounds again. A player is allowed to touch one of the opposite party only each time he quits bounds, and after having touched an adversary, he is exempt from being touched on his return to bounds. Every player who is touched, goes to the prison belonging to his party, where he must remain until one of his own side (who must start from bounds after the prisoner has been within the line of the prison) be able to reach him, without being touched in his run from bounds to prison, by any of the opposite party who may have left their bounds after him. When thus released, neither he nor the player who has relieved him is to touch or be touched in their return to bounds again. The game is won by that side which has all the players of the other in prison at the same time.

SADDLE MY NAG.

Two players toss up for choice of partners; six or eight on each side is the best number: after choosing, the two leaders toss up for innings, he who loses then ranges himself and his associates in the following manner:—One player places himself almost upright, with his hands resting against a wall or tree, a second puts his head against the skirts of the first, the third against the skirt of the second, and so on until they are all ranged. They must either hold by the trowsers of the player who is before them, cross their arms on their breasts, or lean them on their knees. One of the winning party now begins by taking a run, placing his hands upon the back of the outer player on the other side, and leaping as far forward on the range as he possibly can, in order to afford room for his partners behind him, who follow in succession, until all are on the backs of the other party. If they can all remain on without touching the ground with the hand or any other part, while the leader counts twenty, or if any of the other party sink beneath the weight, or touch the ground with their hands or knees to support themselves, the riders keep their innings, and go on again. If on the contrary, or in case there be not room enough for them to leap on, or they cannot keep on the backs of those who are on before them, they lose, and the other party become riders, and they nags.

PUSS IN THE CORNER.

This is a very simple, but at the same time, a very lively and amusing game. It is played by five only; and the place chosen for the sport should be a square court or yard with four corners, or any place where there are four trees or posts, about equi-distant from each other, and forming the four points of a square. Each of these points or corners is occupied by a player; the fifth, who is called Puss, stands in the centre. The game now commences; the players exchange corners in all directions: it is the object of the one who stands out, to occupy any of the corners which may remain vacant for an instant during the exchanges. When he succeeds in so doing, that player who is left without a corner becomes the Puss. It is to be observed that if A and B attempt to exchange corners, and A gets to B's corner, but B fails to reach A's before the player who stands out gets there, it is B and not A who becomes Puss.

WARNING,

This may be played by any number, from ten to a hundred. One begins the game by standing within a line, running parallel for a considerable length with, and about three feet from a wall, and repeating the following words,—" Warning once, warning twice, warning three times over; a bushel of wheat, a bushel of rye, when the cock crows, out jump I!—

Cock-a-doodle-doo!—Warning!" He then runs out, and touches the first he can overtake, who must return to bounds with him. These two then (first crying "Warning" only) join hands, and each of them endeavours to touch another; he also returns to bounds, and at the next sally joins hands with the other two. Every player who is afterward touched by either of the outside ones, does the like, until the whole be thus touched and taken. It is not lawful to touch an out-player after the line is broken, either accidentally, or by the out-players attacking it, which they are permitted to do. Immediately a player is touched, the line separates, and the out-players endeavour to catch those belonging to it, who are compelled to carry those who capture them, on their backs, to bounds. When three are touched, he who begins the game is entitled to join the out-players.

FOLLOW MY LEADER.

Without a bold and active leader this sport is dull and monotonous; with one possessing the necessary qualifications it is quite the contrary. Any number may play at it. A leader is fixed on, and the other players range themselves in a line behind him. He commences the sport, by some feat of agility, such as leaping, hopping, or climbing, and his followers then attempt to perform it in succession. He then goes to another trial of skill; the others, or so many of them as are able to do so, follow his example, and thus the sport proceeds until the parties think fit to cease. The most nimble and active should, of course, be chosen for a leader; he should perform feats of such difficulty as to render the sport interesting, at the same time avoiding such as he knows can only be undertaken by himself, or by one or two of his followers. If one boy can perform a feat, which those who are placed before him in rank fail in attempting, he takes precedence of them until he is, in like manner excelled by any of those who are behind him.

TOUCH.

This is a sport of speed. Six or eight is the best number to play at it. One volunteers to be the player, who is called Touch; it is the object of the other players to run from and avoid him. He pursues them all; or, if he think fit, singles out an individual, and follows until he comes up with and touches him. The player so overtaken becomes Touch, and then endeavours to get near enough to lay his hand upon one of the rest. This is an active and amusing game for boys in cold weather. It is sometimes called Touch-iron or Touch wood; in these cases, the players are safe only while they touch iron or wood, as may be previously agreed. They are liable to be *touched* only when running from one piece of wood or iron to another.

SPORTS WITH TOYS.

The Sports with Toys are very numerous; those which are most usual in the play-ground are with the kite, the hoop, the sucker, the pea-shooter, and two or three others; of each of which we offer our readers a description.

THE POP-GUN.

The Pop-gun is made of a piece of wood, from which the pith has been taken; a rammer must be made, with a handle of a proper length, which should have a shoulder to prevent the slender or ram-rod point going the entire length of the gun; the pellets are made of moistened tow, or brown paper. Put one into one end of the gun, push it with the rod to the other, and then placing a second pellet at the end where the first was inserted, push that toward the opposite end, and it will drive the first pellet out with great force. Pop-guns are also made with quills, the pellets for which are cut by the quills out of slices of raw potato.

THE SLING.

Cut out an oval piece of leather, about two inches wide at the broadest part; at each of the ends, fasten a leathern thong, or piece of cord,—one of these cords, or thongs, should be longer than the other; place a stone in the broadest part of the leather, twist the longest thong twice or thrice round your hand, hold the other lightly between your thumb and fore-finger, whirl it round several times, let go the shorter thong, and the stone will be shot to a great distance. Small lumps of clay kneaded to the point of a pliant switch, may be jerked to a height scarcely credible.

THE PEA-SHOOTER.

By means of a tube of tin or copper, a pea may be propelled from the mouth, by the mere force of the breath, to a very considerable distance. The natives of Macouslie, with a cane tube, about twelve feet long, propel arrows with their breath, with such force and dexterity, as to bring down different sorts of feathered game.

THE KITE.

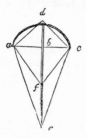

To construct the Kite, you must, in the first place, procure a straight lath of deal for the upright or straighter, and a thin hoop, or a pliant piece of hazel for the bow or bender. Fasten the bender by its centre, with string, to the upright, within a little distance of its top; then notch the two ends of the bow, and fasten them to the upright by a string, which is made fast at each of the ends, and turned once round the upright, as *a, b, c*; the string must then be carried up to the junction of the bow and straighter, and made fast at *d*, and thence to *a*; from *a*, it must pass through a notch at *e*, up to *c*; then down to *f*, where it must be tied in a notch cut for that purpose, and up to *a* again. Your skeleton being now complete, your next task is to paste a sufficient quantity of paper together to cover it, and afford a hem to be pasted over the outer edges.

Next, bore two holes in the straighter, one about a fifth of the whole length from the top, and the other rather less from the bottom; run through these, and fasten, by a knot at the two ends, your belly-band string, to which the ball of string, by which the kite is flown, is afterward fixed. The wings are made of several sheets of writing paper, half cut in slips, rolled up, and fastened at *a* and *c*. The tail, which should be from ten to fifteen times the length of the kite, is made by tying bobs of writing paper, four times folded, about an inch and a half broad, and three inches long, at intervals of three inches and a quarter, on a string, with a large bob, similar to the wings, at the bottom of it. Your kite is now complete, and fit to be flown in the usual manner.

It is well known that the celebrated Doctor Franklin once let up a kite previous to his entering the water to bathe, and then, lying on his back, suffered himself to be drawn across a stream by its power. The master of a respectable academy at Bristol, among whose pupils we have enjoyed many pleasant hours in the pastime of flying kites, has lately succeeded in travelling along the public roads, (we believe, from Bristol to London,) with amazing speed, in a carriage drawn by kites, in the most safe and accurate manner possible, notwithstanding the variations of the wind and the crookedness of the roads.

THE THAUMATROPE.

This very amusing toy is made and exhibited in the following manner: Cut out a circular piece of card, to which fasten six bits of string, as in the

cut. Draw on one side of it a figure with balls, and on the other, two balls only, as represented in the margin; then taking one of the strings between the forefinger and thumb of each hand, close to the card, twist or twirl it rapidly round, and according to which pair of strings you use, the figure will seem to be tossing two, three, or four balls in different directions. Various cards and devices may be used: for instance, you may draw a bird on one side, and a cage on the other; by only using the centre pieces of string, the bird will seem to be in the

cage or aviary; a horse on one side, and a jockey on the other, as in the cut, (taking care to reverse the figures, or draw them upside down to each other,) and by using the different pairs of strings, you may cause the rider to appear upon, leaping under, or by the side of the horse, as you please. For other designs, we suggest a tight rope and a dancer; a body and a head; a candle and a flame; a picture and its frame, &c.

BATTLEDORE AND SHUTTLECOCK.

Battledores and Shuttlecocks are to be obtained cheap at all the bookstores. The game is played by two persons, who, with the battledores, strike the shuttlecock to and fro between them.

Shuttlecock is a boyish sport of long standing. It appears to have been a fashionable game among grown persons in the reign of James the First, and is mentioned as such in an old comedy of that time. Among the anecdotes related of Prince Henry, son to James the First, is the following: "His Highness playing at shuttlecock with one far taller than himself, and hitting him, by chance, with the shuttlecock upon the forehead, 'This is,' quoth he, 'the encounter of David with Goliah.'"

THE SUCKER.

Cut a circular piece out of stout leather; bore a hole through its centre, and pass a string, with a knot to prevent the end escaping, through this hole. Soak the leather well in water before you use it; when thoroughly soaked, place the leather on a stone, press it well down with your foot, and then taking the string, you may, by your sucker, raise a considerable weight.

THE HOOP.

Every body knows how to trundle the Hoop in the usual way; several pairs of tin squares are sometimes nailed to the inner part of the hoop, which produce, in the opinion of some lads, an agreeable jingle. In some parts of England, boys drive their hoops one against the other, and the player whose hoop falls in these encounters, is conquered.

THE WATCH-SPRING GUN.

Neatly cut a bit of wood, about four inches long, into the form of the stock of a pistol or gun; scoop a groove in the upper part of it; in this groove place a large quill, open at both ends, fasten it on with waxed thread, and let it project beyond the point of the stock and reach as far as the middle of it; next, procure an old watch-spring, which may be bought cheap at a watch-maker's, cut off a piece of it about as long as the quill, bend it backward, and tie one end of it firmly to the upper part or but-end of the stock. Then bore a small hole through the middle of the stock about an inch from the mouth of the quill; cut a pin in two, fasten one half of it, by its head, to a bit of thread, the other end of which fasten to the thread that binds on the spring; this is the trigger, and your gun is complete. To use it, place a little arrow, or a shot, in the groove between the mouth of the quill and the hole in the stock; put the pin through this hole, and bend back the spring so that the pin may catch it; take the toy in your right hand, pull the trigger out with the fore-finger, and the spring being thus released, will drive the shot, or arrow, through the quill to a considerable distance. If you use arrows, you may shoot at a little butt or target.

CAT AND MOUSE.

This is a French sport. The toy with which it is played consists of two flat bits of hard wood, the edges of one of which are notched. The game is played by two only; they are both blindfolded, and tied to the ends of a long string, which is fastened in the centre to a post, by a loose knot, so as to play easily in the evolutions made by the players. The party who plays the mouse occasionally scrapes the toys together, and the other, who plays the cat, attracted by the sound, endeavours to catch him.

MISCELLANEOUS SPORTS.

Under this head we intend to describe a variety of amusing sports and recreations, which could not, in strictness, be inserted among any of the preceding classes.

BLIND-MAN'S BUFF.

This popular, old-fashioned, and delightful pastime, is so well known, as to render any description of it unnecessary. There is, however, a variation of it called Shadow Buff, which is less known, but equally amusing. A large piece of white linen is suspended smoothly at one end of a room; at a little distance from it, Buffy, with his face toward the linen, is seated on a low stool. Directly in a line, and about a yard behind him, a table is placed with a candle on it; all the other lights must be extinguished. The players then walk one by one, between the table and Buffy, (who must not turn his head,) limping, hopping, and grimacing as they please, so as to distort their shadows on the linen. If Buffy can tell correctly to whom any shadow belongs, (guessing once only for each person,) the player, whom he so discovers, takes his place.

BASTE THE BEAR.

Lots are drawn for the first bear, who takes his seat on a stone, with one end of a rope, about three yards long, in his hand, the other end of which is held by the bear's master. The other players attack the bear with twisted handkerchiefs, and the master endeavours to touch one of them : if he can do so without letting the rope go, or pulling the bear from his seat, the player so touched takes the place of the bear. Each bear has the privilege of choosing his own master; being bear once, or even oftener, does not exonerate a player, if fairly touched, from becoming so again.

DICK, DUCK, AND DRAKE.

From this game comes the proverb which is frequently applied to a spendthrift. "He is making ducks and drakes of his money." It is played by skimming, or what boys call shying, bits of slate or flat stones along the surface of a river or pond. If the thing thrown touches the water and rebounds once, it is a dick; if twice, a duck; if thrice, a drake. He who makes his slate or pebble rebound the greatest number of times, wins the game.

SLIDING.

Sliding is one of the diversions ascribed to young men of London by Fitzstephen, and, as far as one can judge from his description of the sport, it differed not in the performance from the method used by the boys of our own time. He mentions another kind of pastime upon the ice, which is even now practised by boys in several parts of England; his words are to this effect: "Others make a seat of ice, as large as a mill-stone, and having placed one of their companions upon it, they draw him along, when it sometimes happens, that moving on slippery places, they all fall down headlong."

Sledges are, now-a-days, also used, which being extended from a centre by means of a strong rope, those who are seated in them are moved round with great velocity, and form an extensive circle. Sledges of this kind were set upon the Thames in the time of a hard frost at the commencement of the last century, as the following couplet, taken from a song written upon that occasion, plainly proves.

> "While the rabble in sledges run giddily round,
> And nought but a circle of folly is found."

SKATING.

Skating is by no means a modern pastime, and probably the invention proceeded rather from necessity than the desire of amusement. It is a boast of a northern chieftain, that he could traverse the snow upon skates of wood. Strutt states that he cannot by any means ascertain at what time skating made its first appearance in England, but that some traces of such an exercise are found in the thirteenth century; at which period, according to Fitzstephen, it was customary in the winter, when the ice would bear them, for the young citizens of London to fasten the leg bones of animals under the soles of their feet, by tying them round their ankles, and then taking a pole shod with iron into their hands, they pushed themselves forward by striking it against the ice, and moved with celerity, equal, says the author, to a bird flying through the air, or an arrow from a cross-bow; but some allowance, we presume, must be made for the poetical figure: he then adds, " at times, two of them thus furnished agree to set opposite one to another at a great distance; they meet, elevate their poles, attack and strike each other, when one or both of them fall, and not without some bodily hurt, and even after their fall are carried a great distance from each other by the rapidity of the motion, and whatever part of the head comes upon the ice it is sure to be laid bare."

The wooden skates shod with iron or steel, which are bound about the feet and ankles like the talares of the Greeks and Romans, were, most probably, brought into England from the low countries, where they are said to have originated, and where, it is well known, they are almost universally used by persons of both sexes when the season permits. Some modern writers have asserted that " the metropolis of Scotland has produced more instances of elegant skaters than perhaps any other county whatever; and the institution of a skating club has contributed not a little to the improvement of this amusement." Strutt, in noticing this, observes that when the Serpentine river in Hyde Park was frozen over, he saw four gentlemen there dance, if the expression may be allowed, a double minuet, in skates with as much ease and perhaps more elegance, than in a ball-room; others again, by turning and winding with much adroitness, have readily in succession described upon the ice the form of all the letters in the alphabet.

SWINGING.

The construction of the swing is simple: two ropes of equal lengths, are to be suspended from any branch or cross piece of timber, of adequate strength; at the bottom of these ropes a seat is to be securely fastened, and the party who takes the seat must be propelled by another on the ground; a rope for this purpose must be fastened to the back part of the seat.

FRENCH AND ENGLISH.

This game is played by two parties, whose numbers are equal; they all take hold of a rope, and the object of each party is to pull those belonging to the other across a chalk line on the ground, by means of the rope. When all the players on one side are thus pulled over or made prisoners, the other party wins the game. This is a very lively sport, any number may join in it, and it affords capital exercise and much amusement.

TIP-CAT.

Tip-cat, or, perhaps, more properly, the game of cat, is a rustic pastime well known in many parts of the kingdom. Its denomination is derived from a piece of wood, called a cat, with which it is played; the cat is about six inches in length, and an inch and a half or two inches in diameter, and diminished from the middle to both the ends, in the shape of a double cone; by this curious contrivance, the places of the trap and ball are at once supplied, for when the cat is laid upon the ground, the player, with his cudgel, strikes it smartly, it matters not at which end, and it will rise with a rotatory motion, high enough for him to beat it away as it falls, in the same manner as he would a ball.

There are various methods of playing the game of cat, but we shall only notice the two that follow. The first is exceedingly simple, and consists in making a large ring upon the ground, in the middle of which the striker takes his station; his business is to beat the cat over the ring. If he fail in so doing he is out, and another player takes his place: if he be successful, he judges with his eye the distance the cat is driven from the centre of the ring, and calls for a number, at pleasure, to be scored toward his game; if the number demanded be found, upon measurement, to exceed the same number of lengths of the cudgel, he is out; on the contrary, if he do not, he obtains his call. The second method is to make four, six, or eight holes in the ground, in a circular direction, and as nearly as possible, at equal distances from each other, and at every hole is placed a player with his cudgel; one of the opposite party, who stand in the field, tosses the cat to the batsman who is nearest him, and every time the cat is struck, the players are obliged to change their situations, and run once from one hole to another in succession; if the cat be driven to any great distance, they continue to run in the same order, and claim a score toward their game, every time they quit one hole and run to another; but if the cat be stopped by their opponents, and thrown across between any two of the holes before the player who has quitted one of them can reach the other, he is out.

HOP-SCOTCH.

In some parts of England this game is called Pottle. It is played with an oyster-shell, in the following manner :—Draw, with chalk, on the ground, a figure similar to the cut in the margin. Toss up for innings. He who wins stands at the * and throws the shell into No. 1, which is called the first bed; he then steps with his right foot into that bed, and "scuffles," that is, jerks, with his right foot, the shell out toward the *. He now throws the shell into No. 2; steps, with his left foot into No. 1, and then, placing his right foot in No. 2, scuffles the shell out as before, and steps with one foot back to No. 1, and thence out. He must now throw the shell into No. 3, and step into 1, 2, and 3, scuffle the shell out, and step back through the beds alternately. He must then go to 4, 5, and 6, in succession, and, at each throw, step into every previous bed, with one foot only, and the like when

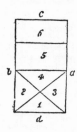

coming back, reversing the numbers. After this, the player puts the shell into No. 1, hops into that bed, scuffles the shell into 2, and so on to 6, and back again in the same manner, bed by bed, to the *. Lastly, he places the shell into No. 1, puts his right foot in the bed, and scuffles the shell through all the beds, beyond the further line of 6, at one jerk. If the player who gets the innings do all this correctly, he wins the game. If, however, he put himself out, as hereafter described, the second player takes the innings; if the latter put himself out, without going through the game, the first takes up his own game, where it was when he went out; the second also does the like with his, if the first gets out a second time. When there are more than one innings, the first who goes through the game, as above stated, wins. A player loses his innings in either of the following cases :— If he throw the shell into the wrong bed, or on the line, or put two feet into one bed, or a foot upon the lines, or do not scuffle the shell out of the bed in which it lies at the first attempt, or put his hands to the ground, or throw or scuffle the shell beyond line *c*, (except in the last, or what is called " the long scuffle,") or outside the lines *a b ;* or if, in going forward, he put his leg into 3 before 2, or the contrary when coming back; or if, when scuffling the shell through on the hop, he drive it beyond the next bed in which it lies; or if, in any part of the game, when he has stepped into a bed, he take more than one hop in order to get near the shell; or if he hop after he has scuffled it; or, lastly, if, in the long scuffle, he do not, at one effort, send it with his foot from beyond the line of *c*. But observe, that when he has cast the shell into No. 2, or any bed beyond it, he is not compelled to scuffle it out, that is, beyond the line *d*, at one effort.

KING OF THE CASTLE.

This is a very unexceptionable and simple, but nevertheless, lively sport. One player places himself on the top of a little mound or hillock ; he is the King of the Castle, and he endeavours to retain possession of his post, as long as possible, against the attacks of his playmates, who endeavour, one at a time, to push him off. If he be driven off the mound or hillock, the player who dethrones him takes his place.

SEE-SAW

A plank is placed across a felled tree, a low wall, or anything similar, and a player seats himself at each end ; by a slight exertion, if the plank be properly balanced, each end rises and sinks alternately. It must be observed, that if the players be of unequal weight, he who is the heavier must, to preserve the due equilibrium, make his end of the plank shorter.

c

WHOOP.

This game is played as follows :—All the players but one, collect at a place called " home," while one goes off to hide himself.

When ready, he shouts "Whoop oh !" the others then sally out to find him ; he who discovers the hidden player, calls out "Whoop oh !" the hidden player then breaks from his concealment, and if he can catch one of the others, the one so caught must carry him on his back to " home." It is then the boy's turn who has made the discovery to go and hide himself, and the others endeavour to discover his lurking place, as before.

HIDE AND SEEK.

This is very like the preceding game ; a handkerchief, or some other trifle, is concealed by one player, and the rest attempt to find it ; the discoverer takes the next turn to hide the article. It is a custom, in this game, for the boy who has hid the article to encourage those who approach it, by telling them that they burn, and to warn them of their departure from it by saying they freeze.

HIPPAS.

The Greeks had a pastime called hippas, which, we are told, was one person riding upon the shoulders of another, as upon a horse : a sport of this kind was in practice with us at the commencement of the fourteenth century, and is still occasionally seen in some parts of the country ; it is performed by two competitors, who struggle one with the other, and he who pulls his opponent from the shoulders of his carrier is the victor. A soft piece of turf is usually chosen for this sport.

THREAD THE NEEDLE.

Thread the needle may be played by a considerable number of boys, who all join hands, and the game commences with the following dialogue between the two outside players at each end of the line : " How many miles to Babylon?" "Threescore and ten." "Can I get there by candlelight?" "Yes, and back again." "Then open the gates without more ado, and let the king and his men pass through." In obedience to this mandate, the player who stands at the opposite end of the line and the one next him, lift their joined hands as high as possible; the other outside player then approaches, runs under the hands thus elevated, and the whole line follows him, if possible, without disuniting. This is threading the needle. The same dialogue is repeated, the respondent now becoming the inquirer, and running between the two players at the other end, with the whole line after him. The first then has his turn again.

DUCK.

Duck should be played by a number exceeding three, but not more than six or eight. A large stone with a smooth top is placed on or fixed into the ground, and an offing marked at eight or ten yards distance. Each of the players being previously provided with a large pebble, or stone, double the size of a cricket ball, or thereabout, one of them, by chance or choice, becomes duck; that is, he places the pebble or stone with which he is going to play, on the large stone, and stands a little on one side. The others then cast their pebbles or ducks at it, in turn, from the offing, each endeavouring to knock it off its place. Each player, as soon as he has cast his duck, watches for an opportunity of carrying it back to the offing, so as to cast again. If the player who is duck, can touch him after he has taken up his pebble, and before he reaches the offing, provided his own pebble remain on the large stone, then the player so touched becomes duck. It sometimes happens that three or four of the out-players' ducks lie so close together, that the player who is duck can stand in a situation to be within reach of all of them; in this case, they cannot, without running the risk of being touched, pick up, until one of those who are at the offing is lucky enough to strike the duck off the large stone; then, before its owner can replace it, which he must do before he can touch a player, they all take up their ducks and run to the offing, where, of course, they are safe.

HUNT THE SLIPPER.

This is usually an in-door game, although there is no other objection to its being played on a dry piece of turf than that the slipper cannot be heard when struck by its momentary possessor, when passing round the joyous ring. Several young persons sit on the ground in a circle, a slipper is given to them, and one, who generally volunteers to accept the office in order to begin the game, stands in the centre, and whose business it is to " chase the slipper by its sound." The parties who are seated, pass it round so as to prevent, if possible, its being found in the possession of any individual. In order that the player in the centre may know where the slipper is, it is occasionally tapped on the ground, and then suddenly handed on to the right or left. When the slipper is found in the possession of any one in the circle, by the player who is hunting it, the party on whom it is so found, takes the latter player's place.

c 2

PALL MALL.

Pall-mall is a game wherein a round piece of box is struck, with a mallet, through a high arch of iron, which he that can do at the fewest blows, or at the number agreed upon, wins. It is to be observed, that there are two of these arches, that is, one at either end of the alley. The game of Mall was a fashionable amusement in the reign of Charles II., and the walk in St. James's Park, now called the Mall, received its name from having been appropriated to the purpose of playing at Mall, where Charles himself, and his courtiers, frequently exercised themselves in the practice of this pastime. The denomination of " Mall," given to this game, is evidently derived from the mallet or wooden hammer used by the players to strike the ball. It will be perceived that this game is rather similar to Goff; we have been told that it still exists in some parts of England; but we must confess that it never fell under our personal observation.

HOP, STEP, AND JUMP.

This is a sport of emulation; the object is to ascertain which of the players concerned can, eventually, go over the greatest portion of ground in a hop, a step, and a jump, performed in succession, and which may be taken either standing or with a run, as may be agreed, at the outset, between the players.

DRAWING THE OVEN.

Several players seat themselves on the ground, in a line, and in such a manner that each may be clasped round the body by the player who is seated behind him. When all are thus united, two others take the one who is at the extremity of the line by the two hands and pull until they separate him from the grasp of the one who is behind him. They then take the second in the same manner, and so on until they have thus drawn the whole line.

THE LAME LAMPLIGHTERS.

Two boys kneel, each on one knee only, holding the other leg off the ground, one opposite the other; a lighted candle is given to one, and another candle, not lighted, to the other; they then attempt to illumine the latter; but, being in equilibrium on one knee, and liable to be thrown off their balance by the least motion, they will find this so difficult a matter as to cause great diversion to the spectators.

THE JUMPING ROPE.

A long rope is swang round by a player at each end of it; when it moves tolerably regular, one, two, or even more boys, step in between those who hold the rope, suffering it to pass over their heads as it rises, and leaping up so that it goes under their feet when it touches the ground, precisely as in the case of a common skipping-rope. The principal difficulty in this sport is, to run between the players at the proper moment of time, that is, just as the rope is at highest elevation, so as to be ready to jump over when, in its circuit, it comes toward the feet. Care must be taken that due time be kept in the leaps, so that they may perfectly accord with the motion of the rope.

There is another mode of playing with the long skipping-rope, namely, by the player at one end of it, advancing a step or two toward the other, keeping the hand which holds the rope on the outside, and then, with the assistance of the player at the other end, turning the rope round, and skipping over it in its circuit.

THE WOODEN BOTTLE.

This is a sport similar to " The Lame Lamplighters," frequently played by the parlour fire-side, in holyday time :—an individual seats himself on a wooden bottle which is placed sideways upon the floor, and endeavours, with a burning candle, which he holds in his right hand, to light another in his left.

DROPPING THE 'KERCHIEF.

A number of players join hands so as to make a circle ; one only stands out ; he walks round the outside of the circle, and drops a handkerchief behind which player in the circle he thinks fit. The party behind whom the handkerchief is thus dropped immediately follows the one who dropped it : those who stood on each side complete the circle by joining hands, and the chace commences. The pursuer is bound to follow precisely the course of the pursued, who winds in and out under the arms of the other players, who elevate them for his accommodation, and endeavours, by all the means in his power, to puzzle and elude him. If he succeed in so doing, that is, if the pursuer make a blunder in his course, he returns to his place in the circle, and the first player prepares to drop the handkerchief behind one of the players again. When he is fairly overtaken by the player behind whom he has last dropped the handkerchief, the latter takes his place, and he joins hands in the circle.

BUCK.

This is a miniature resemblance of " Saddle my Nag ;" but it neither requires speed, nor even agility. It is a sport for two boys only, who should be nearly equal in size and strength. A third, who does not join in the game, stands by as an umpire. The game commences by one of the players giving a back ; that is, placing his arms across his breast, or resting them on his knees, stooping forward so as to bring his back nearly horizontal with his head, which he supports against a post, wall, tree or whatever may be convenient for the purpose. It is usual, but we think quite unnecessary, for the player who gives the back to be blindfolded ; we say unnecessary, because the only object for doing this is to prevent him seeing what is going on behind, or, rather, above his back, which he cannot possibly do, if he keep his head in a fair and proper position ; and the umpire should see that he does so. The first player having thus taken his position, the second leaps, or vaults, astride on his back, holds up as many of the fingers of one hand as he pleases, and says, "Buck, buck, how many horns do I hold up?" The player who gives the back makes a guess; if he name the right number the other player becomes Buck, and gives him a back. If, however, his guess be an incorrect one, the rider gets off, vaults on again, holds up the same or a different number of fingers, and asks the same question as before; this is repeated until the Buck name the true number. It is the business of the umpire to see that there is no foul play on the part of the rider. We should suggest that it would be an improvement on this quiet, simple game, for the umpire to be made a third player; so that when the Buck's guess is correct, the rider should give a back, the umpire become rider, and the Buck umpire: thus, instead of the place of umpire being a mere idle vocation, the game would be productive of amusement and exercise to all three of the boys engaged in it.

THE SNOW STATUE.

In those days, when winter clothes the surface of the earth with a mantle of snow, and many of the amusements of the play-ground are thereby suspended, it is a custom with boys, as some of our young readers, doubtless, very well know, to make that which is an impediment to their old recreations, a material for new ones. Then do snow-balls, harmless if lightly compressed, but otherwise if strongly kneaded, fly about in abundance. Caves, and even pigmy fortresses, are constructed; the rolling ball, which is first rounded by the little hands of a child, becomes, in a few hours, by driving it over the snow, too big for a man to move. When the joyous tenants of the play-ground have become fatigued with rolling the ball, or it has acquired a size and weight superior to their united powers, it is a common practice with them to cut a rude resemblance of a man out of the mass, adding to its height and diminishing its breadth. This is called the Snow Statue; and when complete, the young sculptors retire to a convenient distance, and, with the aid of snow-balls, each tries his utmost to demolish that which they have just taken such pains to construct.

We are well aware that there are other Minor Sports and Pastimes practised in play-grounds in different parts of the country, besides those we have described; it would be impossible for us "to press the endless throng" within our limits. We give a selection of the best, and of those which most required explanation. We are also aware, that the rules of some of the Sports vary in different places;—where this is the case, we have given those which are most generally adopted. Many games and amusements which might have been inserted in this part of the work, will be found placed with greater propriety, under other heads.

THE DEAF AND DUMB ALPHABET.

Though poor and old, she had a golden joy ;
Her dim eye brightened oft, to see her boy,—
Albeit by Heaven deprived of speech and hearing,—
 Throw by his homely toy,
And tell his love, in manner so endearing,
Upon his nimble fingers, that she thought
Him more endowed than those bereft of nought.

THE art of teaching those who are Deaf and Dumb a mode of comprehending whatever it may be desirous to convey to their minds, and of expressing their own wants and ideas to their more happy fellow creatures, is one of the greatest triumphs that humanity can boast. To such perfection may this art be carried, that those beings, to whose benefit the exertions of professors are directed, may be raised nearly to a par with the rest of the world. It has the great advantage of being remarkably simple ; so that a mother, a brother, sister, or school-fellow, by a little perseverance, may give the deaf and dumb youth the means of communicating his wishes on all occasions. He may be led progressively from the alphabet to the construction and signification of words, the composition of sentences, and, ultimately, to such a complete knowledge of language, as will enable him to study other branches of education with as much promise of success as if he had been born with all his senses in perfection. Our limits will not allow us to enter into any detail of the manner of conveying instruction to the Dumb, beyond the acquirement of the Alphabet, to which we add an engraving showing the position of the hands to express each letter.

THE ALPHABET.

A, E, I, O, U. The vowels *a, e, i, o,* and *u,* are expressed by touching, with the fore-finger of the right hand, the thumb, or one of the fingers of the left, according to the letter required to be expressed.

A is made by touching the top of the thumb; *e,* by touching that of the fore-finger; *i,* by touching that of the middle finger; *o,* by touching that of the ring, or fourth finger; and *u,* by touching that of the little finger.

B. Join the fore-finger and thumb of each hand, and place the backs of the two fore-finger nails together.

C. Curve the fingers and thumb toward each other, so as to resemble as much as possible the shape of the letter.

D. Curve the fingers and thumb of the right hand, but not quite so much as for *C,* and place the tops of the fore-finger and thumb against the side of the fore-finger of the left hand, which is to be kept straight.

F. Place the fore-finger of one hand across the back of the two first fingers of the other.

G and *J.* Clench the hands, and place one fist upon the other.

H. Draw the palm of one hand across the palm and fingers of the other, beginning near the ball of the thumb, and going along the hands to the tips of the fingers, precisely as if you were brushing something off the palm of one hand with the other.

K. Curve the fore-finger toward the thumb, and place the second joint of the fore-finger so curved, against the back of the second joint of the fore-finger of the other hand.

L. Lay the fore-finger of the right hand straight upon the palm of the left.

M. Lay the three first fingers of the right hand upon the palm of the left.

N. Lay the two first fingers of the right hand upon the palm of the left.

P. Bend the thumb and fore-finger as for *D,* only make a lesser curve, and place the tops of the thumb and fore-finger to the two first joints of the fore-finger of the other hand.

Q. Place the tops of the fore-finger and thumb together; curve the fore-finger of the other hand, and place it on the inside of the fore-finger and thumb, precisely where they touch each other.

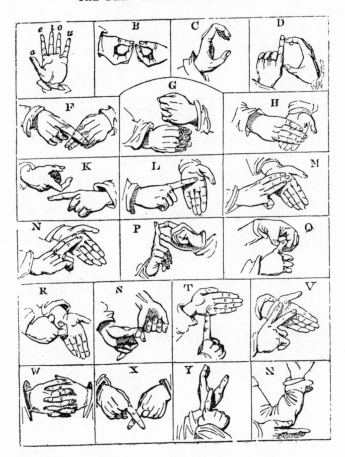

R. Curve the fore-finger of the right hand, and place it on the palm of the left.

S. Curve the little fingers of each hand, and hitch them together.

T. Place the top of the fore-finger of the right hand against the lower edge of the left hand, between the little finger and the wrist.

V. This letter is made nearly as *N,* with this difference only, that for *V,* the two fore-fingers of the right hand are placed apart, upon the palm of the left, instead of close together, as is the case for *N.*

W. Join the hands, with the fingers of one between those of the other.

X. Cross the two fore-fingers at the second joint.

Y. Place the fore-finger of the right hand between the thumb and fore-finger of the left, which must both be extended.

Z. Raise one hand toward the face, and place the palm of the other under the elbow of the arm which is so elevated.

It is usual to mark the conclusion of each word by snapping the middle finger and thumb of the right hand: this, it may readily be imagined, renders the dumb language much more intelligible.

Numbers are counted by the fingers in the most simple way; one finger held up, signifies 1; two fingers, 2; the open hand, 5; the two hands, 10, &c

Thus it will be perceived, that although many persons are by Nature deprived of speech, yet Art has so ameliorated their condition, as not to leave them altogether DUMB.

ARCHERY.

To save his own and Albert's life,
Tell is to shoot an apple from the head
Of his own child!

WILLIAM TELL

IN this island, Archery was greatly encouraged in former times, and many statutes were made for its regulation. The Artillery Company of London, though they have long disused the weapon, are the remains of the ancient fraternity of Bowmen or Archers. As to the time when shooting with the long bow first began amongst the English, there appears no certain account. Richard I, was killed by an arrow, in 1199; after this time, we read nothing of Archery, till that of Edward III. when an order was issued to the sheriffs of most of the English counties, to provide five hundred white bows, and five hundred bundles of arrows, for the then intended war against France. The famous battle of Cressy was fought four years afterward, in which, it is stated, that we had about two thousand archers, opposed to about the same number of French. In the fifth year of the reign of Edward IV. an act was passed, that every Englishman, and Irishman dwelling with Englishmen, should have an English bow of his own height, which is directed to be made of yew, wych, hazel, ash or awburne, or any other reasonable tree, according to their power. The next chapter also directed, that butts should be made in every township, which the inhabitants were obliged to shoot at, every feast day, under the penalty of one half-penny when they should omit this exercise. During the reign of Henry VIII. several statutes were made for the promotion of Archery. An act of parliament, in Elizabeth's reign, regulated the price of bows. Charles I. is said to have been an Archer; and, in the eighth year of his reign, he issued a commission to prevent the fields near London being so enclosed as " to interrupt the necessary and profitable exercise of shooting." So lately as the year 1753, targets were erected in the Finsbury fields, during the Easter and Whitsuntide holydays, when the best shooter was styled " Captain " for the ensuing year, and the second, " Lieutenant." Edward VI, in his journal, says, that one hundred Archers of his guard shot, before him, two arrows each, and afterward, altogether; and that they shot at an inch board, which some pierced quite through with the heads of their arrows, the board being well seasoned timber. The distance of the mark is not mentioned. As a pastime there is none, perhaps, superior to this; it is now, and for years past has been, highly popular in this country; in fact, judging from the past and the present, we may venture to predict that

> The Archer's sport will never be extinct,
> Until the memory of Robin Hood,
> Of Cressy's well-fought field, and Chevy-Chase,
> Be blotted from the tablet of our minds.

THE BOW,

The young archer should, in the first place, select a bow, that is fit and proper for his own size and strength. It is not probable that, let him be ever so skilful, he will be able to achieve such an exploit, as the construction of a good bow himself; bow-making being a trade which requires many years' practice and much attention; in fact, there are few persons, now-a-days, although there are many bowyers, who can manufacture bows of a superior description.

The back of the bow is the flat outside, and the belly the round inside part of it. The round inside part is bent inward; if the bow be pulled the reverse way, it will break; therefore, however a bow may be bent when unstrung, it is invariably to be strung with the round part inward.

ARROWS.

Arrows should be delicately proportioned in length and weight to the bow for which they are intended. They are used blunt or sharp, and varying in their thickness according to the fancy of the Archer. Some are made so as to taper gradually from the feathers to the pile, and some *viceversa ;* others again are thickest in the centre. All arrows should have their nocks or notches cased with horn, and the nocks should be of such a size as to fit the string with exactness, and be neither too tight nor too loose. Three goose or turkey feathers are affixed to arrows; one of these, denominated the cock feather, is of a different color from the other two, and this is always to be placed uppermost.

THE STRING.

That part of the string which receives the nock of the arrow is whipped with sewing silk, to prevent the string being rubbed and weakened. If the silk should come off the string, it ought to be re-whipped without delay; otherwise, it will be in danger of breaking; and this is not the only mischief, for from the breaking of a string oftentimes ensues the snapping of the bow. It is also advisable to whip the noose and eye of the string, although many archers do not trouble themselves to do so. At one end of the bow-string an eye is made; it is left for the archer himself, bows being of different lengths, to make the other : this, to a young archer, will be found rather difficult; his best plan will be to inspect the mode of making the noose on an old string. The young archer will do well, if any of the threads of his string break, to throw it by and use another. He should never, if possible, permit the string to become twisted or ravelled; should such an occurrence take place, before it is put on again it ought to be re-twisted and waxed. A bow, five feet long when braced, should never have the string more than five inches from its centre. This rule will be a guide to the young archer in stringing his bow; whatever be its length he will of course adjust the distance in the same proportion, according to the admeasurement.

THE TASSEL.

This is very necessary to the archer for the purpose of cleaning the arrow from such dirt as generally adheres to it if it enter the ground. This dirt, if suffered to remain, will impede the arrow in its flight, and also render its course untrue. The tassel is suspended on the left side of the archer, and is thus always at hand for use.

THE GLOVE.

The glove consists of places for three fingers, a back thong and a wrist strap to fasten it. The finger-stalls should neither project far over the tops, nor be drawn back to cover the first joint.   The glove is used for the purpose of protecting the fingers from being hurt by the string.

THE BRACE.

The brace is worn on the bow arm to save it from being injured by the string, which, without this protection, would, in all probability, incapacitate the archer from shooting long at a time.   It is made of stout leather, with a very smooth surface, so that the string may glide over it without impediment.

THE QUIVER.

The quiver is for the reception of the arrows, but is never constantly worn except in roving; it is now usually made of tin, although it is occasionally constructed, as was indeed universally the case formerly, of wood or leather.

THE BELT, POUCH, AND GREASE-BOX.

The belt is buckled round the waist; the grease-box is suspended from the middle, and the pouch or bucket on the right side of it.   A composition for greasing the finger of the shooting-glove, and the smooth side of the brace, when occasion may require, is kept in the box : the pouch holds the arrows for immediate use in target shooting.

THE ASCHAM.

This is a large case fitted up with the necessary drawers and compartments for the reception of the bow, stock of arrows, strings, and all the necessary accoutrements of the archer.

BUTTS.

The butt is rather pyramidical in shape, generally speaking, but it may be fashioned according to the fancy of the archer ; for grown up persons, they are seven or eight feet wide, three or four feet thick at the base, and nearly seven feet in height at the middle.   Butts are made of long plats of turf which are to be closely pressed down ; a round piece of pasteboard is placed in the centre of the butt for a mark, which must be increased or decreased in size according to the distance at which the archer shoots : for thirty yards, it should be four inches in diameter; for sixty yards, six inches; and so in proportion for a greater distance.   The mark is fixed to the butt by a peg driven through its centre.   Shots that take place outside the mark are not reckoned, and he who places most shots in the pasteboard during the play is accounted the winner.   Butts are frequently placed at different distances from each other ; a set of butts is four, which are so contrived as not to prevent the players seeing them all at once.   What is called a single end is shooting at one mark only ; a double end is shooting to a mark, and back again from that mark to the one first shot from.

TARGETS.

Targets should be proportioned to the size and skill of the juvenile archer, and to the distance at which he stands from them. The facing is usually made of canvass which is sewn on the bass; the bass is made of straw, worked as a bee-hive. The facing has a gold centre and four circles; namely, the outer white edged with green, the black inner, white and red. Where it is not convenient to keep the targets fixed, it is better to use another kind, made of pasteboard, these being more portable, although by no means so durable, as targets made of the other materials we have mentioned. If one target only be shot at, a great deal of time is wasted in going to fetch the arrows, and again returning to the spot for shooting from : two targets are, therefore, generally used, and the archers shoot from one to the other. In Archery matches, there are generally two prizes ; one for the greatest number of arrows shot into the target,—the other for the shot nearest the gold centre. Hits in the target are sometimes reckoned all alike ; but there is usually a distinction made. The gold centre is the mark, and the circle which approaches nearest to it, being less in size, and consequently, more difficult to hit, and nearer the main mark itself, an arrow shot in that circle is deemed of more value, in reckoning for the prize, than if it were to take place in any of those outside it, and so in proportion with the others. A celebrated society of Archery allows the following numbers for each circle. For the gold, nine ; for the red, seven ; for the inner white, five ; for the black, three ; and for the outer white, one. A writer on this subject, however, seems to think, that the outer circles are overrated, and if nine be allowed for the centre, only three should be scored for the red ; two for the inner white ; and less, in proportion for the two outer circles. When the sport terminates, the value of the number of hits, and not the hits themselves, should be reckoned ; and he whose score is the largest, is, of course, the victor.

As ink is by no means a convenient thing to carry into the field, and marks made with the black-lead pencil are liable to be rubbed out, it is advisable to have a pin suspended from a card, properly divided for each archer's score, and to prick down the hits with it.

STRINGING THE BOW.

The bow is to be taken in the right hand, by the handle, with the flat part toward the person who is about to string it ; his right arm should rest against his side ; the lower end of the bow, which has always the shortest bone, should be placed against the inside of the right foot, which should be turned a little inward to prevent the bow from slipping ; the left foot should at the same time be brought forward ; the centre of the left hand wrist must be placed on the upper limb of the bow below the eye of the string, the forefinger knuckle upon one edge of the bow, and the top of the thumb on the other. The bow is now to be pulled up vigorously, and the upper limb of it pressed down by the right hand, and the wrist of the left which should at the same time slide upward until the eye of the bowstring is safely placed in the nock. The middle, the ring and the little fingers, should all three be stretched out, as they are not wanted in this operation of stringing the bow; moreover, if this be not done, they are liable to be caught between the string and the bow, and thus become severely punished. The young archer should take care that the eye is well placed in the nock before he removes his left hand. He should not become impatient in the action of stringing the bow, but perform it systematically as directed; if he do not succeed, let him lay it by for a few minutes, and when he is cool make a second attempt. To unstring the bow, the short horn is to be placed on the ground; the palm of the left hand receiving the flat side of the upper limb; the string should be upward; the handle is then to be pressed with the right arm so as to slacken the string; when the latter becomes loose enough, the eye is to be brought out of the nock, by the thumb of the left hand.

POSITION.

The face is to be turned toward the mark, but no part of the body, which, if the mark be north, should be turned toward the east; the head

should be rather inclined; the left hand, with the bow in it in a perpendicular position, is to be held out straight toward the mark; the arrow is to be brought well toward the ear and not the eye, on the left side of the bow and under the string; the forefinger of the left hand passes over it; by the other hand the nock is placed in the string at the proper place, with the cock feather uppermost; when this is done, the forefinger of the left hand is removed and placed round the bow. While the left hand is raising the bow, the right should be drawing the string with two or three fingers only and not the thumb; as soon as it reaches the head it should be let loose, for fear of its breaking.

Great care should be taken to acquire a proper position, as represented in the marginal cut, for bad attitudes in Archery appear extremely ridiculous.

FLIGHT-SHOOTING.

Flight-shooting was at one time much more frequently practised with the long bow than it is at present. The object in flight-shooting is simply to ascertain which of a party can shoot to the greatest distance; this must of course, be very detrimental to bows, which are more frequently snapped in flight-shooting than at any other pastime with the long bow. No skill in aiming is requisite in flight-shooting; it is, therefore, by no means improving to the young Archer, who wishes to excel as a marksman. The longest and lightest arrows that the bow will bear are used in flight-shooting; the game is generally seven.

CLOUT-SHOOTING.

Clout-shooting is mostly practised by those who cannot conveniently set up butts or targets near home. The clout, which is quite portable, is made of a round piece of pasteboard, thirty-six inches in circumference, fastened to a stick; or it may be made of white cloth, so contrived as to roll up on a stick which is run through it. In clout-shooting, seven is the game, and all arrows tell that fall within three bows' length of the clout.

ROVING.

This is a very pleasant pastime with the long bow; and is, indeed, by some, preferred even to target-shooting. The parties are not restricted to any particular place, but rove about from field to field for miles around, if they think fit. The mark is any clear and conspicuous object, such as a tree or a bush. The number of the game is, in general, as in flight and clout-shooting, seven; but it may be increased or decreased, according to the inclination of the parties. If there be more than six persons in a roving party, they should divide themselves into companies; and when the first company have shot to, and walked some distance from, the first mark, the second should shoot at it: and so on with those that follow. Arrows that reach within five bows' length of the mark tell; but those which reach nearest cut the others out. In measuring the distance, the Archer does so with his own bow, from a spot in the mark which is one foot from the ground; and the first arrow is the one that is nearest, not to the mark, but to that point or spot of the mark. The Archer may measure to what part of his arrow he pleases. He who shoots nearest has the privilege of indicating the next mark. It is better to use blunt-headed arrows in Roving than sharp ones; as it not unfrequently happens that the latter are driven so firmly into the mark as to make it a matter of difficulty to extract them: should this occur, it is advisable to cut away the wood around the arrow, rather than endeavour to tug it out by violence. Every Rover should carry at least a dozen arrows with him, in order to be prepared against accidents.

D

CONCLUDING REMARKS.

We strongly recommend the young Archer never to shoot with another person's bow; he may, very probably, break it; and in that case, a loss might ensue to the owner, which money could not remedy. When the grass is above the ankle, shoot only at a considerable elevation. After two or three arrows are shot, the Archer should cease awhile, otherwise his aim will get unsteady. If he shoot point-blank at a mark, the arrow, if it miss, will strike along, and so bury itself in the grass, as to defy the keenest eye, in many instances, for a very considerable time, to discover it. This inconvenience may be remedied by shooting at a proper elevation, for then the arrow will descend in such a manner as to leave the feathers visible; they will also be saved, from that injury which frequently occurs to them, by the moisture of the grass, or ground, when shot point-blank. Arrows should not be used of different lengths, nor should the young Archer shoot alone; for in solitary shooting, he falls into habits of negligence and indifference; if he practice with others, he will strive to emulate his companions; and, instead of a careless, unskilful marksman, soon become an adept in the pleasant pastime of ARCHERY.

CRICKET.

The youthful Yeomanry are in the field,—
Their tents are pitched, and every heart beats high
To join the friendly strife :—their stoutest forts
Are slender wickets ;—all their entrenchments,
A popping and a bowling-crease ; their weapons,
Bats ;—their ammunition, a brace of balls,
In leathern and tight-fitting jerkins clad.

This truly English pastime, although long a favorite with the people of this country, never reached to a greater degree of popularity than it possesses at this time. It is a favorite with the peer and the peasant,— the Socior Societatis Artium and the school-boy.. Royalty has heretofore stood bat in hand at the popping-crease, surrounded by those youthful buds of nobility of which our nation has since been proud ; and, strange though it may seem, yet it is no less strange than true,—young matrons have played matches of Cricket against maidens, without impeachment to their usual reputation, and having husbands, brothers, and sweethearts for their spectators. In many counties, Cricket is the universal pastime of the people ; in others, it is rarely played, and in many, scarcely mentioned. The man of Devon, who deems all sports inferior to wrestling, and the inhabitant of Somerset, who doats upon the manly game of back-sword, seldom bestow a thought upon Cricket ; it is, nevertheless, esteemed and enjoyed by the people of other counties, especially those about the metropolis, as a sport paramount, and practised in so great a degree, as nearly to exclude all other manly field recreations of a similar nature.

Cricket is usually played by eleven persons on each side, though a less number is sufficient. Two umpires are to be appointed in order to settle all disputes that may arise; they are to take their stations at each wicket, and should be well acquainted with the laws of the game. The umpire at the striker's wicket should be rather behind it, so as not to be in the way of the players; and the umpire at the bowler's wicket, directly behind it, to see that the striker does not strike the ball with his leg.

BATS, BALLS, WICKETS, &c.

The bat should not be higher than twenty-one inches in the pod, and four inches and a quarter in the widest part; this is the size for men; boys must, of course, have bats in proportion to their size and strength.

The ball, for the use of men, should weigh about five ounces; for youth, however, it should be lighter.

Full-sized wickets are three stumps, which are sufficiently long to leave twenty-four inches out of the ground, with a bail, seven inches long, to fit the top. These, like the bat and ball, must be decreased in size for the young cricketer. They should be placed directly opposite to each other, at the distance of twenty-two yards for men, but varying according to the size of the player.

The bowling-crease should be in a line with the wicket, and have a return crease.

The popping-crease should be three or four feet from the wicket, and exactly parallel with it.

THE BOWLER.

Bowling is a very important part of the game, and requires great steadiness. Bad bowling is often the cause of losing a game. A bowler should not be too systematic, but vary his balls faster or slower, according to the peculiarities of the striker. The bowler and his partner at the opposite wicket should have a secret sign, by which they may hint to each other the propriety of varying the direction or swiftness of the balls. The mode of bowling most generally approved of, is to hold the ball with the seam across, so that the tips of the fingers may touch; it should be held with just a sufficient grasp to keep it steady; by a turn of the wrist, it may be made to cut or twist after it is grounded, which will frequently perplex expert players.

THE STRIKER, OR BATSMAN.

The striker should always be ready for running; when his partner is about to strike, he should stand before the popping-crease, but he must be cautious not to leave the ground before the ball is out of the bowler's hand; for if he do, the bowler may put down his wicket, and he will, of course, be out. As soon as the ball is delivered, the striker may follow it, but should not run too far, so that, if no runs be obtained, he may return in time to save his wicket. The bat should be kept on the outside of the opposite partner, and care taken not to run against him.

THE WICKET-KEEPER.

The wicket-keeper should not suffer the striker to move from his ground without knocking down his wicket, which is called " stumping out."

THE FIRST SHORT-SLIP.

The first short-slip should stand so as to reach within two feet of the wicket-keeper; if the latter should go from the wicket after the ball, the first short-slip should take his place until his return; but no player should take the ball before the wicket-keeper, provided it be coming straight to him.

THE POINT.

The point should place himself in the popping-crease, about seven yards from the striker. In backing up, he should take care to give the slip sufficient room.

LEG, OR SLIP.

Leg, or slip, should stand a little back from the straight line of the popping-crease.

LONG-STOP.

Long-stop should stand a proper distance behind the wicket, to save a run, if the ball should not be stopped by the striker or wicket-keeper. The person who is placed in this situation, should not be afraid of the ball when bowled swift. He should also be able to throw in well, as it is not only to the balls that pass the wicket-keeper, but to such as are just tipped with the edge of the bat, that he will have to attend. He must also be attentive in backing up.

THE LONG-SLIP TO COVER THE SHORT-SLIP.

This player must stand about the same distance from the wicket as the long-stop, in a line with the striker, between the point and the short-slip.

TO COVER THE POINT AND MIDDLE-WICKET.

This player's place is on the off side, so that if the ball should be hit to the point and middle-wicket man, and missed, he will be in readiness to receive it.

THE LONG-SLIP OFF SIDE.

He should be placed on the off side, between the middle wicket-man and the bowler, at a considerable distance in the field, so as to cover them. It is desirable to appoint a person to this situation, who can throw well and judiciously.

LONG-FIELD ON SIDE.

Long-field on side is at some distance wide of the bowler's wicket, so as to prevent a second run.

If there be more players, they may be placed to back up, or save runs, in different situations about the field.

LAWS OF CRICKET.

The bowler should deliver the ball with one foot behind the bowling crease, and within the return crease. He should bowl four balls before a change of wickets, which he is to do but once in the same innings. He must be careful to toss the ball in such a way that the striker can play at it; for if he should toss it above the striker's head, or out of the bounds of the bowling-crease, the party which is in shall be allowed one notch, to be put down to the byes; and such ball is not considered as one of the four balls. When the umpire calls " In ball," the hitter may strike at it, and get all the runs he can. When an exchange of bowler takes place, no more than two balls can be allowed for practice. If the arm be extended straight from the body, or the back part of the hand be uppermost when the ball is delivered, the umpire shall immediately call " No ball."

The striker, or batsman, is always out when the bail is knocked off the stump; when a stump is bowled out of the ground; or, if the ball should, from a stroke over or under his bat, or upon his hands, (but not his wrists,) be held before it touches the ground, even if it should be pressed to the body of the catcher; or if, while he is striking, or at any other time when the ball is in play, both his feet are over the popping-crease, and his wicket put down, except when his bat be on the ground within it. Likewise, if he hit down his own wicket; or, if either of the strikers prevent a ball from being caught, the striker shall be out; or, if the ball be struck up, and the hitter wilfully strike it again; or if, in attempting to run a notch, the wicket be struck down by a throw, or with the ball in hand, before his foot, hand, or bat is grounded over the popping-crease: If the striker remove or take up his ball while in play, without being requested by the opposite party; or if, with his leg or foot, he stop a ball which has been pitched in a straight line to the striker's wicket. If "A lost ball" be called, the striker shall be allowed four notches. If the players have crossed each other in running, he that runs for the wicket which is put down, shall be out; but if they have not crossed each other, he that has left the wicket which is put down, shall be out.

When a ball is caught, no notch shall be reckoned. When a striker is run out, the notch they were running for shall not be reckoned. While the ball is kept in the bowler's or wicket-keeper's hand, it is considered no longer in play, nor are the strikers bound to keep within their bounds, till the umpire has called " Play ;" but if a player should go out of his ground, with intent to run, before the ball is delivered, the bowler may put him out. If a striker be hurt by a ball, or otherwise, during his play, he may retire from his wicket and continue his inning; and another person may be permitted to stand out for him, but not go in. If any player should stop the ball intentionally with his bat, it shall then be considered dead, and the opposite party may add five notches to the score.

If the ball be struck up, the striker may guard his wicket either with his bat or his body. If the striker hit the ball against the wicket of his partner when he is off his ground, he is out, if it have previously touched the bowler's or any of the field-men's hands, but not otherwise.

Two minutes are allowed for each man to come in, and fifteen minutes between each innings; when upon the umpires calling " Play," the party refusing to play, shall lose the match.

The umpire should observe the situation of the bowler's foot when he delivers the ball, and if it be not behind the bowling-crease, and within the return-crease, he shall call " No ball." If the striker should run a notch, the umpire shall call " No notch." The umpire at the bowler's wicket has a right to be first applied to for his decision on the catches.

SINGLE WICKET.

The game of Single Wicket is not so interesting as that of Double Wicket; but it may be played by almost any number of persons, though it is seldom played with more than four or six on a side. The business of a bowler and striker is nearly the same as in Double Wicket.

When the striker runs to the bowler's wicket, and knocks the bail from off two stumps placed there, with his bat, and returns to his own wicket without having it knocked down by the ball, he is entitled to count one notch. After he has run one notch, if he start for another, he must touch the bowling-stump, and turn again, before the ball crosses the play, to entitle him to another notch. He is entitled to three notches for a lost ball.

If four, or a less number are at play, then they should make all hits before the wicket, with bounds, &c. and not move off the ground, except by agreement. Where there are more than four players on a side, there should be no bounds; and all hits, byes, and overthrows, should be allowed. It is, of course, to be understood, that the bowler must bowl at the usual distance from the wicket. No more than one minute is to be allowed between each ball. When the striker hits the ball, one of his feet must be on the ground, and behind the popping-crease; otherwise the umpire shall call "No hit." The field's-man must return the ball, so that it shall cross the play between the wicket and the bowling-stump; or between the wicket and the bounds; the striker may run till the ball shall be so returned. These are the principal rules and regulations adopted by the most experienced Cricket-players, at the game of Single Wicket. The distance between the wickets is precisely the same as at Double Wicket, consequently, the runner has twice the ground to run, in obtaining each notch; but we would suggest, that this evil might be remedied by running only a little more than half the usual distance: by this method, Single Wicket will be rendered much less fatiguing, and far more lively and amusing, at least to the BATSMAN.

GYMNASTICS.

Enroll'd among our Gymnasts, the pale youth
Whose limbs, erewhile, weak and of muscle void,
Totter'd beneath their puny load, soon gains
The bloom of health ; and issues forth, at last,
Robust and hardy as the mountaineer.

GYMNASTIC Exercises have lately attained considerable popularity, not
only in this country, but also in Prussia, and other parts of the Continent.
They may be said to be a series of regular and systematic exercises, adapted
to bring into play, and consequently improve, the strength and activity of
the various muscles in the human frame : imparting a knowledge of the
proper use of each, and teaching the pupil the means of disposing of his
natural powers to the best advantage. They are also calculated to inspire
him with confidence in a moment of danger, and to enable him to extricate
himself, as well as others, from peril, by his increased bodily agility, and
the experience he has acquired, as to the most advantageous mode of its
application. A cotemporary writer on this subject makes the following observations in support of the assertion that Gymnastic Exercises confer
courage and presence of mind. "Courage is generated by confidence, and
confidence is acquired by practice. A hazardous undertaking which we

have often achieved, ceases to be considered as any further dangerous than affording us an occasion to call forth all our energies. The well-taught Gymnast would, in a case of necessity, take a leap which few could perform, if any would venture. Leaps of great distances and heights he has often attempted with success. By him the length, the height, and the intervening obstacles could be measured in a moment. Rehearsals of such situations and circumstances have been his daily amusement. He cannot be dismayed at danger who has often played with it, and the principles of his art have supplied him with means to disarm it of half its power. To illustrate the foregoing remarks, we shall here relate what we consider an instance of the coolness, accuracy, and presence of mind to be acquired by daily practice. Walking out one day near the city of Edinburgh, our attention was attracted to a field where the Royal Company of Archers were practising. A man, hired for the purpose, and trained to the duty, was stationed at the target, with a small flag in his hand to mark the spot where the arrows fell, the distance being very considerable. It is incredible with what accurate perception this man followed the arrow in its rapid passage along the arch it made in the sky; and with what accuracy he seemed to conjecture how near the target, or on what side it would fall. He stood close to the target, almost touching it with his right arm; one arrow flew through the air; he narrowly observed the feathered messenger advancing rapidly in its course—he stepped one step to the left, and the arrow stuck firmly in the ground a few inches to his right, betwixt him and the target. He waved his flag to the spot, and a second arrow was sent; from this he escaped by darting a little to the right. To save himself from the third, he had no occasion to move from his station, as he coolly saw it deposited in the lower part of the target. It is needless to detail the rest. The arrows stuck before, behind, and on each side of him. The exercise at last concluded; and it seemed no less surprising to us, the insensibility of danger which this man, for the sake of a little gain, exhibited, than the confidence which his employers doubtless had in the acuteness of his perception."

The same writer elsewhere observes that " the ancients, particularly the free states of Greece, cultivated the study of Gymnastics as an important oranch of the education of youth. Having frequently to defend their liberties, either against the encroachments of kindred states, or the ambition of powerful foreign enemies, they considered it highly necessary to inure their youth to hardy and even violent exercise, that their minds might not be daunted in the hour of danger, nor their bodies sink under the necessary fatigues of warfare."

GYMNASTIC EXERCISES.

THE necessary fittings-up of a Gymnastic ground are as follows :—An horizontal bar, a vaulting-horse, a leaping-stand, parallel bars, a climbing-stand, and ladders of rope and wood.

The best time for performing Gymnastics is early in the morning. Boys should proceed gradually from the more easy to the more difficult exercises ; and it is most advisable to practise these sports under the eye of an experienced person. Where there is a number of boys, they should be divided into classes, according to their strength. It is advisable to carry no toys in the pockets when practising ; extra clothes should be put on when the exercises are finished ; and the usual precautions adopted to prevent taking cold.

The following observations, which are principally from Salzmann, may be perused with advantage. No person in health is injured by being over-heated ; but drinking when extremely hot, or being cooled too quickly, in whatever manner it happens may prove highly pernicious. It is proper, therefore to take off whatever clothing can be decently spared, before begin-ning to exercise, and put it on again immediately after. Lying down upon the cold ground, too, must not be allowed. On commencing any exercise, begin, not with its more violent degrees, but with the more gentle, and leave off in the same manner ; sudden transitions are always danger-ous.   Never let bodily exertion, or your attempts to harden the frame, be carried to excess : let your object be to strengthen the feeble body, not to exhaust and render it languid.   In all exercises, attention should be paid to such a position of all the parts of the body, that none may be exposed to injury : for example, the tongue must never be suffered to remain be-tween the teeth.   The left hand and arm are commonly weaker than the right ; let them be frequently exercised, therefore, by lifting, carrying, and supporting the weight of the body by suspension, till they become as strong as the others.

Although walking, running, dancing, balancing, vaulting, climbing, jumping, wrestling, riding, swimming, and all other muscular exercises, may be included in the term Gymnastics, the common course adopted at the schools includes only walking, running, jumping, vaulting, balancing, and climbing.

WALKING.

In walking, the arms should move freely by the side, the head be kept up, the stomach in, the shoulders back, the feet parallel with the ground, and the body resting neither on the toe nor heel, but on the ball of the foot. On starting, the pupil should rise one foot, keep the knee and instep straight, the toe bent downward.   When this foot reaches the ground, the same should be repeated with the other.   This should be practised until the pupil walks firmly and gracefully.

RUNNING.

In running, the legs should not be raised too high ; the arms should be nearly still, so that no unnecessary opposition be given to the air by useless motions.   Running in a circle is excellent exercise, but the direc-tion should be occasionally changed, so that both sides may be equally worked.

JUMPING.

The first rule in jumping is, to fall on the toes and never on the heels. Bend the knees, that the calves of the legs may touch the thighs.   Swing the arms forward when taking a spring, break the fall with the hands, if necessary ; hold the breath, keep the body forward, come to the ground with both feet together, and in taking the run, let your steps be short, and in-crease in quickness as you approach the leap.   Begin with a moderate height or breadth, and increase both as you improve.

PARALLEL BARS.

Begin by raising the body by the hands, and then moving the hands alternately backward and forward, until you go along the bars each way

by means only of your hands. Then move or jump with both hands at once. The swing is performed by supporting the body by the arms, with the stomach upward, until the toes are in a straight line with the head; when the pupil can do this with ease, he should throw his body from this position over the bar to the right or left. The movement of lowering the body by bending the elbows is done by drawing up the feet toward the hams, and sinking gradually until the elbows are even with the head; rise again by straightening the arms, and repeat the exercise several times. Many other exercises may be performed on these bars, which will occur to the pupil in the course of his practice.

HORIZONTAL BAR.

The first position is taking hold of the bar with both hands, and raising the body until the chin is on a line with the knuckles. When you can look over the bar in this manner with ease, place the hands on the further

side of the bar from you, and raise the body as before. In the next exercise, the body is raised from the ground by both hands on each side of the bar, and the pupil passes, springs, or moves the hands alternately along the bar. Keep the legs close, lift the feet so as to touch the bar and sink them down again; repeat this several times, and when in this position, pass along the bar by alternately moving the hands; the body may then be supported by the right arm and left leg, and afterward by the left arm and right leg; you may then place yourself in a riding position on the bar. You may also swing with the head downward, take the bar with both hands, and pass the feet between them, until they hang downward; you may either return them the same way, or drop upon your toes to the ground.

THE LONG LEAP.

Make a trench, which widens gradually from one end to the other, so that the breadth of the leap may be increased daily. Keep the feet close together, and take your spring from the toes of one foot, which should be quickly drawn up to the other, and they should descend at the same instant; throw the arms and body forward, especially in descending. Take a run of about twenty paces.

THE DEEP LEAP.

This is performed from a flight of steps, increasing the depth according to the progress of the pupil. The body should be bent forward, the feet close together, and the hands ready to touch the ground at the same time with or rather before the feet. We do not, however, much approve of this exercise.

THE HIGH LEAP.

Get a stand made of two upright posts, bored through with holes, through which you may pass a string at what length you please, with

sand bags of sufficient weight to keep it straight, and yet not so heavy as to prevent your carrying it away with your foot, in case you touch it while leaping; or you may have holes bored to admit movable pegs to support the string, as in the cut. You must take this leap both standing and with a run; for the former, the legs should be kept together, and the feet and knees raised in a straight direction; for the latter, we recommend a short run, and a light tripping step, gradually quickened as the leaper approaches the string. You should be particularly careful not to alight on your heels, but rather on the toes and balls of the feet.

THE HIGH LEAP WITH THE POLE.

Take the pole with the right hand about the height of the head, and with the left about the height of the hips; when put to the ground, spring with the right foot, and pass by the left of the pole, over whatever you have to clear, turning round as you alight, so as to front the place you leap from.

THE DEEP LEAP WITH THE POLE.

This requires strength in the arms and hands. Place the pole the depth you have to leap, lower the body forward, cast off your feet and swing round the pole so as to alight with your face fronting the point you leaped from. Come to the ground, if possible, on the balls of your feet.

THE LONG LEAP WITH THE POLE.

This is performed precisely as the last, only that you spring forward, rather than high; it may be practised across the trench.

VAULTING.

The horse for vaulting is made of a wooden cylinder with rounded ends; two ridges are placed across it, the space between which is called the saddle, and should be wide enough apart for a person to sit between them with ease. The horse may be wadded or not, according to fancy. Leaping on the horse is performed by springing by the hands astride upon it. The body is raised in the same manner, until the feet reach high enough to stand on the horse; the hands are then to be placed on the further ridge, and the body thrown forward into the saddle.

Vaulting into the saddle may be performed with or without a run; place

the hands on one of the ridges, take a spring, and turn the body on one side, so that one leg may pass over the horse, and the performer descend astride into the saddle. To vault sideways over the horse, the hands must be placed as above, and a spring made sufficient to throw the feet over the horse; one hand then leaves its hold, and you descend on the other side. To vault on or over the saddle forward, take hold of each ridge with the hands, and spring between them, so as to rest or to go over the saddle.

TO CLIMB THE ROPE.

In climbing the rope the hands are to be moved alternately, one above the other, the feet drawn up between every movement of the hands, and the rope grasped firmly between them; in descending, move one hand after the other, as the friction, if you slide, would blister them. The best method to climb the slant rope is to lay the sole of one foot flat on the rope, and the other leg over the instep of that foot.

THE PLANK.

The breadth of the plank should be about two feet; its thickness, two inches; to climb it, the hands are to be placed on each side, and the feet  on its surface; ascend by moving them alternately. Elevate the plank by degrees as you improve in the exercise. The progress that may be made in the ascension of the plank is astonishing. We know several Gymnasts who can ascend a plank in a perpendicular position, without difficulty. To do this, the body and feet are in a different position to that represented in the marginal cut, where the figure is merely travelling up an inclined plane; to ascend a perpendicular plank, the body is curved inward more from the shoulders downward, and the legs thrust up so that the higher one is nearly even with the hand.

ASCENDING THE LADDER.

Take hold of each side of the ladder, and ascend by moving the hands alternately. To climb the ladder by rundels, the learner must bring the elbow of the arm which happens to be the lowest, down to the ribs, before he pulls himself up by the other. To climb the ladder by one side, take hold of one side of the ladder with both hands, the palms toward the outer part of the side; move the hands alternately, and keep the legs close and steady.

TO CLIMB THE PERPENDICULAR OR SLANT POLE.

Move the legs and hands alternately, taking care, however, not to place the hands over each other, as in climbing the rope. In descending the pole, the hands are held ready to be used, if necessary, on each side of it; the legs being then a little slackened, you will descend with great ease.

FLYING STEPS.

This is a very beneficial exercise. Fix a beam firmly in the ground, with a strong iron cap, that moves in a circular horizontal position, at the top of it; four ropes are to be fixed to the cap, and bars of wood fastened at the bottom of the ropes, which are to be taken hold of, and the pupils vault round, bearing the weight on the rope, and continually increasing in speed until they touch the ground only at intervals with their toes. (*Vide* cut at the commencement of Gymnastic Exercises.)

GYMNASTIC RECREATIONS.

THE following Recreations of skill and agility, will, we have no doubt, prove highly attractive to our youthful readers; they are, with two or three exceptions, entirely distinct from the usual Gymnastic Exercises; and will be found, on account of their being less formal, more amusing, perhaps, than the preceding ones.

STEPPING THROUGH YOUR OWN FINGERS.

Get a bit of wood, or half of a tobacco-pipe, hold it between the two fore-fingers of each hand, and, without letting it go, after a little practice, you may leap over it, forward and backward, without difficulty: when perfect in this, you may, as the writer of this has frequently done, place the tops of the two middle fingers together, and leap over them both ways, without either separating or touching them with the feet. It is impossible to per-form this trick with high-heeled shoes; and, in fact, the great difficulty consists in clearing the heels.

THE TRIUMPH.

Place the palms of the hands together, behind you, with the fingers down-ward, and the thumbs nearest the back; then, still keeping as much as pos-sible of the palms together, and, at least, the fingers of one hand touching those of the other, turn the hands, by keeping the tops of the fingers close to the back, until the ends are between the shoulders, with the palms together, the thumbs outward, and the tops of the fingers toward the head. This is a very difficult feat, and well deserves its title.

E

THE JAVELIN.

This is a capital Gymnastic Recreation. Get a heavy pole, shod at one end with iron, or a spike, if you think proper; elevate it with the other

hand to the height of the ear, and cast it at a target. At some of the Gymnastic schools, the pupils are taught to cast the pole with their fingers, as they would a reed; this is a bad practice,—the spear should be grasped with the whole hand, the but-end of it coming out between the fore-finger and thumb, and the front or shod part projecting from the little finger, which ought to encircle it as much as its thickness will permit; poise it accurately, and take your aim deliberately before you cast it. When you cast, throw your arm back as far as possible, and deliver the pole with all your force.

DOT AND CARRY TWO.

The person who is to perform this exploit, (whom we shall designate as No. 1,) stands between two others, (whom we shall call Nos. 2 and 3;) he then stoops down and passes his right hand behind the left thigh of No. 2, whose hand he grasps; and his left hand behind the right thigh of No. 3, whose left hand he grasps. Nos. 2 and 3 then pass each one arm round the neck and shoulders of No. 1, and when in this position, No. 1, by raising himself gradually from his stooping position, lifts the others from the ground.

PROSTRATE AND PERPENDICULAR.

Hold your arms on your breast, lie on your back and get up again, without making use of either your elbows or hands.

THE FLYING BOOK.

Place a book, or other convenient thing, between the two feet, in such a way that it is held between the ancles and the inner side of the feet; then kick up, backwards, with both feet, and throw the book over your head.

KNUCKLE DOWN,

An exercise of some difficulty, is performed by putting the toes against a chalk line, kneeling down and rising up again, without any assistance of the hands, or moving the toes from the chalk line.

THE LONG REACH.

A line is to be marked on the floor, to which both feet, or rather, the toes of both your feet are to be brought, and beyond which they must not pass.  One hand, either right or left, at option, is then to be thrown forward (without touching the floor in its passage) so far and no farther than you can spring back again from the horizontal position to the original upright position of the body, without disturbing the stated posture of the feet, or scraping the floor with the hand in the back-spring. The distance, at which different persons can thus spring back from the hand, will, of course, differ according to their length of arm, or their strength and activity.

When you have ascertained the distance at which you can recover without scraping the hand, or changing the original position of your feet, you must stretch forward as far as possible; and whilst your body is supported by the hand on the floor, chalk as far as possible with the other; after this, rise up from your hand and recover your original position, without touching the ground again with either hand. There is great scope for skill and activity in this feat, and there are persons not exceeding five feet, or five feet and a few inches, who will chalk considerably further than others six feet high. The great art is, to bring your body as near to the floor as possible; for which purpose, it is recommended, (and allowable,) to move the feet backward from the line of demarcation, as far as you can, which will bring the body much lower than it is in the figure, and enable you to chalk, at least, the full length of yourself, which is considered pretty good chalking, although there are persons who will exceed the distance very considerably. Those who perform this trick the best, contrive, when on the stretch, that the body may rest upon the elbow.

CHAIRING THE LEG.

Place the left foot on the lower back rail of a chair, then pass your right leg over the back of the chair, and bring it to the floor between the chair and your left leg. This is to be done without touching the chair with your hand.

In doing this trick, the chair should not stand upon a slippery floor, as it may move from under you, and cause a fall; a heavy chair should also be selected, and great care taken while performing it.

E 2

THE TURN-OVER.

In performing this feat, it is necessary to take a run of half-a-dozen paces. The trick is to place the toe of the right foot against the wall,

about the height of the knee from the ground, and to throw the left leg over it, making an entire revolution, so that when your left leg reaches the ground, your back will be to the wall. The toe of the right foot is the point upon which you must turn; and it must not quit the wall during the performance of the exploit. To perform the turn-over appears to be a matter of considerable difficulty, at the first glance of the description; but it may be attempted by a lad of tolerable activity, who has made himself master of the instructions, without danger, and, in a short time, accomplished with facility. Ordinary care must, of course, be taken during the early attempts.

TRIAL OF THE THUMB.

This feat is very simple. Place the inside of the thumb against the edge of a table, and then move your feet backward as far as you can

from the table, so as to be able to recover your upright position by the spring of your thumb without moving your feet. You may accomplish this feat with much greater ease, if, previously to springing from the thumb, you make two or three bends to and fro with your body. Neither the fingers, nor any part of the hand, except the thumb, should touch the table. It is advisable to begin by making the spring with your feet at a short distance only from the table at first, and to draw them further from it gradually as you improve in the performance of the feat. The table from which you spring ought to be a heavy one, or the opposite end of it placed close against a wall, otherwise you may push it back when making your spring; in which case, a fall on the hands and knees would be almost inevitable.

THE PALM-SPRING.

A feat, which affords excellent exercise, something similar to the Thumb-trick, is performed by standing with your face toward a wall

and throwing yourself forward, until you support yourself from falling, by the palm of one of the hands being placed, with the fingers upward, against the wall; when in this position, you must recover your former erect station by springing from your hand, without bringing your feet forward. According to the greater or less distance you stand from the wall, the more or less difficult the feat will be. As in the feat of the Trial of the Thumb, it is better to begin the performance of the Palm-spring at a short distance only from the wall, at first; by practice, if you are active and resolute, you may, at last, rise with ease with your feet placed full two-thirds of your own height distant from the wall.

THE STOOPING STRETCH.

This feat, in which considerable agility may be acquired by practice, is performed in the following manner: draw a line on the floor, against

which place the outer edge of the right foot; at a moderate distance behind the right heel, place the left heel against the line. Take a piece of chalk in the right hand, stoop a little forward, pass the right hand between the legs immediately under the right knee, and chalk the floor as far beyond the line as you can, so that you can recover yourself without moving the toes of the feet, or touching the ground with either of your hands. In this case there is no spring from the hand, as the chalk only, which is held between the two fore-fingers, touches the floor. Your knee and body may project over the chalk-line, if your feet keep their proper place, as above directed, on the outer side of it,

TUMBLE-DOWN DICK.

This feat must be performed with a long-backed chair; place the knees on the extremity of the feet of the chair, in the position indicated by the  cut, and, with your two hands, take hold about the seat rail; bring your face down to touch the back of the chair, upon which, at the extremity, or as near as you can come without falling forward, or suffering the top of the chair to touch the floor, a piece of money, or &c. is placed, which is to be removed with the mouth. Much of the management in this trick depends upon properly regulating the position of the hands, which may be shifted as you find necessary, up or down the upright pieces which form the back of the chair. strong, old-fashioned kitchen chair is the best for this purpose.

THE FINGER-FEAT.

Your arms must be horizontally placed across the breast, and close to it; the fore-fingers of each hand must then be brought into contact. In this position another person must endeavour to separate your fingers by pulling at each arm. However much stronger he may be than you, he will not be able to detach your fingers, if you hold them properly. It must be agreed, previously, that the person who attempts to separate the fingers of the other shall not use a sudden jerk, but a regular force

TWO TO ONE.

With the skipping-rope several excellent exercises may be performed; the best, perhaps, is the following. Skip in the common way for a few seconds, constantly increasing your velocity of movement, and, at length, leap tolerably high, and whirl the rope round so fast that it may pass twice under your feet before they touch the ground; continue this until you can repeat it several times in succession, and, at last, pass the rope three times, instead of twice, under your feet during the leap.

LIFTING AT ARM'S LENGTH.

Elevating a pole at arm's length has long been accounted a superior feat; to do this, the arm must be stretched out at full length, the pole (the poker will do to begin with) grasped with the nails upward, and elevated in a right line with the arm.

LEAP BEFORE YOU LOOK.

Much care must be taken in this, as well as in " The Tumble-down Dick " feat, lest you hurt yourself.

Procure a chair that is strong, and, at the same time, so narrow in the back that you can bestride it with ease ; stand on the seat, push with your hands against the top rail, and your knees against the middle one, until you get it tilted on its back legs ; but before you lose your footing, leap from the seat, so as to alight on the ground, still holding the top rail in your hand, and the back of the chair between your legs. We repeat that great caution is necessary at first, but after a little practice, the feat is very easy. Without confidence in your own powers, it can never be performed ; to give you this necessary confidence, be assured that hundreds have succeeded in achieving it.

THE GREAT WOODEN BALL.

Casting the wooden ball is a very good recreation. A large wooden bowler, in which several holes are bored, is used for this purpose. Place your thumb in one of these holes, and your middle, or fore-finger, in another, and cast it, under-handed, either at a mark or for a distance. The common bowl used in skittle-alleys, (we do not mean those used for nine-pins,) will afford a pattern ; the maker must, however, remember that its dimensions are to be decreased, it being too heavy, and the finger-holes too far apart for the use of boys. It ought to be adapted in size, to the age of those persons for whose use it is intended.

THE TANTALUS TRICK.

An amusing scene may be produced by requesting a person to stand with his back close against the wall, and, when in this position, placing a piece of money on the ground, a short distance before him, and offering it to him if he can pick it up without moving his heels from the wall. This, he will find, is impossible, as, on stooping forward, a part of the body goes back beyond the heels, which, in this case, the wall will, of course, prevent.

TO TAKE A CHAIR FROM UNDER YOU WITHOUT FALLING.

The figure represents a youth with the back part of his head resting on one stout chair, and his heels upon another, and a third chair, which

ought to be of rather a lighter make, is placed under him. He must stiffen his body and limbs, throw up the chest, keep the shoulders down, and disengage the middle chair, which he must carry round over his body until he deposit it again under him on the opposite side. This is another of those feats which seem very difficult, but which are, in fact, easy of execution. Be assured that if you do not succeed in it, provided the middle chair be not too heavy for your strength, it is because you have not sufficiently attended to the instructions.

THE POKER PUZZLE.

This feat is to be performed with a common fire-poker, which you must hold near the top, between the fingers and thumb, as shown in the annexed cut. You must then, by the mere motion of the fingers and thumb, work or screw the poker upward, until the slender part is moved up to the hand, whilst the poker remains perpendicular during the whole process. For the first few times that this is attempted to be done, considerable difficulty will be met with, as it not only requires strength in the fingers, proportionate to the weight of the poker, but also a certain knack, which is only to be acquired by practice. We have seen some persons perform the poker puzzle, apparently without the least exertion, while others of equal strength have tried their utmost, and failed in the execution of it at last.

THE PULLEY.

Fasten a common pulley to a horizontal piece of wood, or the branch of a tree; run a cord through it, with a cross piece of wood at each end; two boys take hold of these cross pieces,—one lies on his back, and the other pulls him up, sinking himself as he raises his companion; he, in turn, is elevated in the same manner, and thus each sinks and is raised alternately.

BREAST TO MOUTH.

Many persons find much difficulty in performing this feat. Measure the distance between the outside of the elbow and the extremity of the  longest finger: mark that distance on a walking-stick or ruler, as shown by Fig. 2. This stick must be held horizontally before you, as in the annexed sketch, Fig. 1; the middle finger being placed exactly over the mark; the fingers must be kept at right angles with the stick, and the thumb placed over them, as shown by the fist grasping the stick. (Fig. 2.) Holding the stick in this position you must, without changing the place of your fingers, lowering your head, or removing your elbow from your side, endeavour to raise the left end of the stick from your breast to your mouth.

THE CATCH-PENNY.

This is a trick with which many of our young friends are, doubtless, well acquainted; there are others of them who never heard of it, and we  therefore give a sufficiently minute description of the manner of doing it, for the benefit of those who are in the latter case.

Place two, three, or even four penny pieces, in a heap, on your elbow, as in cut; drop your elbow suddenly, and bring your hand to a little below where your elbow was, and you may catch them all. It is impossible, however, to accomplish this, unless you bring your hand exactly beneath the place of your elbow, and perform the motion with quickness.

STILTS.

Walking on stilts is practised by the shepherds of the Landes, or desert, in the South of France. The habit is acquired early, and the smaller the

boy is, the longer it is necessary to have his stilts.   By means of these odd
additions to the natural leg, the feet are kept out of the water, which lies
deep during winter on the sands, and from the heated sand during the summer; in addition to which, the sphere of vision over so perfect a flat is materially increased by the elevation, and the shepherd can see his sheep much
further on stilts than he could from the ground.   Stilts are easily constructed: two poles are procured, and at some distance from their ends, a loop of
leather or rope is securely fastened; in these the feet are placed, the poles
are kept in a proper position by the hands, and put forward by the action of
the legs.   A superior mode of making stilts is by substituting a piece of wood,
flat on the upper surface, for the leather loop; the foot rests on and is fastened by a strap to it; a piece of leather or rope is also nailed to the stilt,
and passed round the leg just below the knee; stilts made in this manner
do not reach to the hands, but are managed entirely by the feet and legs.
In many parts of England, boys and youth frequently amuse themselves by

Walking on Stilts.

SWIMMING.

"This is the purest exercise of health,
The kind refresher of the summer heats."

THOMSON.

MAN, it is supposed, possesses all the requisite powers for swimming, and could traverse deep waters like other animals, were he not deprived of the use of such powers by fear, the effect of prejudice, precipitation or impatience. Courage has frequently enabled persons to swim at the first attempt, while excessive timidity has prevented others, for a long time, from being able to keep themselves, even for a few moments, afloat. Swimming has now become an art, and certain rules may be given for its attainment, by the aid of which, and a little practice, the most timid may eventually acquire the delightful power of "sporting in the silver flood." "In addition to its advantages as a healthy and bracing exercise, humanity alone, the pleasure of being not only able to preserve our own lives, but those of others, ought certainly to be sufficient inducement to acquire a dexterity in this most useful art. When it is considered that ours is a country having the ocean for its frontier, and that in the interior there is none in the world more abounding in rivers, brooks, lakes, and artificial canals; and when it is recollected that England is the first maritime nation in the world, it may seem surprising that such a proportionately small number of its inhabitants can swim. It might have been much more naturally inferred, that every inhabitant of our island felt almost as much at ease in the water as on dry ground. The upsetting of the slender boats of the natives of Otaheite, is to them a subject of merriment; they swim about, take hold of the light vessel, right her again, and paddle away, never considering they have been in any danger. Were the practice of swimming universal in this country, and it might be so, we should hardly ever read of deaths by drowning." It would be useless to enlarge further upon the advantages to be derived from acquiring this art; they must be evident to the most inexperienced.

Before we proceed to those rules by which our youthful readers may be enabled to attain proficiency, we conceive that we shall be conferring a benefit on them by offering to their notice some extracts from Doctor Buchan's remarks, and the excellent advice of the celebrated philosopher, Doctor Franklin, on this subject.

DOCTOR BUCHAN'S REMARKS.

"Immersion in cold water is a custom which lays claim to the most remote antiquity; indeed, it must be coeval with man himself. The necessity of water for the purpose of cleanliness, and the pleasure arising from its application to the body in hot countries, must have very early recommended it to the human species. Even the example of other animals was sufficient to give the hint to man; by instinct many of them are led to apply cold water in this manner; and some, when deprived of its use, have been known to languish, and even to die.

"The cold bath recommends itself in a variety of cases, and is peculiarly beneficial to the inhabitants of populous cities, who indulge in idleness, and lead sedentary lives. It accelerates the motion of the blood, promotes the different secretions, and gives permanent vigor to the solids. But all these important purposes will be more essentially answered by the application of salt water. This ought not only to be preferred on account of its superior gravity, but likewise for its greater power of stimulating the skin, which promotes the perspiration, and prevents the patient from catching cold.

"It is necessary, however, to observe, that cold bathing is more likely to prevent than to remove obstructions of the glandular or lymphatic system; indeed, when these have arrived at a certain height, they are not to be removed by any means. In this case, the cold bath will only aggravate the symptoms, and hurry the unhappy patient into an untimely grave; it is, therefore, of the utmost importance, previously to the patient's entering upon the use of the cold bath, to determine whether or not he labors under any obstinate obstruction of the lungs or other viscera: and, where this is the case, cold bathing ought strictly to be prohibited.

" In what is called a plethoric state, or too great fulness of the body, it is likewise dangerous to use the cold bath, without due preparation. In this case, there is great danger of bursting a blood-vessel, or occasioning an inflammation.

" The ancient Greeks and Romans, we are told, when covered with sweat and dust, used to plunge into rivers without receiving the smallest injury. Though they might escape danger from this imprudent conduct, yet it was certainly contrary to sound reason. Many robust men have thrown away their lives by such an attempt. We would not, however, advise patients to go in the cold water when the body is chilled; as much exercise, at least, ought to be taken, as may excite a gentle glow all over the body, but by no means so as to overheat it.

" To young people, and particularly to children, cold bathing is of the utmost importance; it promotes their growth, increases their strength, and prevents a variety of diseases incidental to childhood.

" It is, however, necessary here, to caution young men against too frequent bathing; as many fatal consequences have resulted from the daily practice of plunging into rivers, and continuing there too long.

" The most proper time of the day for using the cold bath, is, no doubt, the morning, or, at least, before dinner; and the best mode, that of quick immersion. As cold bathing has a constant tendency to propel the blood, and other humors, towards the head, it ought to be a rule always to wet that part as soon as possible. By due attention to this circumstance, there is reason to believe, that violent headaches, and other complaints which frequently proceed from cold bathing, might be often prevented.

" The cold bath, when too long continued in, not only occasions an excessive flux of humors toward the head, but chills the blood, cramps the muscles, relaxes the nerves, and wholly defeats the intention of bathing. Hence, by not adverting to this circumstance, expert swimmers are often injured, and sometimes, even lose their lives. All the beneficial purposes of cold bathing are answered by one immersion at a time; and the patient ought to be rubbed dry the moment he comes out of the water, and should continue to take exercise for sometime after."

DOCTOR FRANKLIN'S ADVICE TO SWIMMERS.

" The only obstacle to improvement, in this necessary and life-preserving art, is fear; and it is only by overcoming this timidity, that you can expect to become a master of the following acquirements. It is very common for novices in the art of swimming to make use of corks or bladders to assist in keeping the body above water; some have utterly condemned the use of them; however, they may be of service for supporting the body, while one is learning what is called the stroke, or that manner of drawing in and striking out the hands and feet, that is necessary to produce progressive motion.

But you will be no swimmer till you can place confidence in the power of the water to support you ; I would, therefore, advise the acquiring that confidence in the first place ; especially as I have known several, who, by a little practice necessary for that purpose, have insensibly acquired the stroke, taught as if it were by nature.   The practice I mean is this : choosing a place where the water deepens gradually, walk coolly into it till it is up to your breast ; then turn round your face to the shore, and throw an egg into the water between you and the shore ; it will sink to the bottom, and be easily seen there if the water be clean.   It must lie in the water so deep that you cannot reach to take it up but by diving for it.   To encourage yourself, in order to do this, reflect that your progress will be from deep to shallow water, and that at any time you may, by bringing your legs under you, and standing on the bottom, raise your head far above the water ;.then plunge under it with your eyes open, which must be kept open before going under, as you cannot open the eyelids for the weight of water above you ; throwing yourself toward the egg, and endeavouring, by the action of your hands and feet against the water, to get forward, till within reach of it.   In this attempt you will find that the water buoys you up against your inclination ; that it is not so easy to sink as you imagine, and that you cannot, but by active force get down to the egg.   Thus you feel the power of water to support you, and learn to confide in that power, while your endeavours to overcome it, and reach the egg, teach you the manner of acting on the water with your feet and hands, which action is afterward used in swimming to support your head higher above the water, or to go forward through it.

"I would the more earnestly press you to the trial of this method, because, though I think I shall satisfy you that your body is lighter than water, and that you might float in it a long time with your mouth free for breathing, if you would put yourself into a proper posture, and would be still, and forbear struggling ; yet, till you have obtained this experimental confidence in the water, I cannot depend upon your having the necessary presence of mind to recollect the posture and the directions I gave you relating to it. The surprise may put all out of your mind.

"Though the legs, arms, and head of a human body being solid parts, are, specifically, somewhat heavier than fresh water, yet the trunk, particularly the upper part, for its hollowness, is so much lighter than water, as that the whole of the body, taken altogether, is too light to sink wholly under water, but some part will remain above, until the lungs become filled with water, which happens from drawing water to them instead of air, when a person, in the fright, attempts breathing, while the mouth and nostrils are under water.

"The legs and arms are specifically lighter than salt water, and will be supported by it, so that a human body cannot sink in salt water, though the lungs were filled as above, but from the greater specific gravity of the head.

Therefore, a person throwing himself on his back in salt water, and extending his arms, may easily lay so as to keep his mouth and nostrils free for breathing; and, by a small motion of his hand, may prevent turning, if he should perceive any tendency to it.

" In fresh water, if a man throw himself on his back, near the surface, he cannot long continue in that situation but by proper action of his hands on the water; if he use no such action, the legs and lower part of the body will gradually sink till he come into an upright position, in which he will continue suspended, the hollow of his breast keeping the head uppermost.

" But if, in this erect position, the head be kept upright above the shoulders, as when we stand on the ground, the immersion will, by the weight of that part of the head that is out of the water, reach above the mouth and nostrils, perhaps a little above the eyes, so that a man cannot long remain suspended in water, with his head in that position.

" The body continuing suspended as before, and upright, if the head be leaned quite back, so that the face look upward, all the back part of the head being under water, and its weight, consequently, in a great measure supported by it, the face will remain above water quite free for breathing, will rise an inch higher every inspiration, and sink as much every expiration, but never so low as that the water may come over the mouth.

" If, therefore, a person unacquainted with swimming, and falling accidentally into the water, could have presence of mind sufficient to avoid struggling and plunging, and to let the body take this natural position, he might continue long safe from drowning, till, perhaps, help should come; for, as to the clothes, their additional weight when immersed is very inconsiderable, the water supporting it; though, when he comes out of the water, he would find them very heavy indeed.

" But, as I said before, I would not advise you, or any one, to depend on having this presence of mind on such an occasion, but learn fairly to swim, as I wish all men were taught to do in their youth; they would, on many occasions, be the safer for having that skill; and, on many more, the happier, as free from painful apprehensions of danger, to say nothing of the enjoyment in so delightful and wholesome an exercise. Soldiers particularly should, methinks, all be taught to swim; it might be of frequent use, either in surprising an enemy or saving themselves; and if I had now boys to educate, I should prefer those schools (other things being equal) where an opportunity was afforded for acquiring so advantageous an art, which, once learned, is never forgotten.

" I know by experience, that it is a great comfort to a swimmer, who has a considerable distance to go, to turn himself sometimes on his back, and to vary, in other respects, the means of procuring a progressive motion.

" When he is seized with the cramp in the leg, the method of driving it away is, to give the parts affected a sudden, vigorous, and violent shock, which he may do in the air as he swims on his back.

" During the great heats in summer there is no danger in bathing, however warm we may be, in rivers which have been thoroughly warmed by the sun. But to throw one's self into cold spring water, when the body has been heated by exercise in the sun, is an imprudence which may prove fatal. I once knew an instance of four young men, who, having worked at harvest in the heat of the day, with a view of refreshing themselves, plunged into a spring of cold water; two died upon the spot, a third next morning, and the fourth recovered with great difficulty. A copious draught of cold water, in similar circumstances, is frequently attended with the same effect, in North America.

" The exercise of swimming is one of the most healthy and agreeable in the world. After having swam for an hour or two in the evening, one sleeps coolly the whole night, even during the most ardent heats of summer. Perhaps the pores being cleansed, the insensible perspiration increases and occasions this coolness. It is certain that much swimming is the means of stopping a diarrhœa, and even of producing a constipation. With respect to those who do not know how to swim, or who are affected with a diarrhœa at a season which does not permit them to use that exercise, a warm bath, by cleansing and purifying the skin, is found very salutary, and often effects a radical cure. I speak from my own experience, frequently repeated, and that of others to whom I have recommended this.

" When I was a boy, I amused myself one day with flying a paper kite, and approaching the banks of a lake, which was near a mile broad, I tied the string to a stake, and the kite ascended to a very considerable height above the pond, while I was swimming. In a little time, being desirous of amusing myself with my kite, and enjoying at the same time the pleasure of swimming, I returned, and loosing from the stake the string with the little stick which was fastened to it, went again into the water, where I found that, lying on my back, and holding the stick in my hand, I was drawn along the surface of the water in a very agreeable manner. Having then engaged another boy to carry my clothes round the pond, to a place which I pointed out to him, on the other side, I began to cross the pond with my kite, which carried me quite over without the least fatigue, and with the greatest pleasure imaginable. I was only obliged occasionally to halt a little in my course, and resist its progress, when it appeared that, by following too quick, I lowered the kite too much ; by doing which occasionally I made it rise again. I have never since that time practised this singular mode of swimming, though I think it not impossible to cross, in this manner, from Dover to Calais. The packet-boat, however, is still preferable."

PRACTICAL INSTRUCTIONS.

We will now suppose one of our young friends by the side of a stream, and anxious to take his first lesson in the art of swimming. If he have any friend or companion with him, who is at once competent and willing to give him the necessary directions, he will do well to follow them; as example in this, and similar cases, is much better than precept. But if he should not be so fortunate, he can either adopt the excellent method mentioned by Doctor Franklin, as stated in a preceding page, or follow the instructions which we are about to give him on the subject.

ENTERING THE WATER.

Our young pupil must not, at first, venture into the water in the bold and dashing manner of experienced swimmers. He must wait patiently until he can do so without danger. Let him remember that there has been a time when the best swimmer alive, tottered, step by step, into the water, and sounded the depth with one foot before he lifted the other from the bottom of the stream. Leander himself, with whose history and fate our juvenile readers who are tolerably advanced in the classics are, doubtless, acquainted,—Leander himself, we repeat, who so often swam across the Hellespont, once paddled in a pond; and those who, under our directions, make their first attempt to buoy themselves up by their own natural powers, in a shallow brook, may, hereafter, become lusty swimmers enough to perform the same feat of which Lord Byron was so proud, namely, crossing the Hellespont, as Leander did in the days of " hoar antiquity." We recommend our young friend to be patient, as well as persevering, during his probation in the art of swimming. He must not feel disgusted and disheartened, because he seems to make comparatively but little progress: let him remember that he is gradually acquiring a new and most important power; he is, by degrees, obtaining a mastery over the waters. It was well observed by a writer of great discernment, that nothing which is worth learning is compassed without some difficulty and application; that it is well worth some pains and trouble to render one's self fearless of falling into a river, in which two out of three of our fellow-countrymen would, in a similar situation, without assistance, be drowned, must be admitted;—let not that trouble, therefore, be grudged.

Previously to entering the water, the head and neck should be well wetted; the pupil should then advance, by a clear shelving bank, in some stream, the depth of which he has ascertained by plumbing or otherwise, until he is breast high; then let him face about toward the bank, and prepare to make his first essay in this art, as directed in the next paragraph.

STRIKING OUT.

With his face turned toward the bank, as above directed, let the pupil lie down gently on his breast, keep his head and neck upright, his breast

advanced, and his back bent inward. Then, let him withdraw his legs from the bottom, and immediately strike them out, not downward, but behind him; strike out the arms forward, with the palms closed, and the backs uppermost, a little below the surface of the water; draw them back again, while he is gathering up his legs for a second attempt, and thus push forward, making use of his hands and feet alternately. It will, perhaps, happen, that he will swallow water in his first efforts, but this should not discourage him: neither should he fancy that, because he makes but little advances, he is not as capable of learning to swim as others; the same little mishaps occur to all young beginners.

CORKS AND BLADDERS.

The use of corks and bladders, for those who are learning to swim, is as strongly recommended by some persons, as it is deprecated by others. That the necessary action with the arms and legs may be acquired more easily with than without them, is clear enough; nevertheless, we are convinced by experience, that it is better to learn how to keep one's self afloat, and to be able to swim ten or a dozen yards, at least, no matter how clumsily, without them. We have seen several young persons who, after having attained the necessary action, in a very superior manner, by the use of corks or bladders, were totally unable to keep their heads above the water when they relinquished their aid, and were thus left precisely in the same situation in which they would have been, had they not made a single attempt in the art of swimming. We have, it is true, known some trifling exceptions, but they have been rare indeed. Corks and bladders, we think, may be useful, but they should not be commenced with. After the learner has made some progress, and is able to cross a narrow stream, corks and bladders may be occasionally adopted, for a short time, in order that the pupil, by means of their support, may, at his ease, perfect himself in the action necessary for superior swimming, especially with the arms and hands. The action of the legs may be much better acquired by means of the plank, as hereafter directed. The best swimmers we have ever met never made use of corks for this purpose, but still they may be

considered of advantage in the manner we have stated. If therefore, our reader should think fit to use corks or bladders, let him attend to the following hints.

Swimming corks are made thus: three or four round slices of cork, increasing progressively in circumference, are run, by a hole made in their centres, on each end of a piece of stout rope, which is long enough to reach across the breast, and beyond the arm-pits; the same number of corks is placed at each side of the rope, and they are kept from slipping off by knots at the two extremities. When bladders are used, they are blown full of air, tied at the necks, and fastened by strings to the ends of the rope, instead of corks.

The manner of using corks or bladders is as follows:—the pupil places his breast across the rope between the corks or bladders as they float; he raises his legs from the ground, and rests his whole weight on the rope, so that the corks or bladders swim between his arms and his sides. In this position he strikes out, and propels himself forward with his legs and feet. The action of the hands and arms supports a swimmer only, so that he would advance almost as much when using corks if he kept them still as if he moved them; nevertheless, their action may be perfected, while the body is supported by the corks, and the young swimmer may acquire that graceful, steady, and powerful manner of striking out, which he may, subsequently, by degrees, bring into practice, when he has thrown the corks aside. The writer of these pages has buffeted the billows at a mile or two from land, where the waters have been moved by, what an angler calls, a curling breeze, with a pleasure which those, and those alone, who have revelled in the strong bosom of the sea, can imagine; and what is more difficult, he has swam the still torpid deeps of an inland lake, in a dead calm; and although, perhaps, not an excellent, has been a very tolerable, swimmer in his time, and this is the manner which he has always followed, and which he recommends his young friends to adopt, of striking out with the arms.   The fingers are to be closed, and the thumbs kept close to the hand, which should be straightened, or rather, a little hollowed in the palm; the hands are then to be brought together, the two thumbs touching, or palm to palm, it is little matter which, and raised just under the chin; they are then to be struck vigorously forward, and when the arms are at their full stretch, parted, and carried slowly and regularly, a little below the surface of the water, at the full stretch of the arms, backward, as far as convenience will permit; they should then sink toward the hips; by a slight pressure on the water, as they descend, the body will be raised, the head may be thrown back, and the breath drawn in for the next stroke.   When the hands are at, or near, the hips, they should be raised, with the thumbs or edges, but by no means the backs, upward, to the first position; while doing this, the legs are to be drawn up as near the body as possible, and the soles of the feet struck out against the water with reasonable force, at the same moment the hands are thrust forward again.   This is, in fact, the whole principle of swimming:—the arms are first thrust forward, and the body propelled by the force of the soles of the feet, striking against the water; the air in the lungs is expired or breathed forth during this action; the hands are then stretched out and carried round so as to lift the body (which wants no support during the time it is propelled by the legs, and the lungs are nearly full of air,) while the legs are drawn up, and the lungs filled with air for a second effort.   These very simple motions will seem difficult and complicated to the young swimmer at first, but by degrees he will learn to perform them with facility. Above all things, let him endeavour to do them deliberately and without being flurried.   It is a fact, that a swimmer, who is apparently slow in his action, makes more progress by half than one who is quick.   The former is deliberate and vigorous; the latter hurried, less effectual, and soon becomes fatigued.   A tyro in the art will make ten efforts during the time occupied by an adept in performing one, and at the same time will scarcely make one half the progress.

We seriously recommend our young readers never to venture out of their depths with corks, if they cannot swim without them. We once knew a very promising youth who was nearly drowned, when in deep water, by the corks slipping from his breast to below his waist, so that his loins, and, at last, his legs, were above water, while his head was beneath; he was extricated from this perilous situation by a youth of his own age, who had begun to learn the art of swimming, but without corks, on precisely the same day as the lad who was thus in danger of being drowned. It would be well, if a string were tied by its middle to each end of the rope, close to the largest cork, and one end of it brought over the shoulder at the back, the other in front, and fastened securely together; this would, at least, prevent the corks from getting out of their proper places.

THE PLANK.

The plank is useful in a bath, to perfect the young swimmer in the manner of properly throwing out his legs and feet. A piece of plank, about  ten or twelve feet in length, two inches thick, and a foot and a half, or two feet broad, is the best size. It is to be thrown into the water, and the pupil, after he has acquired the art of supporting himself for a short time, without any artificial aids, should take hold of one of its ends with both hands; his body will thus be supported, and he should strike out with his legs in the manner before directed, and endeavour to drive the plank before him, taking care to hold fast and follow it closely, otherwise he may suffer rather an unpleasant feeling by the plank darting forward, and leaving him to sink, unexpectedly, over head and ears in the water. . Of the utility of the plank for the purpose above mentioned, we have frequently been witness, and can, therefore, most confidently recommend it to those of our young readers who have an inclination to learn the art of swimming by occasional or preliminary artificial aids.

THE ROPE, AND OTHER AIDS.

The rope for swimmers is usually fastened to the end of a stout piece of wood, which is fixed into a wall or elsewhere, so as to project over the water; the rope descends to its surface, or it may be long enough for a foot or sixteen inches of its extremity to sink. The use of the rope is to support the learner while practising the action with the legs; but it is very inferior for this purpose to the plank; as, while the pupil keeps himself up, by holding the rope, his body remains in too perpendicular a position, so that he strikes downward rather than backward. The pupil should accustom himself, as much as possible, to keep his legs near the surface; for those who swim with the lower extremities deep in the water never make such rapid way as others who adopt the proper position, which should be within a few degrees of horizontal. The plank has another advantage over the rope; it is more steady in the water, and offers sufficient resistance to induce, and even to assist, the young beginner, as a *point d'appui*, to strike out vigorously with his legs. The rope is, in fact, of more utility to those who go into the water to bathe, than those who are learning to swim; for by means of the support which it affords, the bather may raise

his legs from the bottom, and exercise himself most beneficially by tossing, stretching, and turning to and fro in the water; he may thus luxuriate in a manner which would be entirely out of his power without the aid of the rope.

The aid of the hand is chiefly applied to very young learners, who have the advantage of bathing with a grown-up swimmer. It is by far superior as an aid, to corks or bladders; because it can be withdrawn gradually, and at last, altogether, so that the learner may feel almost insensible of its departure, and restored in an instant, if exertion renders him too weak to support himself. A tall, strong youth, or a grown-up person, takes the little learner in his arms, and goes into the water breast-high with him; he then places the pupil nearly flat upon the water, supporting him by one hand under the breast, and encouraging and directing him to strike out boldly, and, at the same time, correctly. After two or three lessons, on different days, the support of the hand may occasionally be, in some degree, withdrawn; and, in the course of a week or ten days, the little swimmer will, in all probability, have no further need of its service. Oh! what a happy, triumphant moment is that, when a boy first floats upon the water, independent of all other aids but those which Nature has provided in his own person. He soon becomes exhausted, but, from that time, he feels a confidence in himself, and his progress is generally most rapid.

The aid of the rope and hand we do not so much approve as that of the hand alone. A rope is fastened about the learner's body, a grown person holds the other end of it, and supports the pupil while he acquires the mode of striking out. The aid, in this case, cannot be applied with such precision to the proper part, nor afforded and withdrawn with such nicety as where the hand alone is used.

SWIMMING OUT OF DEPTH.

We will now suppose our pupil to have made some progress in swimming, and to feel anxious to go into deep water. If he feel quite conscious of his own powers, he may venture a few strokes out of his depth, across a stream, for instance, which is overhead only for a few feet in the centre, with shelving banks on each side. Young swimmers sometimes feel alarmed when they are aware that they have ventured where they can no longer put their

legs on the ground; this feeling flurries them, they strike quick, their hurry increases, trepidation ensues, and they have great difficulty in returning to the shore. We earnestly caution our pupil against giving way to anything of this sort. Before he ventures out of his depth, let him calculate his own powers, and attempt such a distance only as is in proportion with them. Is he able to swim half-a-dozen yards without dropping his feet to the ground? If so, he may confidently cross a deep place which is only half that breadth. Let him not imagine that he is not quite as capable of swimming in deep as in shallow water; the contrary is the fact, for the deeper the water, the better he can swim. Above all things, let him not hurry himself, but strike slowly and evenly, and keep good time with the motions of his arms, his legs, and his lungs. Boys frequently fall into an error, which is invariably attended with unpleasant consequences, when first attempting to swim, as well as when they begin to venture out of depth, by losing their presence of mind, and breathing at the wrong time. They draw breath at the moment when they are striking out with their legs, instead of at the time their body is elevated by the hands, when at the full stretch of the arm backward, or in descending toward the hips. During this action of the legs, the head partially sinks, the face is driven against the water, and the mouth thus becomes filled, which creates a very unpleasant nausea and momentary suffocation. When the hands are in the position above mentioned, the progress of the body forward ceases, the face is no longer driven against the water, but is elevated above the surface; then is the time to draw in the breath, which should be expired while the body at the next stroke is sent forward by the action of the legs. During this time, if your mouth be even with or partly under the surface, no water can enter it, the air which you are driving between your lips effectually preventing it. " Keep time," is one of the swimmer's golden rules. Unless the pupil pay attention to it, he will make but little progress, and must inevitably, now and then, take in a mouthful of the stream in which he is swimming. To those who have never swam " in the silver flood," a circumstance of this sort will be thought very lightly of indeed ; but we speak the general feelings of swimmers, when we say, that the same person who would relish a draught from a stream, when sitting dressed upon its bank, would feel the greatest disgust at taking a mouthful of the same water, when swimming in it.

After the pupil has ventured out of his depth, and feels satisfied with the success of his attempt, he grows emboldened, and increases his distances daily.

TO TREAD WATER.

All that is necessary for treading water, is to let your legs drop in the water until you are upright ; then keep yourself afloat in that position by treading downward with your feet, alternately ; and, if necessary, paddling with your palms at your hips.

TO SWIM ON THE SIDE.

Lower your left side, and at the same time elevate your right ; strike forward with your left hand, and sideway with your right ; the back of the latter being in front instead of upward, the thumb side of the hand downward, so as to serve precisely as an oar. You will thus, by giving your body an additional impetus, advance much more speedily than in the common way ; it will also relieve you considerably when you feel tired of striking out forward. You may also turn on the right side, strike out with the right hand, and use the left as an oar. In either case, the action of the legs is the same as usual.

TO SWIM LIKE A DOG.

Strike with each hand and foot alternately ; that is, begin with the right hand and foot, draw the hand toward the chin, and the foot toward the body at the same time ; and then simultaneously kick backward with the foot, and strike out in a right line with the hand ; then do the like with the left hand and foot, and so on. The hands are not to be carried backward as in the ordinary way of swimming, but merely thrust out with the palms downward, a little way below the surface, in front only; as they are brought back to the breast again, they should be rather hollowed, and the water grasped or pulled toward the swimmer. Much progress cannot be made by swimming in this manner, but still it is worth learning, as every change of method, in going a distance, recruits the swimmer's strength.

THE PORPOISE.

This is a very pleasant and most advantageous change of action. The right arm is lifted entirely out of the water, the shoulder thrust forward, and the swimmer, while striking out with his legs, reaches forward with his hand, as far as possible. At the utmost stretch of the arm the hand falls, a little hollowed, into the water, which it grasps or pulls toward the swimmer in its return to the body, in a transverse direction, toward the other armpit. While it is passing through the water in this manner, the legs are drawn up for another effort, and the left arm and shoulder elevated and thrust forward as above directed for the right. This is the greatest advancing relief in swimming, except swimming on the back; floating on the back rests the whole of the body as well as the limbs, but while floating, no progress is made; whereas, during the time a person swims in the manner above directed, he will not only relieve himself considerably, but also make as great an advance in the water, as if he were proceeding in the ordinary way.

TO SWIM AND FLOAT ON THE BACK.

To do this, you must turn yourself on your back as gently as possible, elevate your breast above the surface, put your head back, so that your

eyes, nose, mouth and chin only are above water. By keeping in this position with the legs and arms extended, and paddling the hands gently by the side of the hips, you will float. If you wish to swim, you must strike out with the legs, taking care not to lift your knees too high, nor sink your hips and sides too low; but keeping in as straight a line as possible. You may lay the arms across the breast; keep them motionless at the sides; or, if you wish, strike out with them to help you on.

To swim with your feet forward, while on your back, lift up your legs one after another, let them fall into the water, and draw them back with all the force you can, toward your hams; thus you will swim feet forward, and return to the place whence you came.

To turn from your breast to your back, raise your legs forward, and throw your head backward, until your body is in a right position : to change from the back to the breast, drop your legs, and throw your body forward on your breast.

TO TURN WHEN SWIMMING.

If you wish to turn while on your back, keep one leg still, and embrace the water beside you with the other ; thus, you will find yourself turn to that side on which your leg by its motion embraces the water, and you will turn either to the right or left, according to which leg you use in this manner.

To turn while swimming in the ordinary way requires no further effort than to incline your head and body to the side you would turn to ; and, at the same time, move and turn your legs, in the same manner as you would do, to turn the same way on land.

TO SHOW THE FEET.

While on your back, bend the small of it downward ; support yourself by moving your hands to and fro just above your breast, and stretch your feet above the water.

TO BEAT THE WATER, &c.

When swimming on your back, lift your legs out of the water one after another, and strike the water with them alternately. Those who are most expert at this, bring their chins toward their breasts at each stroke of the legs.

There is a variety of similar feats performed by expert swimmers, such as treading water with both hands raised over the head ; floating on the back with the arms above the surface ; taking the left leg in the right hand, out of the water, when swimming on the back ; pulling the right heel by the right hand, toward the back, when swimming in the common way ; throwing somersets in the water, backward and forward, &c. &c., for which no particular directions are necessary, as the pupil, when he has grown expert in the various modes of swimming which we have described, will be able to do these things, and any tricks which his fancy may suggest, without difficulty.

DIVING.

Diving, by practice, may be carried to astonishing perfection. Pearls are brought up from the bottom of the sea by divers who are trained to remain a considerable time under water. In ancient times, divers were employed in war to destroy the ships of the enemy ; and many instances are related, by respectable authors, of men diving after, and fetching up nails and pieces of money thrown into the sea, and even overtaking the nail or coin before it has reached the bottom.

Diving may be performed from the surface of the water when swimming, by merely turning the head downward, and striking upward with

the legs. It is, however, much better to leap in, with the hands closed above the head, and head foremost, from a pier, boat or raised bank. By merely striking with the feet, and keeping his head toward the bottom, the diver may drive himself a considerable distance beneath the surface. If he reach the bottom, he has only to turn his head upward, spring from the ground with his feet, and he will soon arrive at the surface. If desirous of making a more rapid ascent, he should strike downward with his feet, pulling the water above him toward his head with one hand, and striking it downward by his side with the other. In diving, the eyes should be open; you must, therefore, take care that you do not close them, as they reach the surface, when you commence your descent. It is almost needless to add, that the breath should be held, the whole time that you are under water.

SWIMMING UNDER WATER.

Swimming between top and bottom may be accomplished by the ordinary stroke, if you take care to keep your head a little downward, and strike a little higher with your feet than when swimming on the surface; or, you may turn your thumbs downward, and perform the stroke with the hands in that position, instead of keeping them flat.

THE CRAMP.

Our practical directions in the art of swimming would be incomplete were we to omit saying a few words as to the cramp. Those who are at all liable to it, ought, perhaps, to abandon all idea of swimming; men of the greatest skill, as swimmers, and of presence of mind in danger, having fallen victims to this, which has been well enough called, "the bathers' bane." The cramp may, however, seize a person for the first time in his life, when at a distance from land; we have frequently known this to occur; and in every case that has come within our personal knowledge, with one exception, the sufferer has saved himself by acting as we are about to advise our young reader, if ever he should be seized with this terrible contraction. Be assured that there is no danger, if you are only a tolerable swimmer, and do not flurry yourself. The moment you feel the cramp in your leg or foot, strike out the limb with all your strength, thrusting the heel out, and drawing the toes upward as forcibly as possible, totally regardless of the momentary pain it may occasion. If two or three efforts of this nature do not succeed, throw yourself on your back, and endeavour to keep yourself afloat with your hands until assistance reach you; or, if there be no hope of that, try to paddle ashore with your palms. Should you be unable to float on your back, put yourself in the position directed for treading water, and you may keep your head above the surface by merely striking the water downward with your hands at your hips, without any assistance from your legs. In case you have the cramp in both legs, you may also endeavour to make some progress in this manner, should no help be at hand. If you have one leg only attacked, you may drive yourself forward with the other. In order to endow you with confidence in a moment of danger from an attack of the cramp, occasionally try to swim with one leg, or a leg and a hand, or the two hands only, and you will find that it is by no means difficult.

We feel rather astonished that none of the treatises on swimming, which have fallen into our hands, recommend the practice of boys attempt-

ing to carry one another in the water; when both can swim, this is an excellent and safe method of learning how to support another who is in danger on account of cramp, weakness, ignorance of swimming, or other causes. In the annexed sketch, the foremost figure is in the act of swimming, and carrying with him another person, who is borne up, simply by applying one hand to each hip of his companion. A person, it is said, had the pleasure of saving a friend from drowning, by these means: it is attended, however, with considerable risk, especially if the person you venture to rescue should lose his presence of mind, which is too often the case with those who are in danger of being drowned. It will surprise any swimmer, who first tries the experiment, to find with what ease he can support a person attached to him in this manner. The person, who rests upon the hips of his companion, is represented as passive, as he is supposed to be unable to swim; but two swimmers, performing this experiment, may strike out together with their legs.

TIMES AND PLACES FOR SWIMMING.

Of all places to swim in, the sea is best, running waters next, and ponds the worst. The best time for swimming is in the months of May, June, July, and August. There are, however, some years, wherein it is not healthy to go into the water during these months; as when the weather, and consequently the water, is colder than ordinary for the season. One ought not to go into the water when it rains; for the rain, if it last any time, chills the water, and endangers catching cold, by wetting one's clothes. The night is also improper for this exercise. Beware of weeds, as although you have company with you, yet, you may be lost beyond the possibility of help, if your feet get entangled among them. The bottom ought to be of gravel, or smooth stones, so that you may stand thereon as firmly as on the earth, and be neither in danger of sinking in the mud, nor wounding the feet: care ought also to be taken that it be even, and without holes; and, above all, that you know the depth, especially when you begin to learn; for as it is then easy to tire one's self when struggling and making the first efforts, you should, therefore, be sure that the bottom is not out of your depth, when you have occasion to rest, and take breath. It is impossible to be too cautious when you are alone, or have no one in company that knows the pond or stream. When you have found out a place fit to learn in, do not venture anywhere else till you are considerably advanced in the art; and, till then, it will be the best way to exercise with some one who is already expert in swimming.

CONCLUDING REMARKS.

In entering the water, the head should be wetted first, either by plunging in head foremost, or pouring water on it. Before you adopt the first method, ascertain if the water be sufficiently deep to allow you to dive without touching the bottom, otherwise you may injure yourself against it. Do not remain in the water too long, but come out as soon as you feel tired, chilly or numbed. It is a good plan to make a plunge, so as to wet the body all over, to return to shore immediately, and an instant afterward enter the water at your ease, and take your lesson or your swim. You do not feel so chilly if you do this, as if you dash in and swim off at once. Never be alarmed at having a few mouthfuls of water, when learning to swim; be not discouraged at difficulties, but bear in mind, that millions have done what you are attempting to do. Beware of banks which have holes in them, and venture out of your depth only by degrees.

If one of your companions be in danger of drowning, be sure that, in endeavouring to save him, you make your approaches in such a manner, as will prevent him from grappling with you; if he once get a hold of your limbs, you both will almost inevitably be lost.

Although it has been said, that the weight of one's clothes will make but little difference in the water, yet we strongly advise the young swimmer, when he has become expert in the art, and confident of his own prowess, to swim occasionally with his clothes on; for this purpose, of course he need only use an old worn-out suit: by so doing, he will be satisfied that dress does not make so much difference as he might imagine, and thus he will have more courage and presence of mind if he should at any time afterward fall into the water, or leap in to save another.

ARITHMETICAL AMUSEMENTS.

Cocker and Dilworth, Walsingame and Vyse,
In their own sphere, by BIDDER were outshone:
They, or with pen or pencil, problems solved,—
He, with no aid but wond'rous memory;
They, when of years mature, acquired their fame,—
He, "lisped in numbers, for the numbers came."

THE delightful and valuable science of Arithmetic first arrived at any degree of perfection in Europe, among the Greeks, who made use of the letters of the alphabet to express their numbers. A similar mode was followed by the Romans, who, besides characters for each rank of classes, introduced others for five, fifty, and five hundred, which are still used for chapters of books, and some other purposes. The common arithmetic, in which the ten Arabic figures, 1, 2, 3, 4, 5, 6, 7, 8, 9, 0, are used, was unknown to the Greeks and Romans, and came into Europe, by way of Spain, from the Arabians, who are said to have received it from the Indians. It is supposed to have taken its origin from the ten fingers of the hand, which were made use of in computations, before arithmetic was brought into an art.

The Indians are very expert at computing without pen or ink; and the natives of Peru, in South America, who do all by the arrangement of grains of maize, excel the European, with the aid of all his rules and implements for writing. But the dexterity of those people cannot for a moment be compared with the feats of mental arithmetic exhibited by GEORGE BIDDER, the youth, whose portrait stands at the head of this article. This astonishing boy, at a very early age, and without education, was capable of solving very intricate questions in arithmetic, without the use of pen, pencil, or writing implements of any sort, but entirely in his own mind, as correctly and quickly as the most expert person could in the common way. We have, personally, witnessed his ability in this respect, and among many other complicated questions, which were put to him, we recollect the following :— Supposing the sun to be 95 millions of miles from the earth, and that it were possible for an insect, whose pace should be 7½ inches per minute, to travel that pace how long would it take to reach the sun ? This he mentally solved in a very short time.

Several other mental arithmeticians have appeared within these few years; among the rest, JEDIDIAH BUXTON, an illiterate peasant, who was never taught to read or write, appears to have been eminent. Several of the questions answered by this man have been recorded; among others, we recollect the following :—How many times will a coach-wheel, whose circumference is 6 yards, turn in going 204 miles ? In thirteen minutes, BUXTON answered,—59,840 times. Then he was asked :—And, supposing sound travels at the rate of 1142 feet per second, how long will it be before the report of a cannon is heard 5 miles off ? His answer was,—23 seconds, 7 thirds, and 46 remain. On being required to multiply 456 by 378, he gave the product in a very short time ; and, when requested to work the question audibly, so that his method might be known, he multiplied 456 first by 5, which produced 2280 ; this he again multiplied by 20, and found the product 45,600, which was the multiplicand multiplied by 100 ; this product he again multiplied by 3, which produced 136,800, the product of the multiplicand by 300 ; it remained, therefore, to multiply this by 78, which he effected by multiplying 2280, (or the product of the multiplicand multiplied by 5,) by 15, as 5 times 15 are 75. This product, being 34,200, he added to 136,800, which was the multiplicand multiplied by 300, and this produced 171,000 which was 375 times 456. To complete his operation, therefore, he multiplied 456 by 3, which produced 1368, and having added this number to 171,000, he found the product of 456 multiplied by 378, to be 172,368. By this it appears, that he was so little acquainted with the common rules, as to multiply 456 first by 5, and the product by 20, to find what sum it would produce, multiplied by 100 ; whereas, had he added two ciphers to the figures, he would have obtained the product at once.

TO TELL ANY NUMBER THOUGHT OF.

Desire any person to think of a number, say a certain number of shillings; tell him to borrow that sum of some one in the company, and add the number borrowed to the amount thought of. It will here be proper to name the person who lends him the shillings, and to beg the one, who makes the calculation, to do it with great care, as he may readily fall into an error, especially the first time. Then, say to the person,—'I do not lend you, but give you 10, add them to the former sum.' Continue in this manner :—'Give the half to the poor, and retain in your memory the other half.' Then add :—'Return to the gentleman, or lady, what you borrowed, and remember that the sum lent you, was exactly equal to the number thought of.' Ask the person if he knows exactly what remains; he will answer 'Yes.' You must then say,—'And I know also the number that remains; it is equal to what I am going to conceal in my hand.' Put into one of your hands 5 pieces of money, and desire the person to tell how many you have got. He will answer 5; upon which, open your hand, and show him the 5 pieces. You may then say,—'I well knew that your result was 5; but if you had thought of a very large number, for example, two or three millions, the result would have been much greater, but my hand would not have held a number of pieces equal to the remainder.' The person then supposing that the result of the calculation must be different, according to the difference of the number thought of, will imagine that it is necessary to know the last number in order to guess the result : but this idea is false; for, in the case which we have here supposed, whatever be the number thought of, the remainder must always be 5. The reason of this is as follows :—The sum, the half of which is given to the poor, is nothing else than twice the number thought of, plus 10 ; and when the poor have received their part, there remains only the number thought of, plus 5 ; but the number thought of is cut off when the sum borrowed is returned, and, consequently, there remain only 5.

It may be hence seen, that the result may be easily known, since it will be the half of the number given in the third part of the operation; for example, whatever be the number thought of, the remainder will be 36, or 25 according as 72 or 50 have been given. If this trick be performed several times successively, the number given in the third part of the operation must be always different; for if the result were several times the same, the deception might be discovered. When the five first parts of the calculation for obtaining a result are finished, it will be best not to name it at first, but to continue the operation, to render it more complex, by saying, for example :—'Double the remainder, deduct two, add three, take the fourth part,' &c.; and the different steps of the calculation may be kept in mind, in order to know how much the first result has been increased or diminished. This irregular process never fails to confound those who attempt to follow it.

A SECOND METHOD.

Bid the person take 1 from the number thought of, and then double the remainder; desire him to take 1 from this double, and to add to it the number thought of; in the last place, ask him the number arising from this addition, and, if you add 3 to it, the third of the sum will be the number thought of. The application of this rule is so easy, that it is needless to illustrate it by an example.

A THIRD METHOD.

Desire the person to add 1 to the triple of the number thought of, and to multiply the sum by 3; then bid him add to this product the number thought of, and the result will be a sum, from which if 3 be subtracted, the remainder will be ten times of the number required; and if the cipher on the right be cut off from the remainder, the other figure will indicate the number sought.

Example:—Let the number thought of be 6, the triple of which is 18; and if 1 be added, it makes 19; the triple of this last number is 57, and if 6 be added, it makes 63, from which if 3 be subtracted, the remainder will be 60: now, if the cipher on the right be cut off, the remaining figure, 6, will be the number required.

A FOURTH METHOD.

Bid the person multiply the number thought of by itself; then desire him to add 1 to the number thought of, and to multiply it also by itself; in the last place, ask him to tell the difference of these two products, which will certainly be an odd number, and the least half of it will be the number required.

Let the number thought of, for example, be 10; which, multiplied by itself, gives 100; in the next place, 10 increased by 1 is 11, which, multiplied by itself, makes 121; and the difference of these two squares is 21, the least half of which, being 10, is the number thought of.

This operation might be varied by desiring the person to multiply the second number by itself, after it has been diminished by 1. In this case, the number thought of will be equal to the greater half of the difference of the two squares.

Thus, in the preceding example, the square of the number thought of is 100, and that of the same number, less 1, is 81; the difference of these is 19; the greater half of which, or 10, is the number thought of.

TO TELL TWO OR MORE NUMBERS THOUGHT OF.

If one or more of the numbers thought of be greater than 9, we must distinguish two cases; that in which the number of the numbers thought of is odd, and that in which it is even.

In the first case, ask the sum of the first and second; of the second and third; the third and fourth; and so on to the last; and then the sum of the first and the last. Having written down all these sums in order, add together all those, the places of which are odd, as the first, the third, the fifth, &c.; make another sum of all those, the places of which are even, as the second, the fourth, the sixth, &c.; subtract this sum from the former, and the remainder will be the double of the first number. Let us suppose, for example, that the five following numbers are thought of, 3, 7, 13, 17, 20, which when added two and two as above, give 10, 20, 30, 37, 23: the sum of the first, third, and fifth is 63, and that of the second and fourth is 57; if 57 be subtracted from 63, the remainder, 6, will be the double of the first number, 3. Now, if 3 be taken from 10, the first of the sums, the remainder, 7, will be the second number; and by proceeding in this manner, we may find all the rest.

In the second case, that is to say, if the number of the numbers thought of be even, you must ask and write down, as above, the sum of the first and the second; that of the second and third; and so on, as before: but instead of the sum of the first and the last, you must take that of the second and last; then add together those which stand in the even places, and form them into a new sum apart; add also those in the odd places, the first excepted, and subtract this sum from the former, the remainder will be the double of the second number; and if the second number, thus found, be subtracted from the sum of the first and second, you will have the first number; if it be taken from that of the second and third, it will give the third; and so of the rest. Let the numbers thought of be, for example, 3, 7, 13, 17: the sums formed as above are 10, 20, 30, 24; the sum of the second and fourth is 44, from which if 30, the third, be subtracted, the remainder will be 14, the double of 7, the second number. The first, therefore, is 3, the third 13, and the fourth 17.

When each of the numbers thought of does not exceed 9, they may be easily found in the following manner :—

Having made the person add 1 to the double of the first number thought of, desire him to multiply the whole by 5, and to add to the product the second number. If there be a third, make him double this first sum, and add 1 to it; after which, desire him to multiply the new sum by 5, and to add to it the third number. If there be a fourth, proceed in the same manner, desiring him to double the preceding sum; to add to it 1; to multiply by 5; to add the fourth number; and so on.

G 2

Then, ask the number arising from the addition of the last number thought of, and if there were two numbers, subtract 5 from it; if there were three, 55; if there were four, 555; and so on; for the remainder will be composed of figures, of which the first on the left will be the first number thought of, the next the second, and so on.

Suppose the number thought of to be 3, 4, 6; by adding 1 to 6, the double of the first, we shall have 7, which, being multiplied by 5, will give 35; if 4, the second number thought of, be then added, we shall have 39, which doubled, gives 78; and, if we add 1, and multiply 79, the sum, by 5, the result will be 395.   In the last place, if we add 6, the number thought of, the sum will be 401; and if 55 be deducted from it, we shall have, for remainder, 346, the figures of which, 3, 4, 6, indicate in order the three numbers thought of.

THE MONEY GAME.

A person having in one hand a piece of gold, and in the other a piece of silver, you may tell in which hand he has the gold, and in which the silver, by the following method :—Some value, represented by an even number, such as 8, must be assigned to the gold, and a value represented by an odd number, such as 3, must be assigned to the silver; after which, desire the person to multiply the number in the right hand by any even number whatever, such as 2 ; and that in the left by an odd number, as 3 ; then bid him add together the two products, and if the whole sum be odd, the gold will be in the right hand, and the silver in the left; if the sum be even, the contrary will be the case.

To conceal the artifice better, it will be sufficient to ask whether the sum of the two products can be halved without a remainder; for in that case the total will be even, and in the contrary case odd.

It may be readily seen, that the pieces, instead of being in the two hands of the same person, may be supposed to be in the hands of two persons, one of whom has the even number, or piece of gold, and the other the odd number, or piece of silver.   The same operations may then be performed in regard to these two persons, as are performed in regard to the two hands of the same person, calling the one privately the right and the other the left.

THE GAME OF THE RING.

This game is an application of one of the methods employed to tell several numbers thought of, and ought to be performed in a company not exceeding nine, in order that it may be less complex.   Desire any one of the company to take a ring, and put it on any joint of whatever finger he may think proper.   The question then is, to tell what person has the ring, and on what hand, what finger, and on what joint.

For this purpose, you must call the first person 1, the second 2, the third 3, and so on. You must also denote the ten fingers of the two hands, by the following numbers of the natural progression, 1, 2, 3, 4, 5, &c. beginning at the thumb of the right hand, and ending at that of the left, that by this order of the number of the finger may, at the same time, indicate the hand. In the last place, the joints must be denoted by 1, 2, 3, beginning at the points of the fingers.

To render the solution of this problem more explicit, let us suppose that the fourth person in the company has the ring on the sixth finger, that is to say, on the little finger of the left hand, and on the second joint of that finger.

Desire some one to double the number expressing the person, which, in this case, will give 8; bid him add 5 to this double, and multiply the sum by 5, which will make 65; then tell him to add to this product the number denoting the finger, that is to say, 6, by which means you will have 71; and, in the last place, desire him to multiply the last number by 10, and to add to the product the number of the joint, 2; the last result will be 712; if from this number you deduct 250, the remainder will be 462; the first figure of which, on the left, will denote the person; the next, the finger, and consequently, the hand; and the last, the joint.

It must here be observed, that when the last result contains a cipher, which would have happened in the present example, had the number of the finger been 10, you must privately subtract from the figure preceding the cipher, and assign the value of 10 to the cipher itself.

THE GAME OF THE BAG.

To let a person select several numbers out of a bag, and to tell him the number which shall exactly divide the sum of those he has chosen:—Provide a small bag, divided into two parts, into one of which put several tickets, numbered 6, 9, 15, 36, 63, 120, 213, 309, &c.; and in the other part put as many other tickets, marked No. 3 only. Draw a handful of tickets from the first part, and, after showing them to the company, put them into the bag again, and, having opened it a second time, desire any one to take out as many tickets as he thinks proper; when he has done that, you open privately the other part of the bag, and tell him to take out of it one ticket only. You may safely pronounce that the ticket shall contain the number by which the amount of the other numbers is divisible; for, as each of these numbers can be multiplied by 3, their sum total must, evidently, be divisible by that number. An ingenious mind may easily diversify this exercise, by marking the tickets in one part of the bag, with any numbers that are divisible by 9 only, the properties of both 9 and 3 being the same; and it should never be exhibited to the same company twice without being varied.

THE NUMBER NINE. (*See opposite page.*)

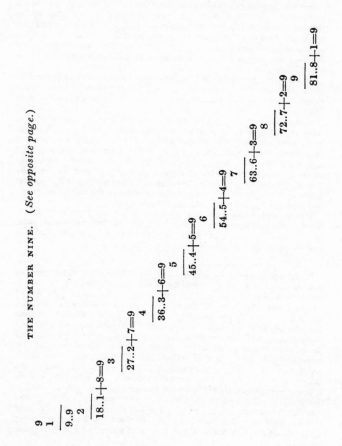

$$9$$
$$1$$
$$\overline{9..9}$$
$$2$$
$$\overline{18.1+8=9}$$
$$3$$
$$\overline{27..2+7=9}$$
$$4$$
$$\overline{36.3+6=9}$$
$$5$$
$$\overline{45..4+5=9}$$
$$6$$
$$\overline{54..5+4=9}$$
$$7$$
$$\overline{63.6+3=9}$$
$$8$$
$$\overline{72..7+2=9}$$
$$9$$
$$\overline{81..8+1=9}$$

THE NUMBER NINE. (*See opposite page.*)

The following discovery of remarkable properties of the number 9 was accidentally made, more than forty years since, though, we believe, it is not generally known :—

The component figures of the product made by the multiplication of every digit into the number 9, when added together, make NINE.

The order of these component figures is reversed, after the said number has been multiplied by 5.

The component figures of the amount of the multipliers, (*viz.* 45) when added together, make NINE.

The amount of the several products, or multiples of 9, (*viz.* 405) when divided by 9, gives, for a quotient, 45 ; that is, 4+5=NINE.

The amount of the first product, (*viz.* 9) when added to the other product, whose respective component figures make 9, is 81 ; which is the square of NINE.

The said number 81, when added to the above-mentioned amount of the several products, or multiples of 9 (*viz.* 405) makes 486 ; which, if divided by 9, gives, for a quotient, 54 : that is, 5+4=NINE.

It is also observable, that the number of changes that may be rung on nine bells, is 362,880 ; which figures, added together, make 27 ; that is, 2+7=NINE.

And the quotient of 362,880, divided by 9, will be 40,320 ; that is 4+0+3+2+0=NINE.

To add a figure to any given number, which shall render it divisible by Nine :—Add the figures together in your mind, which compose the number named ; and the figure which must be added to the sum produced, in order to render it divisible by 9, is the one required. Thus—

Suppose the given number to be 7521 :—

Add those together, and 15 will be produced ; now 15 requires 3 to render it divisible by 9 ; and that number, 3, being added to 7521, causes the same divisibility :—

$$7521$$
$$3$$
$$\overline{}$$
$$9)7524(836$$

This exercise may be diversified by your specifying, before the sum is named, the particular place where the figure shall be inserted, to make the number divisible by 9 ; for it is exactly the same thing, whether the figure be put at the head of the number, or between any two of its digits.

THE CERTAIN GAME.

Two persons agree to take, alternately, numbers less than a given number, for example, 11, and to add them together till one of them has reached a certain sum, such as 100. By what means can one of them infallibly attain to that number before the other?

The whole artifice in this, consists in immediately making choice of the numbers, 1, 12, 23, 34, and so on, or of a series which continually increases by 11, up to 100. Let us suppose, that the first person, who knows the game, makes choice of 1; it is evident that his adversary, as he must count less than 11, can, at most, reach 11, by adding 10 to it. The first will then take 1, which will make 12: and whatever number the second may add, the first will certainly win, provided he continually add the number which forms the complement of that of his adversary, to 11; that is to say, if the latter take 8, he must take 3; if 9, he must take 2; and so on. By following this method, he will infallibly attain to 89; and it will then be impossible for the second to prevent him from getting first to 100; for whatever number the second takes, he can attain only to 99; after which the first may say—"and 1 makes 100." If the second take 1 after 89, it would make 90, and his adversary would finish by saying—"and 10 make 100." Between two persons who are equally acquainted with the game, he who begins must necessarily win.

MAGICAL CENTURY.

If the number 11 be multiplied by any one of the nine digits, the two figures of the product will always be alike, as appears in the following example:—

| 11 | 11 | 11 | 11 | 11 | 11 | 11 | 11 | 11 |
1	2	3	4	5	6	7	8	9
11	22	33	44	55	66	77	88	99

Now, if another person and yourself have fifty counters apiece, and agree never to stake more than ten at a time, you may tell him, that if he permit you to stake first, you will always complete the even century before him.

In order to succeed, you must first stake 1, and remembering the order of the above series, constantly add to what he stakes as many as will make one more than the numbers 11, 22, 33, &c. of which it is composed, till you come to 89; after which your opponent cannot possibly reach the even century himself, or prevent you from reaching it.

If your opponent have no knowledge of numbers, you may stake any other number first, under 10, provided you subsequently take care to secure one of the last terms, 56, 67, 78, &c.; or you may even let him stake first, if you take care afterward to secure one of these numbers.

This exercise may be performed with other numbers; but, in order to succeed, you must divide the number to be attained, by a number which is a unit greater than what you can stake each time; and the remainder will then be the number you must first stake. Suppose, for example, the number to be attained be 52, (making use of a pack of cards instead of counters,) and that you are never to add more than 6; then, dividing 52 by 7, the remainder, which is 3, will be the number which you must first stake; and whatever your opponent stakes, you must add as much to it as will make it equal to 7, the number by which you divided, and so in continuation.

THE CANCELLED FIGURE GUESSED.

To tell the figure a person has struck out of the sum of two given numbers :—Arbitrarily command those numbers only, that are divisible by 9; such, for instance, as 36, 63, 81, 117, 126, 162, 261, 360, 315, and 432.

Then let a person choose any two of these numbers; and, after adding them together in his mind, strike out from the sum any one of the figures he pleases.

After he has so done, desire him to tell you the sum of the remaining figures; and it follows, that the number which you are obliged to add to this amount, in order to make it 9 or 18, is the one he struck out. Thus :—

Suppose he chooses the numbers 162 and 261, making altogether 423, and that he strike out the centre figure, the two other figures will, added together, make 7, which, to make 9, requires 2, the number struck out.

THE DICE GUESSED UNSEEN.

A pair of dice being thrown, to find the number of points on each die without seeing them :—Tell the person, who cast the dice, to double the number of points upon one of them, and add 5 to it; then, to multiply the sum produced by 5, and to add to the product the number of points upon the other die. This being done, desire him to tell you the amount, and, having thrown out 25, the remainder will be a number consisting of two figures, the first of which, to the left, is the number of points on the first die, and the second figure to the right, the number on the other. Thus :—

Suppose the number of points of the first die which comes up, to be 2, and that of the other 3; then, if to 4, the double of the points of the first, there be added 5, and the sum produced, 9, be multiplied by 5, the product will be 45; to which, if 3, the number of points on the other die, be added, 48 will be produced, from which, if 25 be subtracted, 23 will remain; the first figure of which is 2, the number of points on the first die, and the second figure 3, the number on the other.

THE SOVEREIGN AND THE SAGE.

A sovereign being desirous to confer a liberal reward on one of his courtiers, who had performed some very important service, desired him to ask whatever he thought proper, assuring him it should be granted. The courtier, who was well acquainted with the science of numbers, only requested that the monarch would give him a quantity of wheat equal to that which would arise from one grain doubled sixty-three times successively The value of the reward was immense; for it will be found, by calculation, that the sixty-fourth term of the double progression divided by 1 : 2 : 4 : 8 : 16 : 32 : &c., is 9223372036854775808. But the sum of all the terms of a double progression, beginning with 1, may be obtained by doubling the last term, and subtracting from it 1. The number of the grains of wheat, therefore, in the present case, will be 18446744073709551615. Now, if a pint contain 9216 grains of wheat, a gallon will contain 73728; and, as eight gallons make one bushel, if we divide the above result by eight times 73728, we shall have 31274997411295 for the number of the bushels of wheat equal to the above number of grains : a quantity greater than what the whole surface of the earth could produce in several years, and which, in value, would exceed all the riches, perhaps, on the globe.

THE HORSE-DEALER'S BARGAIN.

A gentleman, taking a fancy to a horse, which a horse-dealer wished to dispose of at as high a price as he could; the latter, to induce the gentleman to become a purchaser, offered to let him have the horse for the value of the twenty-fourth nail in his shoes, reckoning one farthing for the first nail, two for the second, four for the third, and so on to the twenty-fourth. The gentleman, thinking he should have a good bargain, accepted the offer; the price of the horse was, therefore, necessarily great.

By calculating as before, the twenty-fourth term of the progression, 1 : 2 : 4 : 8 : &c., will be found to be 8388608, equal to the number of farthings the purchaser gave for the horse; the price, therefore, amounted to £8738. 2s. 8d.

THE DINNER PARTY.

A club of seven persons agreed to dine together every day successively, as long as they could sit down to table differently arranged. How many dinners would be necessary for that purpose? It may be easily found, by the rules already given, that the club must dine together 5040 times, before they would exhaust all the arrangements possible, which would require above thirteen years.

COMBINATIONS OF AN ANAGRAM.

If any word be proposed, for instance, AMOR, and it be required to know how many different words could be formed of these four letters, which will give all the possible anagrams of that word, we shall find by multiplying together 1, 2, 3, and 4, that they are in number, 24, as represented in the following table:—

AMOR	MORA	ORAM	RAMO
AMRO	MOAR	ORMA	RAOM
AOMR	MROA	OARM	RMAO
AORM	MRAO	OAMR	RMOA
ARMO	MAOR	OMRA	ROAM
AROM	MARO	OMAR	ROMA

THE BASKET AND THE STONES.

If a hundred stones be placed in a straight line, at the distance of a yard from each other, the first being at the same distance from a basket, how many yards must the person walk who engages to pick them up, one by one, and put them into the basket? It is evident that, to pick up the first stone, and put it into the basket, the person must walk two yards; for the second, he must walk four; for the third, six; and so on, increasing by two, to the hundredth.

The number of yards, therefore, which the person must walk, will be equal to the sum of the progression, 2, 4, 6, &c. the last term of which is 200, (22.) But the sum of the progression is equal to 202, the sum of the two extremes, multiplied by 50, or half the number of terms: that is to say, 10,100 yards, which makes more than $5\frac{1}{2}$ miles.

THE ARITHMETICAL MOUSETRAP.

One of the best, and most simple mousetraps in use, may be constructed in the following manner:—Get a slip of smooth board, about the eighth of an inch thick, a quarter of an inch broad, and of a sufficient length to cut out the following parts of the trap. First, an upright piece, three or four inches high, which must be square at the bottom, and a small piece be cut off the top to fit the notch in No. 2, (see No. 1 in the margin.) The second piece must be of the same length as the first, with a notch cut across nearly at the top of it, to fit the top of No. 1, and the other end of it trimmed to catch the notch in No. 3, (see No. 2.) The third piece should be twice as long as either of the others; a notch, similar to that in No. 2, must be cut in one end of it, to catch the lower end of No. 2. Having

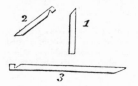

proceeded thus far, you must put the pieces together, in order to finish it, by adding another notch in No. 3, the exact situation of which you will discover as follows :—Place No. 1, as it is in the cut, then put the notch of No. 2 on the thinned top of No. 1; keep it in the same inclination as in the cut; then get a flat piece of wood, or slate, one end of which must rest on the ground, and the centre of the edge of the other on the top of No. 2. You will now find the thinned end of No. 2 elevated by the weight of the flat piece of wood or slate; then put the thinned end of it in the notch of No. 3, and draw No. 2 down by it, until the whole forms a resemblance of a figure 4 : at the exact place where No. 3 touches the upright, cut a notch, which, by catching the end of No. 1, will keep the trap together. You may now bait the end of No. 3 with a piece of cheese ; a mouse, by nibbling the bait, will pull down No. 3, the other pieces immediately separate, and the slate or board falls upon the mouse. We have seen numbers of mice, rats, and birds, caught by this

Figure of 4 Trap.

OPTICAL AMUSEMENTS.

What wonders may be brought to pass,
By the optician's magic glass!
A barley-corn of painted paper,
Illumin'd by a farthing taper,
Into a spacious plain extendeth,
Whereon Dan Sol his hot glance bendeth.
The leech's paltry, dark green potion
Is magnified into an ocean:
His little, crabb'd, perspective scrawl,
Into th' hand-writing on the wall:
Look one way, and a blow-fly's nose
To elephant's proboscis grows:
Turn t'other end, hippopotamus
Becomes a gnat compared with a mouse.

THE science of optics affords an infinite variety of amusements, which cannot fail to instruct the mind as well as delight the eye. By the aid of optical instruments we are enabled to lessen the distance to our visual organs between the globe we inhabit and " the wonders of the heavens above us;" to observe the exquisite finish, and propriety of construction, which are to be found in the most minute productions of the earth;—to trace the path of the planet in its course round the magnificent orb of day, and to detect the pulsation of the blood, as it flows through the veins of an insect. These are but a small portion of the powers which this science offers to man; to enumerate them all would require a space equal to the body of our work: neither do we propose to notice, in the following pages, the various instruments and experiments which are devoted solely, or rather, chiefly, to purposes merely scientific; it being our intention merely to call the attention of our juvenile readers to such things as combine a vast deal of amusement with much instruction; to inform them as to the construction of the various popular instruments; to show the manner of using them, and to explain some of the most attractive experiments which the science affords. By doing thus much, we hope to offer a sufficient inducement to push inquiry much further than the information which a work of this nature will enable us to afford.

THE CAMERA OBSCURA.

We give our young friends a brief description of this optical invention; though very common, it is extremely amusing; almost every one has seen

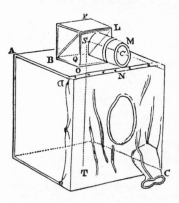

it, but few persons know how to construct it. A C represents a box of about a foot and a half square, shut on every side except at D C; O P is a smaller box, placed on the top of the greater; M N is a double convex lens, whose axis makes an angle of forty-five degrees with B L, a plane mirror, fixed in the box, O P; the focal length of the lens is nearly equal to C S + S T, *i. e*, to the sum of the distances of the lens from the middle of the mirror, and of the middle of the mirror from the bottom of the large box. The lens being turned toward the prospect, would form a picture of it, nearly at its focus; but the rays, being intercepted by the mirror, will form the picture as far before the surface as the focus is behind it, that is, at the bottom of the larger box; a communication being made between the boxes by the vacant space, Q O. This instrument is frequently used for the delineation of landscapes: for which purpose, the draughtsman, putting his head and hand into the box, through the open side,

D C, and drawing a curtain round to prevent the admission of the light, which would disturb the operation, can trace a distinct outline of the picture that appears at the bottom of the box.

There is another kind of camera obscura, for the purposes of drawing, constructed thus : in the extremity of the arm, P Q, that extends from the side of a small square box, B L, is placed a double convex lens, whose axis is inclined in an angle of forty-five degrees, to a plane mirror, B O ; the focal length of the lens is equal to its distance from the side of the box, O T ; therefore, when the lens is turned toward the illuminated prospect, it would project the image on the side, O T, if the mirror were removed ; but this will

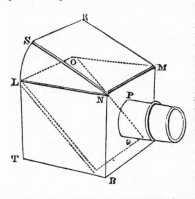

reflect the image to the side, M L, which is as far distant from the middle of the mirror as this is from the side, O T. It is there received on a piece of glass, rough at the upper side, and smooth at the lower, and appears in its proper colors on the upper side of the plate. It is evident that in each of these instruments the image is inverted with respect to the object. M S is a lid to prevent the admission of light during the delineation of the picture ; and others, for the same purpose, are applied to the sides, M R and N L.

You may also construct the camera obscura in a room, thus :—you first darken the room, by closing the shutters, and every place where the external light can be admitted. You then cut a circular hole in the shutter, or a board placed against the window, in which you place a lens, or convex-glass, the focus of which is at the distance of not less than four, nor more than fifteen or twenty feet : from six to twelve feet is the best distance. At this distance, also, place a pasteboard, covered with the whitest paper, with a black border, to prevent any of the side rays from disturbing the picture ; let it be two feet and a half long, and eighteen or twenty inches high ; bend the length of it inward, to the form of part of a circle, the diameter of which is equal to double the focal distance of the glass : then fix it on a frame of the same figure, and place it upon a movable foot, that it may be easily fixed at that exact distance from the glass where the objects paint themselves to the greatest perfection. When it is thus placed, all the objects which are in the front of the window will be painted upon the paper, in an inverted position, with the greatest regularity, and in the most natural colors.

There is another method of making the camera obscura, by a scioptric ball; that is, a ball of wood, through which a hole is made, in which hole a lens is fixed: this ball is placed in a wooden frame, in which it turns freely round; the frame is fixed to the hole in the shutter, and the ball, by turning about, answers, in great part, the use of the mirror on the outside of the window. If the hole in the window be not bigger than a pea, the objects will be represented without any lens.

If you place a movable mirror without the window, by turning it more or less, you will have upon the paper all the objects which are on each side of the window.

The inverted position of the images may be deemed an imperfection, but it is easily remedied; for, if you stand above the board, on which they are received, and look down upon it, they will appear in their natural position; or, if you stand before it, and, placing a common mirror against your breast, in an oblique direction, look down in it, you will there see the images erect, and they will receive an additional lustre from the reflection of the glass; or, place two lenses in a tube that draws out; or, lastly, if you place a large concave mirror at a proper distance before the picture, it will appear before the mirror in the air, and in an erect position.

If, instead of putting the mirror without the window, you place it in the room, and above the hole, (which must then be made near the top of the shutter,) you may receive the representation on a paper placed horizontally on a table, and draw all the objects that there appear painted.

THE MAGNIFYING CAMERA OBSCURA.

Let the rays of light that pass through the lens in the shutter be thrown on a large concave mirror, properly fixed in a frame. Then take a slip or thin plate of glass, and sticking any small object to it, hold it in the incident rays, at a little more than the focal distance from the mirror, and you will see, on the opposite wall, amidst the reflected rays, the image of that object, very large, and extremely clear and bright.

THE PRISMATIC CAMERA OBSCURA.

Make two holes, F, f, (Fig. 1,) in the shutter of a dark chamber, near to each other; and against each hole, a prism, A B C, and $a\ b\ c$, in a perpendicular direction, that their spectrums, M N, may be cast on the paper in a horizontal line, and coincide with each other; the red and violet of the one being in the same part with those of the other. The paper should be placed at such a distance from the prisms that the spectrum may be sufficiently dilated. Provide several papers nearly of the same dimensions with the spectrum, cross these papers, and draw lines parallel to the divisions of the colors: in these divisions cut out such figures as you may find will have an agreeable effect, as flowers, trees, animals, &c. When you have placed one of these papers in its proper position, hang a black cloth or paper behind it, that none of the rays that pass through may be reflected, and confuse the phenomenon: the figure cut on the paper will then appear strongly illuminated with all the original colors of nature.

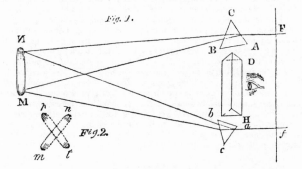

Fig. 1.

Fig. 2.

If, while one of the prisms remains at rest, the other be revolved on its axis, the continual alteration of the colors will afford a pleasing variety: which may be farther increased, by turning the prism round in different directions. When the prisms are so placed that the two spectrums become coincident in an inverted order of their colours, the red end of one falling on the violet end of the other, if they be then viewed through a third prism, D H, held parallel to their length, they will no longer appear coincident, but in the form of two distinct spectrums, $p\,t$ and $n\,m$, (fig. 2,) crossing one another in the middle, like the letter X. The red of one spectrum, and the violet of the other, which were coincident at N M, being parted from each other by a greater refraction of the violet to p and m, than that of the red to n and t.

This recreation may be farther diversified by adding two other prisms, that shall form a spectrum in the same line, and contiguous to the other; by which not only the variety of figures, but the vicissitude of colors, will be considerably augmented.

CAMERA LUCIDA.

Opposite to the place or wall where the appearance is to be, make a hole of at least a foot in diameter; or, if there be a high window with a casement of that dimension in it, this will do much better, without such hole or casement opened. At a convenient distance, to prevent its being perceived by the company in the room, place the object or picture intended to be represented, but in an inverted situation. If the picture be transparent, reflect the sun's rays by means of a looking-glass, so that they may pass through it toward the place of representation; and, to prevent any rays from passing aside it, let the picture be encompassed with some board or cloth. If the object be a statue, or a living creature, it must be enlightened by casting the sun's rays on it, either by reflection, refraction, or both. Between this object and the place of representation put a broad convex glass, ground to such a convexity as that it may represent the object distinctly in such place. The nearer this is situated to the object, the more will the image be magnified upon the wall, and the further, the less; such diversity depending on the difference of the spheres of the glasses. If the object cannot be conveniently inverted, there must be two large glasses of proper spheres, situated at suitable distances, easily found, by trial, to make the representation correct. This whole apparatus of object, glasses, &c. with the persons employed in the management of them, are to be placed without the window or hole, so that they may not be perceived by the spectators in the room, and the operation itself will be easily performed.

THE POLEMOSCOPE.

By a polemoscope you may see what passes in another place without being seen from thence yourself: it may be made by fixing, in a common opera-glass, a small mirror, inclined to an angle of forty-five degrees, and adjusting a proper object-glass; by this, while appearing to look straight forward, you may see what passes on one side of you. This instrument may also be so constructed that the tube may turn round, and the mirror be elevated or depressed, that you may see successively, and at pleasure, all the objects that you would perceive, if you were at the top of the wall against which the instrument is placed.

THE KALEIDOSCOPE.

To construct this instrument procure a tube of tin, brass, pasteboard, or any other material, eight or ten inches long, and one and a half or two inches in diameter; place a cap upon one end, with a small hole in the centre, at the circumference of the circle, *d*, in the annexed figure, which is a view of the right end of the instrument, from which the cap has been removed. The circle is the edge of the tube, the lines, *a c* and *b c*, are the edges of the two reflecting surfaces, which are nearly of the same length as the tube: they may be made of

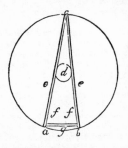

two pieces of looking-glass, or of plate-glass or crown-glass, which have been blackened on one side at *e e*, the surfaces *f f*, being well polished. The blackening may be effected with the smoke of a lamp simply, or upon varnish, or with any other black matter which effectually resists the rays of light; and the two reflectors must be kept apart at *g*, by means of a piece of cork, or any other substance, placed at each end of the tube. At *c*, where the reflectors join, they should be straight, and adapted to each other; or they may be placed differently, or even parallel, as in the figure following. At the other end of the tube, (the object end,) where the two reflecting surfaces, *a c b c*, terminate, a circular piece of ground glass is to be fitted into the tube, and retained there by means of a piece of wire, which is to be bent to a circle, and placed upon the glass to keep it steady. Over this end let another tube be fitted, an inch or two in length

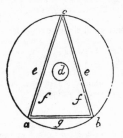

at least, capable of being turned round; and, at its end, let another circular piece of glass, smooth, be fitted in, similarly to the preceding. Into this outer cap, or tube, put the objects to be viewed, which may consist of any semi-transparent colored substances, as glass, beads, shells, or pearls, and the like, but not too many at a time. Place the cap on, and then, advancing the tube to the eye, still keeping the side, *a b*, upward, look through at *d*, and you will have a brilliant symmetrical repetition of the objects which are placed between the two glasses and visible through the angular aperture, *a b c*. Turn round the cap, more or less, in which the objects are so placed, and you will perceive a change in the combinations of the images; new forms will present themselves, entirely different from the former, sometimes arising out of the centre, at others vanishing there, and occasionally playing round it in double and opposite oscillations. Standing still, however, the draughtsman may copy off upon paper the *shapes* that present themselves, if he cannot hope to equal the varied tints, which are developed in succession; each new one delighting the eye by the perfection of its forms and the brilliancy of its coloring, both of which depend upon previously managing the objects to be viewed, and the angle at which the two reflectors, *d c*, and *b c*, are fixed.

Instead of *two* reflectors, this instrument may be constructed with three or more such planes, which may be arranged differently as regards each other : but the perfection of the kaleidoscope is to be found in procuring the reflection of distant natural objects, and in reducing them to the size proper for pictorial representation. This may be accomplished by fixing upon the object end a convex lens, fastened to the *slider tube*, which must then be nearly as long as the inner one, in order that the right focus may be found, which is adapted to the particular object ; so two or three lenses may be kept, of several focal lengths, which should be always less than its greatest distance from the sight-hole, and will be found, generally, at from one-fourth to a third of that distance. A further variation, however, may be obtained, by introducing two lenses ; one fixed to the inner tube, the other to the slider ; and approaching to or receding from these, by means of the slider, the focus will be found.

As a matter of economy to those who may possess a telescope, it is suggested, that the size of the kaleidoscope may be made to correspond with that instrument, so that its glasses may be occasionally borrowed. A concave glass, placed at the sight-hole, (*d*, fig. 2,) will throw the objects off, and reduce their size by taking care that the focal length be equal to the length of the *reflectors*.

Supposing the instrument to contain twenty small pieces of glass, &c. and that you make ten changes in each minute, it will take the inconceivable space of 462,880,899,576 years and 360 days, to go through the immense variety of changes it is capable of producing, amounting (according to our frail idea of the nature of things) to an eternity. Or, if you take only twelve small pieces, and make ten changes in each minute, it will then require 33,264 days, or 91 years and 49 days, to exhaust its variations.

THE MAGIC LANTERN.

The object of this ingenious instrument is to represent, in a dark room, on a white wall or cloth, a succession of enlarged figures, of remarkable, natural, or grotesque objects. The figure in the next page is a representation of one. It consists of a tin box, with a funnel on the top, represented by *e*, and a door on one side of it. This funnel, by being bent, as shown in the figure, serves the double purpose of letting out the smoke, and keeping in the light. In the middle of the bottom of the box is placed a movable tin lamp, *a*, which must have two or three good lights, at the height of the centre of the polished tin reflector, *c*. In the front of the box, opposite the reflector, is fixed a tin tube, *m*, in which there slides another tube, *n*. The

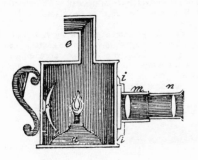

sliding tube has, at its outer extremity, a convex lens, of about two inches diameter; the tube, *m*, also has a convex lens fixed in it, as shown in the figure, of three inches diameter. The focus of the smaller of these lenses may be about five inches. Between the tube, *m*, and the lamp, there must be a slit or opening, (as at *i i*) to admit of the passage of glass sliders, mounted in paper or wooden frames, such as are represented below; upon which slid-ers it is that the miniature figures are painted, which are intended to be shown upon the wall. The distinctness of the enlarged figures depends not only upon the goodness of the magnifying glass, but upon the clearness of the light yielded by the lamp, *a*. It may be purchased ready made of any optician.

To paint the glasses. Draw on a paper the subject you desire to paint. Lay it on a table or any flat surface, and place the glass over it: then draw the outlines, with a very fine pencil, in varnish mixed with black paint, and, when dry, fill up the other parts in their proper colors. Transparent colors must be used for this purpose, such as carmine, lake, Prussian blue, verdigris, sulphate of iron, tincture of Brazil wood, gamboge, &c.; and these must be tempered with a strong white varnish, to prevent their peeling off. Then shade them with black, or with bistre, mixed with the same varnish.

To exhibit the Magic Lantern. The lamp being lighted, and the room darkened, place the machine on the table, at some distance from the white wall or suspended sheet, and introduce into the slit, $i\ i$, one of the sliders represented above, with the figures inverted. If the movable tube, n, be then pushed in or drawn out, till the proper focus be obtained, the figures on the slider will be reflected on the wall, in their distinct colors and proportions, with the appearance of life itself, and of any size, from six inches to seven feet, according to the distance of the lantern from the wall. Movements of the figures are easily made by painting the subject on two glasses, and passing the same through the groove.

To represent a tempest. Provide two plates of glass, whose frames are so thin, that they may both pass freely through the groove of the common magic lantern at the same time. On one of these, paint the appearance of the sea, from the slightest agitation to the most violent commotion : representing, first, a calm ; afterward a small agitation, with some clouds ; and so on to the end, which should exhibit a furious storm.

These representations are not to be distinct, but run into each other, that they may form a natural gradation ; and great part of the effect depends on the perfection of the painting, and the picturesque appearance of the design.

On the other glass, paint vessels of different forms and dimensions, and in different directions, together with the appearance of clouds in the tempestuous parts.

Both glasses being done, pass the first slowly through the groove ; and when you come to that part where the storm begins, move it gently up and down, which will produce the appearance of a sea that begins to be agitated ; and so increase the motion till you come to the height of the storm. At the same time introduce the other glass with the ships, and moving that in like manner, they will exhibit a natural representation of the sea, and of ships in a calm and in a storm. As the glasses are drawn slowly back, the tempest will seem to subside, the sky grow clear, and the ships glide gently over the waves.

By means of two glasses, disposed in the before-mentioned manner, numberless other subjects may be represented.

THE APPARITION.

Inclose a small magic lantern in a box large enough to contain a small swing dressing-glass, which will reflect the light thrown on it by the lantern in such a way, that it will pass out at the aperture made at the top of the box, which aperture should be oval, and of a size adapted to the cone of light to pass through it. There should be a flap with hinges, to cover the opening, that the inside of the box may not be seen. There must be holes in that part of the box which is over the lantern, to let the smoke out; and over this must be placed a chafing-dish, of an oblong figure, large enough to hold several lighted coals. This chafing-dish, for the better carrying on the deception, may be inclosed in a painted tin box, about a foot high, with a hole at top, and should stand on four feet, to let the smoke of the lantern escape. There must also be a glass planned to move up and down in the groove, *a b*, and so managed by a cord and pulley, *c d e f*, that it may be raised up and let down by the cord coming through the outside of the box. On this glass, the spectre (or any other figure you please) must be painted, in a contracted or squat form, as the figure will reflect a greater length than it is drawn.

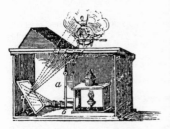

When you have lighted the lamp in the lantern, and placed the mirror in a proper direction, put the box on a table, and, setting the chafing-dish in it, throw some incense in powder on the coals. You then open the trap door and let down the glass in the groove slowly, and when you perceive the smoke diminish, draw up the glass that the figure may disappear, and shut the trap door.

This exhibition will afford a deal of wonder: but observe, that all the lights in the room must be extinguished; and the box should be placed on a high table, that the aperture through which the light comes out may not be seen.

THE NEBULOUS MAGIC LANTERN.

The light of the magic lantern, and the color of images, may not only be painted on a cloth, but also reflected by a cloud of smoke. Provide a box of wood or pasteboard, about four feet high, and seven or eight inches square at bottom, but diminishing as it ascends, so that its aperture at top be but six inches long, and half an inch wide. At the bottom of this box there must be a door that shuts quite close, by which you are to place in the box a chafing-dish with hot coals, on which is to be thrown incense, whose smoke goes out in a cloud at the top of the box : on this cloud, you are to throw the light that comes out of the lantern, and which you bring into a smaller compass by drawing out the movable tube. The common figure will here serve.

It is remarkable in this representation, that the motion of the smoke does not at all change the figures; which appear so conspicuous that the spectator thinks he can grasp them with his hand. In the experiment, some of the rays passing through the smoke, the representation will be much less vivid than on the cloth; and if care be not taken to reduce the light to its smallest focus, it will be still more imperfect.

THE PHANTASMAGORIA.

In the exhibition of the common magic lantern, the spectators see a round circle of light with the figures in the middle of it ; but, in the Phantasmagoria, they see the figures only, without any circle of light. The exhibition is produced by a magic lantern, placed on that side of a half-transparent screen which is opposite to that on which the spectators are, instead of being on the same side, as in the ordinary exhibition of the magic lantern. To favor the deception, the sliders are made perfectly opaque, except in those places that contain the figures to be exhibited, and in these light parts the glass is covered with a more or less transparent tint, according to the effect required. The easiest way is to draw the figures with water colors on thin paper, and afterward varnish them. To imitate the natural motions of the objects represented, several pieces of glass, placed behind each other, are occasionally employed. By removing the lantern to different distances, and, at the same time, altering, more or less, the position of the lens, the images are made to increase and diminish, and to become more or less distinct at the pleasure of the exhibitor; so that, to a person unacquainted with the effect of optical instruments, these figures appear actually to advance and recede.

To make transparent screens for the Phantasmagoria. Transparent screens are prepared by spreading white wax, dissolved in spirits of wine or oil of turpentine, over thin muslin : a screen so prepared may be rolled up without injury. A clearer screen may be produced, by having the muslin always strained upon a rectangular frame, and preparing it with turpentine, instead of wax : but such a screen is not always convenient, and cannot be rolled without cracking, and becoming, in a short time, useless ; therefore, nothing can be better for the purpose than the former.

SOLAR MICROSCOPE.

The solar microscope is constructed in the following manner. In the inside of a tube is placed a convex lens, A B, and at a distance a little greater than its focal length, but less than double of it, is fixed some transparent colored object, Q P, at the focus conjugate to the place of the object.

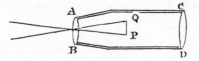

A broad lens, C D, is placed before the object, to collect the solar rays, for the purpose of illuminating it more strongly, and, consequently, making the image more distinct and vivid.

TO CONSTRUCT A LANTERN WHICH WILL ENABLE A PERSON TO READ BY NIGHT AT A GREAT DISTANCE.

Make a lantern of a cylindric form, or shaped like a small cask placed lengthwise, so that its axis may be horizontal, and fix in one end of it a parabolic or spheric mirror, so that its focus may fall about the middle of the axis of the cylinder. If a small lamp or taper be placed in this focus, the light passing through the other end will be reflected to a great distance, and will be so bright that the very small letters on a remote object may be read, by looking at them with a good telescope. Those who see this light, if they be in the direction of the axis of the lantern, will think they see a large fire.

THE CHINESE SHADOWS, (OMBRES CHINOISES.)

Make an aperture in a partition wall, of any size; for example, four feet in length and two in breadth, so that the lower edge may be about five feet from the floor, and cover it with white Italian gauze, varnished with gumcopal. Provide several frames of the same size as the aperture, covered with the same kind of gauze, and delineate upon the gauze different figures, such as landscapes and buildings, analogous to the scenes which you intend to exhibit by means of small figures representing men and animals.

These figures are formed of pasteboard, and their different parts are made movable, according to the effect intended to be produced by their shadows, when moved backward and forward behind the frames, and at a small distance from them. To make them act with more facility, small wires, fixed to their movable parts, are bent backward, and made to terminate in rings, through which the fingers of the hand are put, while the figure is supported by the left, by means of another iron wire. In this manner they may be made to advance or recede, and to gesticulate, without the spectators observing the mechanism by which they are moved; and, as the shadow of these figures is not observed on the paintings till they are opposite those parts which are not strongly shaded, they may thus be concealed, and made to appear at the proper moments, and others may be occasionally substituted in their stead.

It is necessary, when the figures are made to act, to keep up a sort of dialogue, suited to their gestures, and even to imitate the noise occasioned by different circumstances. The paintings must be illuminated from behind, by means of a reverberating lamp, placed opposite to the centre of the painting, and distant from it about four or five feet. Various amusing scenes may be represented in this manner, by employing small figures of men and animals, and making them move in as natural a way as possible, which will depend on the address and practice of the person who exhibits them.

THE MARVELLOUS MIRROR.

In the wainscot of a room make two openings, of a foot high, and ten inches wide, and about a foot distant from each other: let them be at the common height of a man's head; and, in each of them, place a transparent glass, surrounded with a frame, like a common mirror. Behind this partition place two mirrors, one on the outward side of each opening, inclined to the wainscot in an angle of forty-five degrees; let them be both eighteen inches square; let all the space between them be enclosed by boards or pasteboard, painted black, and well closed, that no light may enter; let there be also two curtains to cover them, which may be drawn aside at pleasure. When a person looks into one of these supposed mirrors, instead of seeing his own face he will perceive the object that is in the front of the other; so that, if two persons present themselves at the same time before these mirrors, instead of each one seeing himself they will reciprocally see each other. There should be a sconce with a candle or lamp placed on each side of the two glasses in the wainscot, to enlighten the faces of the persons who look in them, otherwise this experiment will have no remarkable effect.

This recreation may be considerably improved by placing the two glasses in the wainscot, in adjoining rooms, and a number of persons being previously placed in one room, when a stranger enters the other, you may tell him his face is dirty, and desire him to look in the glass, which he will naturally do; and on seeing a strange face he will draw back; but returning to it, and seeing another, another, and another, like the phantom kings in Macbeth, what his surprise will be is more easy to conceive than express. After this, a real mirror may be privately let down on the back of the glass, and if he can be prevailed on to look in it once more, he will then, to his farther astonishment, see his own face; and may be told, perhaps persuaded, that all he thought he saw before was mere imagination.

When a man looks in a mirror that is placed perpendicularly to another, his face will appear entirely deformed. If the mirror be a little inclined, so as to make an angle of eighty degrees, (that is, one-ninth part from the perpendicular,) he will then see all the parts of his face, except the nose and forehead : if it be inclined to sixty degrees, (that is, one-third part,) he will appear with three noses and six eyes : in short, the apparent deformity will vary at each degree of inclination ; and when the glass comes to forty-five degrees, (that is, half-way down,) the face will vanish. If, instead of placing the two mirrors in this situation, they are so disposed that their junction may be vertical, their different inclinations will produce other effects ; as the situation of the object relative to these mirrors is quite different.

INGENIOUS ANAMORPHOSIS.

This recreation shows how to draw, on a flat surface, an irregular figure, which shall appear, when seen from a proper point of view, not only regular, but elevated. Provide a thin board, about two feet long and one foot wide, as A B C D, and place thereon a circular piece of card or stiff drawing paper, on which a distorted figure is to be drawn, that, being viewed from the point, H, shall appear regular, and exactly resembling that which is placed at M F.

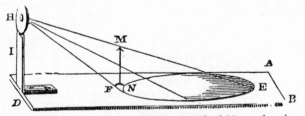

Fix, at the end of the board, an upright piece, I, of thin wood or tin, at the top of which is a sight-hole, H, of two-tenths of an inch in diameter.

Prepare a lamp, or candlestick, the light of which may be raised or lowered at pleasure, and to which is fixed a brass arm, bearing a sort of conical funnel, D, and whose opening at the end next the light is not more than three or four tenths of an inch in diameter.

Draw the subject you would represent on a piece of glass of equal height with the space, M F, with a very light stroke, and with any color that is quite opaque. Then remove the upright piece, I, and place the lamp, so prepared, in such a manner that the light may be exactly where the sight-hole, H, was. Its rays then passing through the glass at M F, will enlighten the surface of your paper, and there show, in a distorted form, the subject that is painted on the glass.   Then draw, with a pencil, all the strokes

of the shadow as they appear, and, taking away the light, replace the upright side-piece, I, and see if what you have drawn correspond with the subject on the glass, correcting what imperfections there may happen to be.   In the last place, color the subject, so traced, with the utmost attention, inspecting your work, from time to time, from the point of view, before you give it the finishing stroke.   When the figure, that is drawn and painted on your paper, is viewed from the sight, H, it appears to be at the same point where the glass, M F, was placed, and in the same form that it was painted on the glass.   It appears to the eye even elevated above the surface of the board on which the drawing is placed, and thereby receives a remarkable and pleasing illusion.

SINGULAR ILLUSION.

Affix to a dark wall a round piece of paper an inch or two in diameter; and, a little lower, at the distance of two feet on each side, make two marks; then place yourself directly opposite to the paper, and hold the end of your finger before your face in such a manner, that when the right eye is open, it shall conceal the mark on the left, and, when the left eye is open, the mark on the right; if you then look with both eyes to the end of your finger, the paper, which is not at all concealed by it from either of your eyes, will, nevertheless, disappear.

ANOTHER.

Fix, at the height of the eye, on a dark ground, a small round piece of white paper, and a little lower, at the distance of two feet to the right, fix up another, of about three inches in diameter; then place yourself opposite to the first piece of paper, and, having shut the left eye, retire backward, keeping your eye still fixed on the first object: when you are at the distance of nine or ten feet, the second will entirely disappear from your sight.

THE MULTIPLIED MONEY.

Take a large drinking-glass, of a conical form, that is, small at bottom, and wide at top, and, having put into it a shilling, let it be half filled with water; then place a plate upon the top of the glass, and turn it quickly over, that the water may not get out: a piece of silver as large as half-a-crown will immediately appear on the plate, and, somewhat higher up, another piece of the size of a shilling.

CHEMICAL AMUSEMENTS.

They play such merry pranks, that some would think
They entertained an imp to conjure for them.
Yet 'tis not so :—their few hours of pastime,
These young disciples of the Alchymist
Adorn with feats, which, to the unlearned eye,
Show oft like magic :—but grandam Wisdom
Knows them as recreations of young Science,
In sportive mood, upon a holyday.

CHEMISTRY has been called, by its votaries, a fascinating science, and
with some truth, for it certainly affords more recreation than any other :
that it is the most useful of all sciences cannot be denied, nor can there
be a doubt that it has a tendency almost to enchant those who devote their
attention to it. Its powers are almost infinite, and, in some instances, produce effects which appear magical: a great number of those conjuring
tricks, which have astonished our cotemporaries as much as our forefathers,
have been effected solely by its agency. It is not, of course, our intention
to teach our readers chemistry in all its branches, but merely to direct the

inquiring mind of youth to skim lightly and agreeably over its surface : for this purpose, we have selected a series of experiments for their amusement, not doubting but that they will consider the time profitably spent in perusing them, and we flatter ourselves that they will be an inducement to carry their inquiries much further than our limits will afford. For those who wish to be instructed as well as amused, we have added some explanations of the decompositions, or chemical changes, which take place, in order to show that, although almost magical in appearance, they are dependent upon some fixed and unerring law of nature. Without any further prefatory observations, we shall now commence our Chemical Recreations.

CRYSTALLIZATION OF SALTS.

1. Dissolve one ounce of sulphate of soda (Glauber's salts) in two ounces of boiling water ; pour it while hot, into a phial, and cork it close. In this state it will not crystallize when cold ; but if the cork be removed, the crystallization will commence and proceed rapidly.

The presence of atmospheric air is necessary in the process of crystallization ; the experiment will occasionally fail when under unfavorable circumstances : should this be the case, drop into the fluid a crystal of Glauber's salt, and the whole will immediately commence shooting into beautiful crystals.

2. Repeat the above experiment with a small thermometer immersed in the solution, and corked up with it. When cold, remove the cork, and the thermometer will be seen to rise. This experiment shows that heat is given out in the act of crystallization.

3. Take half an ounce of caustic soda, (common soda,) and dissolve it in about its own weight of water ; then pour into the solution half an ounce of sulphuric acid (oil of vitriol :) when the mixture is cold, crystals of sulphate of soda will be found in the liquor.

4. Take caustic soda, and pour upon it muriatic acid : this will produce muriate of soda, our common table salt.

5. Take of carbonate of ammonia, (the common volatile smelling salts,) and pour upon it muriatic acid until the effervescence cease. The produce will be a solid salt, viz. muriate of ammonia, or crude salammoniac of the shops. Caustic substances corrode matter in consequence of their tendency to unite with it ; they continue to act upon it until they are saturated by the combination.

6. Mix two ounces of semi-vitrified oxyd of lead (litharge) with three drachms of muriate of ammonia, and submit the whole to a strong heat in a crucible. The heat will drive off the ammonia, and the muriatic acid

will combine with the lead, forming a muriate of lead. When the operation is complete, pour the ingredients into a metallic vessel to cool and crystallize. This is the patent yellow used by painters.

In this experiment, the lead is dissolved by the muriatic acid, which has been disengaged by the heat driving off the ammonia with which it was previously combined.

SYMPATHETIC INKS.

1. Write with a diluted solution of muriate or nitrate of cobalt, and the writing will be invisible; but, upon being held to the fire, it will appear perfectly distinct, and of a blue color : if the cobalt should be adulterated with iron, the writing will appear of a green color. When taken from the fire, the writing will again disappear. If a landscape be drawn and all finished with common colors, except the leaves of the trees, the grass and the sky, and the latter be finished with this sympathetic ink, and the two former with the adulterated solution just mentioned, the drawing will seem to be unfinished, and have a wintry appearance ; but, upon being held to the fire, the grass and the trees will become green, the sky blue, and the whole assume a rich and beautiful appearance.

2. Write with a diluted solution of muriate of copper, and the writing will be invisible when cold ; but, on being held to the fire, it will appear of a yellow color. A landscape may be drawn and finished, as in the last experiment, and, in addition to the sympathetic inks there used, corn fields may be painted or finished with this sympathetic ink. The whole will have a very drear and bleak aspect till held before a fire, when it will instantly assume a cheerful and lively appearance, as if by magic. If human beings be drawn in common colors, as if in the act of reaping, the whole will appear more curious and interesting. These landscapes will, at any time, exhibit the same appearance.

3. Write with a weak solution of alum in lemon-juice, and the characters will remain invisible until wetted with water, which renders them of a grayish color, and quite transparent. A letter written with a solution of rock-alum alone, being dried, and having a small quantity of water poured over it, will appear of a whiter color than the paper.

4. Write with a weak solution of sulphate of iron, (green vitriol ;) when dry it will appear invisible ; but if wetted over with a brush, dipped in tincture of galls, or a strong decoction of oak bark, the writing will be restored, and appear black.

5. Write with the above solution ; when dry, wash it over with a solution of prussiate of potash, and the writing will be restored to a beautiful blue.

In all secret or sympathetic writing, as it is called, there is a chemical decomposition : this is more particularly striking in the two last experiments ; in the former of which, the gallic acid unites with the iron, forming a black ; and in the latter, the prussic acid unites with the iron, forming a blue, or prussiate of iron.

HEAT AND COLD.

1. Take one ounce of muriate of ammonia, the same quantity of nitrate of potash, (saltpetre,) and two ounces of sulphate of soda : reduce these salts separately into powder, and mix them gradually with four ounces of water ; the result will be, that as the salts dissolve, cold will be produced. A thermometer, immersed in the mixture, will sink at or below the freezing point. If a test tube be filled with water, and immersed in the mixture, the water will soon be frozen.

The above mixture is frequently used at the tables of the great, to cool wine when ice cannot be procured.

2. Put a small quantity of sulphuric acid (oil of vitriol) into a glass or cup, and pour upon it about half its quantity of cold water ; upon stirring it, the temperature will rise to many degrees above boiling water. In mixing sulphuric acid with water, great care should be taken not to do it too suddenly, as the vessel may break from the increased heat, and the acid be spilled on the hands, clothes, &c. ; the greatest caution is necessary in using it, as it will burn almost anything it touches.

3. Dissolve a little lime in muriatic or nitric acid, then pour some of the liquid into a glass, and add to it a few drops of sulphuric acid ; the whole will become nearly a solid mass, and, at the same time, give out a strong heat.

4. Set a quart pot upon a stool, on which a little water has been previously thrown, before the fire ; put a handful of snow into the pot, and also a handful of common salt. Hold the pot fast with one hand, and with a short stick stir the contents with the other, as if you were churning butter ; in a few minutes the pot will freeze so hard to the stool, that with both hands you can scarcely disengage it.

5. The most powerful of all freezing mixtures is a mixture of muriate of lime and snow : to produce the greatest effect by this mixture, equal weights of the salt, finely powdered, and newly-fallen snow, must be quickly mixed together. This is the mixture that is employed to freeze quicksilver.

Whenever substances become more condensed by mixture, heat is given out ; when they expand, cold is produced : or perhaps, it would be more proper to say, the compound has more or less capacity for heat than the separate ingredients.

6. Fill a common thermometer tube with cold water, and suspend it in the air by a string : if the tube be continually sprinkled with ether, the water will presently become ice.

All liquids require a great portion of heat to convert them into vapour, and all evaporation produces cold. The quick evaporation of ether, in the above experiment, carries away the heat from the water, and converts it into ice. An animal might be frozen to death in the midst of summer, by being repeatedly sprinkled with ether.

COMBUSTION AND EXPLOSION.

1. Bruise, and slightly moisten with water, a few crystals of nitrate of copper ; then roll them up quickly in a piece of tin-foil : in about a minute the tin-foil will begin to smoke, and soon after, take fire and explode with a slight crackling noise.

2. Throw a few grains of chlorate of potash, (oxmuriate of potash,) and a very small bit or two of phosphorus, into a cup containing a little sulphuric acid, the phosphorus will instantly burst into flame.

3. Take five parts of nitrate of potash, (saltpetre,) three of sub-carbonate of potash, (salt of tartar,) and one of sulphur, all quite dry, and mix them together in a warm mortar : if a little of this powder be placed upon a shovel, over a hot fire, it first begins to blacken, and, at last, melts and explodes with a loud report. A small quantity only should be used ; for although there is no danger in the mixture, yet some nervous persons may be alarmed at the loudness of the report.

4. Put a small quantity of calcined or pure magnesia into a cup, and pour over it a sufficient quantity of sulphuric acid to cover it : almost immediately combustion will commence, and sparks will be thrown out in all directions.

5. Put a little dry pulverized charcoal into a warm tea-cup, and pour over it some nitric acid, when combustion will take place, as in the preceding experiment.

6. Pour a table-spoonful of oil of turpentine into a cup, and place it in the open air ; then put about half the quantity of nitric acid, mixed with a few drops of sulphuric, into a phial, fastened to the end of a long stick ; pour it upon the oil, and it will immediately burst into flames, and continue to give out much light and heat.

7. Rub a few grains of chlorate of potash, and about half the quantity of sulphur, together in a mortar, and a crackling detonation will be produced, accompanied with flashes of light. If a small quantity of the same

I

mixture be wrapped in paper, laid upon an anvil, and smartly struck with a hammer, a report will be produced, which will be loud in proportion to the quantity used.

8.   Take a little of the composition mentioned in the last experiment, on the point of a knife, and drop it into a wine glass containing sulphuric acids; a beautiful column of flame will be the consequence immediately it comes in contact with the acid.

9.   Mix a few grains of chlorate of potash with twice their quantity of loaf sugar reduced to powder; place this mixture upon a plate, dip a piece of wire in sulphuric acid, and let a single drop fall from its end upon the mixture; it will immediately burst into flame, and continue to burn till the whole is consumed.

10.   Take a metal button, and rub it for a short time against a piece of wood or stone, then touch a small piece of phosphorus with it, the latter will immediately take fire and burn.

11.   Hold the end of a rod of glass to a grindstone while it is revolving; in a very short time it will become so hot, that phosphorus, gunpowder, and other combustible bodies, may be inflamed by it.   Wood rubbed against wood will also produce great heat.   The natives of New Holland light their fires by these means.

12.   Put a small piece of German tinder into the lower end of a syringe, then draw up the piston and force it suddenly down by giving it a smart blow against a wall or table, when the tinder will be ignited, either from the sudden condensation of the air, or the friction occasioned by the movement of the piston.   Syringes for this purpose are sold in London at about half-a-guinea each.

13.   Take two pieces of common bonnet cane and rub them strongly against each other in the dark, and a considerable quantity of light will be produced.   Two pieces of borax have the same property in a more eminent degree.   In this, and the three preceding experiments, the effects described being produced by friction, they ought, in strict propriety, perhaps, to be called electrical rather than chemical experiments.

14.   *Combustion by concentrating the sun's rays.*   Hold a double convex glass, of about two inches diameter, to the sun, about mid-day when shining very bright, at its focal distance from a piece of coin, which will soon become so hot that it cannot be touched with the finger.   The intensity of the heat produced will depend upon the size and convexity of the glass, and also on the season of the year.   Gunpowder, phosphorus, &c may be set on fire in this manner; and, with a very powerful glass, most of the metals may be melted.

15. Put a small quantity of spirits of wine into a glass with a halfpenny or a shilling, then direct the rays of the sun, by means of a glass, upon the coin, and, in a short time, it will become so hot as to inflame the spirits.

COMBUSTION IN AND UNDER WATER.

1. Mix one grain of phosphorus with three or four grains of chlorate of potash, and put this mixture into a glass with a narrow bottom; then put the small end of a funnel into the glass, in contact with the mixture, and fill the glass nearly full of water, but not by means of the funnel; then pour a few drops of sulphuric acid down the funnel, and the combustion of the phosphorus will immediately commence, and continue till the whole is consumed.

2. *The Well of Fire.* Add, gradually, one ounce, by measure, of sulphuric acid to five or six ounces of water, contained in an earthenware basin; throw in an ounce of granulated zinc, and a small bit or two of phosphorus, when phosphuretted hydrogen gas will be produced, which takes fire immediately it comes in contact with atmospheric air; so that, in a short time, the whole surface will become luminous, and continue so long as gas is generated, which may be seen darting from the bottom through the fluid with great rapidity.

3. Fill a saucer with water, and let fall into it a grain or two of potassium; the potassium will instantly burst into flame with a slight explosion, and burn vividly on the surface of the water, darting, at the same time, from one side of the vessel to the other, with great violence, in the form of a beautiful red-hot fire ball.

4. *Will-o'-the-wisp.* Take a glass tumbler three parts filled with water, and drop into it two or three lumps of phosphuret of lime; a decomposition will take place, and phosphuretted hydrogen gas be produced, bubbles of which will rise through the water, and take fire immediately they burst through the surface, terminating in beautiful ringlets of smoke, which will continue until the phosphuret of lime is exhausted.

This gas is generated at the bottom of stagnant shallow pools, in marshes and boggy places, and is frequently seen hovering over the surface of burial grounds; it is what we call the *ignis fatuus* or *Will-o'-the-wisp.*

5. *Green Fire under Water.* Put into a glass tumbler two ounces of water, and add, first, a piece or two of phosphorus about the size of a pea, then thirty or forty grains of chlorate of potash; then pour upon the mass, by means of a funnel with a long neck reaching to the bottom of the glass, five or six drachms of sulphuric acid. As soon as the acid comes in contact with the ingredients, flashes of fire begin to dart from under the surface

of the fluid. When this takes place, drop into the mixture a few pieces of phosphuret of lime; this will immediately illumine the bottom of the vessel, and cause a stream of fire, of an emerald green color, to pass through the fluid.

The effects produced in the foregoing experiments, are occasioned by the sudden chemical decomposition which takes place; and here it may be necessary to caution our young friends not to exceed the quantities we have directed to be used; for although we have avoided everything that is dangerous, yet an excess of quantity, in some cases, might be attended with inconvenience, and create alarm from the sudden effects that are produced. When phosphorus is used, it should be handled with great care, lest any portion of it get under the finger nails, a small bit of which would occasion considerable pain for sometime.

LUMINOUS WRITING IN THE DARK.

Fix a small piece of solid phosphorus in a quill, and write with it upon paper; if the paper be then removed to a dark room, the writing will appear beautifully luminous.

GREEN FIRE.

Put a small quantity of highly-rectified spirits of wine, mixed with a little boracic acid, into an earthenware vessel, and set them on fire, when a very beautiful green flame will be produced.

RED FIRE.

Proceed as in the last experiment, using nitrate or muriate of strontites, instead of boracic acid, and a beautiful red flame will be produced.

YELLOW FIRE.

Proceed as above, mixing nitrate or muriate of barytes with the spirits, and a brilliant yellow flame will be produced.

The above methods have been used in our theatres to heighten the effect of some of those horrifying spectacles with which the city has been treated, such as Der Freyschutz, &c.

METALLIC DISSOLVENTS.

Gold. Pour a small quantity of nitro-muriatic acid upon a small piece of gold, or gold leaf, and, in a short time, it will completely disappear, and the solution will have a beautiful yellow color.

Silver. Pour a little nitric acid upon a small piece of pure silver, or silver leaf, and it will be dissolved in a few minutes.

Copper. Pour a little diluted nitric acid upon a small piece of copper, and, in a short time, the copper will be dissolved, and the solution will have a beautiful blue color.

Lead. Pour a little diluted nitric acid upon a small piece or two of lead, which will first convert it into a white powder, and then dissolve it.

Iron. Pour some sulphuric acid, diluted with about four times its bulk of water, upon a few iron filings ; a violent effervescence will ensue, and, in a little time, the filings will be dissolved.

These experiments are intended to show how easily we can dissolve metals when we submit them to a proper menstruum.

METALLIC VEGETATION.

Mix together equal parts of saturated solutions of silver and mercury, diluted with distilled water : in this mixture suspend five or six drachms of pure mercury in a piece of fine linen rag doubled. The metallic solutions will soon shoot into beautiful needle-shaped crystals, and attach themselves, and adhere strongly, to the bag containing the mercury. When the arborization ceases to increase, the bag, loaded with beautiful crystals, may be taken out of the vessel where it was formed, by means of the thread by which it is suspended, and hung under a glass jar, where it may be preserved as long as may be thought proper.

THE LEAD TREE.

Put into a common wine decanter about half an ounce of super-acetate of lead, (sugar of lead,) and fill it to the bottom of the neck with distilled or rain water ; then suspend, by a bit of silk, or thread, fastened also to the cork or stopper, a piece of zinc wire, two or three inches long, so that it may hang as nearly in the centre as possible ; then place the decanter where it may not be disturbed. The zinc will very soon be covered with beautiful crystals of lead which are precipitated from the solution, and this will continue until the whole becomes attached to the zinc, assuming the form of a tree or bush, whose leaves or branches are laminal, or in plates of metallic lustre.

THE TIN TREE.

Into the same, or a similar vessel, to that used for the lead tree, pour distilled or rain water, as before, and put in three drachms of muriate of tin, and about ten drops of nitric acid. When the salt is dissolved, suspend a piece of zinc wire, as in the last experiment, and set the whole aside to precipitate without disturbance. In a few hours the effect will be similar to that produced by the lead, only that the tree of tin will have more lustre. In these experiments it is wonderful to see the lamina, or thin plates, shoot out ; as it were, from nothing.

THE SILVER TREE.

Put into a decanter four drachms of nitrate of silver, and fill up the decanter with distilled or rain water; then drop in about an ounce of mercury,

and place the vessel where it may not be disturbed: in a short time the silver will be precipitated in the most beautiful arborescent form, resembling real vegetation.

The above experiments show the precipitation of one metal by another, owing to the affinity that exists between them. The metal in solution having a greater affinity for the pure metal suspended in it, precipitates itself from the solution, and becomes firmly attached thereto. The Silver Tree, produced as above described, is frequently called Arbor Dianæ, or the Tree of Diana.

TRANSMUTATION OF COLORS.

To produce a blue by mixing two colorless fluids. Pour a little of the solution of sulphate of iron into a glass, then add to it a few drops of a solution of prussiate of potash, and the whole will assume a beautiful blue color.

In this experiment a decomposition takes place; the sulphuric acid leaving the iron to unite with the potash, and the prussic acid leaving the potash to unite with the iron, forming prussiate of iron, and sulphate of potash; the sulphate of potash remaining in solution, while the prussiate of iron is slowly precipitated, falling to the bottom in the state of a fine powder. This is the prussian blue of the shops.

To produce a yellow from two colorless fluids. Pour a little of the solution of nitrate of bismuth into a glass, then add to it a small quantity of solution of prussiate of potash, and a yellow color will be immediately produced.

In this experiment, as in the last, we have a decomposition; nitrate of potash and prussiate of bismuth are formed, the prussiate of bismuth giving it the yellow color.

To produce a brown from two colorless fluids. Pour a little of the solution of sulphate of copper into a glass, then add to it a small quantity of a solution of prussiate of potash, and a reddish brown will be produced.

In this experiment we have a sulphate of potash and a prussiate of copper, which gives the brown color, according to the principle just laid down.

To make black ink from two colorless fluids. Put into a glass a quantity of water, and add to it some tincture of galls; then put in a small quantity of a solution of sulphate of iron, and the whole will immediately become black.

Here, as in the preceding experiments, a decomposition is effected; the gallic acid uniting with the iron, forms our common writing ink.

A blue color produced from two colorless fluids. Put into a glass a quantity of water, and dissolve therein a few crystals of sulphate of copper, then pour in a small quantity of liquid ammonia, and the whole will immediately be changed to a beautiful blue.

In this experiment the ammonia unites to the copper, forming ammoniate of copper, which is of a beautiful blue, approaching to violet.

Another way. Take any chalybeate water, (that is, water containing iron in solution,) and add to it a little of the solution of prussiate of potash, which will change it to a blue color, as in a previous experiment.

Prussiate of potash is one of the best tests for iron that we are acquainted with, and will detect its pressure, however minute the quality.

To change a blue liquid to a red. Pour a little of the infusion of litmus, or blue cabbage, into a wine glass, and add to it a drop or two of nitric or sulphuric acid, which will immediately change it to a red color.

One of the characteristics of acid is that it changes most of the vegetable colors to red. This experiment is an instance.

To change a blue liquid to green. Pour a little of the infusion of violets into a wine glass, and add to it a few drops of a solution of potash or soda, when it will be changed to a beautiful green; to which, indeed, alkalies change most of the vegetable colors.

To change a red liquid into various colors. Put a little of the infusion of red cabbage into three different glasses; to the first, add a little muriatic or nitric acid; to the second, a little of the solution of potash; and to the third, a little of the solution of sulphate of alumin and potash, (alum.) The liquid in the first glass will be converted to a fine crimson, that in the second to a beautiful green, and that in the third to a purple.

In this experiment the changes take place as in the preceding ones, and may be explained on the same principles of decomposition.

THE MAGIC SHRUB.

Place a sprig of rosemary, or any other garden herb, in a glass jar, so that when it is inverted, the stem may be downward, and supported by the sides of the vessel ; then put some benzoin acid upon a piece of hot iron, so hot that the acid may be sublimed, which will rise in form of a thick white vapour. Invert the jar over the iron, and leave the whole untouched until the sprig be covered by the sublimed acid in the form of a beautiful hoar frost.

Sublimation is the same as distillation, only we call it sublimation when the product is collected in a solid form ; the term distillation is applied to liquids. In the above experiment we have a beautiful instance of sublimation, the fumes of the acid rise and are condensed on the cold leaves of the plant.

A LAMP WITHOUT FLAME.

Procure six or eight inches of platinum wire, about the hundredth part of an inch in thickness ; coil it round a small cylinder ten or twelve times, then drop it on the flame of a spirit lamp, so that part may touch the wick and part remain above it. Light the lamp, and when it has burned a minute or two, put it out ; the wire will then be ignited, and continue so long as any spirit remains in the lamp.

Lamps manufactured on this principle are sold by some of the chemists in London.

THE EXPLODING TAPER.

If the light of a taper be blown out, and the taper be let down into a jar of oxygen gas while the snuff (which should be a thick one) remains red hot, it rekindles instantly with an explosion. When the taper is relighted, it continues to burn with a rapidity, a brilliancy of flame, and an evolution of light truly wonderful.

THE GLOW-WORM IN GAS

Place a glow-worm within a jar of oxygen gas, in a dark room ; the insect will become more active, and shine with greater brilliancy, than it does in common air. Oxygen gas communicates a stimulus to the animal system ; and it is, probably, owing to this, that the glow-worm becomes more beautiful in consequence of its being more active, as its luminous appearance is supposed to depend entirely on the will of the animal.

THE CANDLE INVISIBLY EXTINGUISHED.

Place a lighted candle in the bottom of a jar which has its open part uppermost, (the jar being filled with atmospheric or common air,) then take a jar filled with carbonic acid gas, and invert it over the jar in which the candle is placed; the effect is very striking; the invisible fluid, being heavier than atmospheric air, descends like water, and extinguishes the flame. The whole, to spectators who have no idea of substance without sensible matter, having the appearance of magic.

TO MAKE WATER BOIL BY COLD AND CEASE TO BOIL BY HEAT.

Half fill a Florence flask with water, place it over a lamp, and let it boil for a few minutes, then cork the mouth of the flask as expeditiously as possible, and tie a slip of moist bladder over the cork to exclude the air. The water being now removed from the lamp, the ebullition will cease, but may be renewed by pouring cold water gradually upon the upper part of the flask; but, if hot water be applied, the boiling instantly ceases. In this manner the ebullition may be renewed, and again made to cease, alternately, by the mere application of hot and cold water.

We shall, in this place, be more elaborate than usual, and give our young friends the theory of what causes the above phenomenon. Be it known, then, to all who are not previously acquainted with the fact, that water boils at 212 degrees under the common pressure of our atmosphere: now, if the atmosphere, or a part of it, were removed, the pressure on the surface would be less, and the consequence would be that water would boil at a much lower temperature; and this leads us to an explanation of what takes place in the foregoing experiment. We fill a flask half full of water, and boil it for a few minutes over a lamp, the steam which rises forces out the atmospheric air, and occupies its place; we then remove the lamp, and secure the flask so as to prevent the readmission of atmospheric air. If cold water be now poured over that part of the flask occupied by the steam, the cold will condense the steam, which will trickle down the sides of the flask, and mix with the liquor below; the steam being thus condensed, a vacuum is formed above the surface. The water, having then no pressure of atmospheric air or steam, commences boiling afresh; but if hot water be now poured upon it, the steam again occupies the surface, and the boiling ceases.

A LIQUID PRODUCED FROM TWO SOLIDS.

Mix equal portions of sulphate of soda and acetate of lead, both in fine powder: let them be well rubbed together in a mortar, when the two solids will operate upon each other, and a fluid will be produced.

A SOLID PRODUCED FROM TWO LIQUIDS.

If a saturated solution of muriate of lime be mixed with a saturated solution of carbonate of potash, (both transparent liquids,) the result is the formation of an opaque and almost solid mass.   If a little nitric acid be added to the product, the solid mass will be changed to a transparent fluid.

These two last experiments were formerly called chemical miracles, but the present scientific age no longer consider them so, it being now well ascertained that the changes which take place are occasioned by chemical decomposition, or the action of one salt upon another.

THE LITTLE GAS-FACTOR.

Put a little coal into the bowl of a common tobacco-pipe, stop the mouth of it up with clay, and place the bowl in a fire ; as soon as the coal becomes heated, a small stream of gas will issue from the top of the pipe.   If he put a candle to it, the gas will light and burn for sometime, sufficiently brilliant to illuminate the study of

The little Gas=factor.

DRAUGHTS, OR CHECKERS.

To teach his grandson Draughts, then,
  His leisure he'd employ,
Until at last the old man
  Was beaten by the boy.

DRAUGHTS is a game which it is well to learn prior to commencing chess; though by far inferior to that noble pastime, it is at once unobjectionable and amusing. As in the case of chess, bets are seldom made upon the game of Draughts; it cannot therefore, be deemed, in any measure, conducive to gambling, which we most earnestly entreat our young readers, on all possible occasions, to avoid, as they value their present comfort and future welfare.

The game of Draughts is said to be of great antiquity, but we cannot discover that it was much known in Europe until the middle of the sixteenth century. In the year 1668, an elaborate treatise on the game was published by a Parisian professor of mathematics, named Mallet. Mr. Payne, a celebrated writer on this subject, is said to have copied many of Mallet's games; but both Payne and Mallet have been materially improved upon by a later writer, Mr. Sturges. The present treatise, we trust, will render any

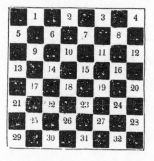

reference to the above, or any other writers upon Draughts, superfluous, except to the most curious and finished adepts in the game.

RULES FOR PLAYING.

In playing Draughts, the table must be placed with an upper white corner toward the right hand; and for the sake of playing the following games and preliminary practice, the numbers may be written upon the board itself, near a corner of each square; or a table may be drawn upon a card, and the squares numbered, as in the figure: such a table will be a ready guide to any move directed.

The game is played by two persons, each of whom takes a set of twelve men of different colors, generally white and black, but they may be of any colors, according to the fancy. One player, of course, takes all the men of one color, and the other all those of the other color. The black pieces are to be placed on the first twelve white squares, and the white on the last twelve white squares, or *viceversa*.

When the pieces are thus placed, each player alternately moves one of his men forward, angularly, to the next white square; and when moved to a square adjoining to an enemy, and another square next angularly behind the man so moved is unoccupied at that time, or afterward becomes so, then the man so placed or left unguarded must be captured by the enemy, whose man leaps over to the vacant square, and the prisoner is taken off the board. The same practice is immediately to be repeated in case the man effecting a capture thereby gets situated angularly fronting an enemy, and is unguarded behind. When any man gets onward to the last row opposite to that from whence his color started, then he becomes a king, and is crowned by his adversary placing another man, previously taken prisoner, upon him; he may then move and take either backward or forward.

In order that the moves may be more perfectly understood, we request attention to the following directions: the men should be placed on the board precisely as they appear in the cut in the next page, with this difference only, that the white pieces may be placed where the black stand, and the black where the white are, according to the fancy of the players. The men being thus posted, we will suppose that white has the first move. As only one of the front rank can be moved, he must either move the man on 21, to 17; that on 22, to 17 or 18; that on 23, to 18 or 19; or, that on 24, to 19 or 20. From 22 to 18 is supposed to be the best first move; we will, therefore, imagine that white makes it. It is black's turn to move a piece; he, like his adversary, can only advance one of his front rank men; he may move the man on 9, to 13 or 14; that on 10, to 14 or 15; that on 11, to 15 or 16; and that on 12, to 16 only. The white having moved from 22 to 18, the black then may move, if he please, from 11 to 15. In the next move, the

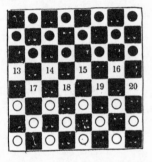

white man on 18, will take the man so placed by black on 15, by leaping over his head into 11. It is now black's turn to move, and he, in return, can take white's man which stands in 11, by either of the men standing on 7 or 8. In case he makes the capture with 7, he jumps over the head of the man to be taken, into 16; if he prefer taking him with 8, the move, for that purpose, is from 8 to 15. An opportunity, here occurs, of giving a practical explanation of the huff. Supposing, when black had moved from 11 to 15, white had omitted to take him, in the manner we have just explained, and made some other move, white, in this case, would have "stood the huff:" that is, black might have taken away the white man that stood on 18, or compelled white to have taken him, which he pleased. This is "standing the huff;" and, be it recollected, that so taking off the man from 18, is not to be considered as a move, black having his move after having so done, before white can move again.

In case the game were in a more advanced state, and that the black man, which, at the beginning, stood on 4, had been removed, the white man on 18, instead of taking only the black man on 15, would have taken the black man on 8, in addition, by leaping over 15 into 11, and over 8 into 4, which would be reckoned as one move. In this case, the man in 4, having reached one of the back squares of the enemy, (1, 2, 3, and 4,) he becomes a king; and black crowns him, by placing one of white's captured men on his head. The piece can now move, and take either backward or forward, and *is* of great importance. As many of the black men as, in their turn, reach either of the squares, 29, 30, 31, 32, immediately become kings, as in the case of the white men reaching 1, 2, 3, or 4, and, of course, have equal powers.

We will now give a practical example or two of the "kingly powers" of these "crowned heads." Supposing a black king stood on 29, a white king on 25, a white man on 18, another white king on 19, and a third white king, or a white man, on 27,—if it were black's move, and the board was clear, except only of the pieces that are mentioned, he would take them all thus : from 29 to 22, taking 25 ; from 22 to 15, taking 18 ; from 15 to 24, taking 19 ; and from 24 to 31, taking 27. If, however, the black king only take the first, second, or third of these pieces, he would stand the huff, (i. e.) the adversary might remove the black king off the board, or compel him to take the piece or pieces in his power, at his, the adversary's, pleasure.

To show the difference between the moves of a man and a king more clearly, suppose, instead of a king, black had only a man on 29, in that case, the man might go to 22, taking 25, and from 22 to 15, taking 18 ; but here his exploits would end, as he could not move backward from 15 to take 19, but, on the contrary, he must rest on 15 ; and, at the next move, would himself be taken, by the white king, on 19, jumping over his head into 10.

When all the men, on one side, are taken, or so hemmed in by the opposite color, that they cannot move, the person who has played them is beaten If, at the latter end of the game, one, two, or three, more or less, of each color, be left on the board, and neither can prevail on the other to risk, or if one who is weaker than, or has not the move of the other, be determined to go to and fro in safe squares, where he can never be taken, the game is called drawn, and given up, neither party winning. The way to give the finishing stroke to a game, where one color has two kings, and the other but one, or where one is, in any respect, a little stronger than the other, will be found in the following pages ; as also hints for a weak color making a drawn game, when the stronger adversary is in such a situation, as to be unable to get out his pieces to make an attack on the weaker party.

LAWS OF DRAUGHTS.

The following are a set of laws for the game, which have been sanctioned by the first players of Draughts in the kingdom.

1. Each player takes the first move alternately, whether the last game be won or drawn.

2. Any action which prevents the adversary from having a full view of the men is not allowed.

3. The player who touches a man must play him.

4. In case of standing the huff, which means omitting to take a man when an opportunity, for so doing, occurred, the other party may either take the man, or insist upon his man, which has been so omitted by his adversary being taken.

5. If either party, when it is his turn to move, hesitate above three minutes, the other may call upon him to play; and if, after that, he delay above five minutes longer, then he loses the game.

6. In the losing game, the player can insist upon his adversary taking all the men, in case opportunities should present themselves for their being so taken.

7. Persons not playing are not to advise, or in any manner interfere with the game of either party.

8. To prevent unnecessary delay, if one color have no pieces but two kings on the board, and the other no piece but one king, the latter can call upon the former to win the game in twenty moves : if he do not finish it within that number of moves, the game is to be relinquished as drawn.

9. If there be three kings to two on the board, the subsequent moves are not to exceed forty.

GAMES FOR PRACTICE.

It is now time for us to lead our pupil from theory to practice; for this purpose we shall proceed to lay before him a few games and situations, which he can either play alone, or with another, on a marked board, such as we have previously described. And here we feel it necessary to remark, that it will not be sufficient merely to go over the moves indicated in the following pages; by so doing, much time will be lost, and little learned: it is indispensable, if the learner be desirous of obtaining any benefit from these games, that he should carefully look to each series of moves, and, if possible, improve upon them as he goes on. The position of a single piece may totally defeat the best attacks, and it is not to be supposed that any two players will ever, except by some extraordinary accident, make all the identical moves, set down in the ensuing games. Still, however, much may be done by a few schemes of moves; especially, as toward the end, the positions of the men are very frequently similar, and we feel convinced, that by playing the following few games, (provided proper attention is given to them) an insight into the game may be acquired sooner than by the longest essay on the subject. We strongly recommend the young Draught-player, if he be desirous of speedily acquiring some proficiency in the game, to make himself a perfect master of the ends of, as well as any nice situations that occur in, the following games, so as to be able to play them, as it were, whenever an opportunity may occur. It is the advice of many experienced Draught-players, that learners should provide themselves with a common-place book for noting down any particular situations that may happen in their progress, or such masterly moves, by older hands, as they may have the good fortune to witness. Books for this purpose, containing representations of the board, so that the men placed in the proper positions for the moves can be marked in, may be had, reasonably, at the ivory turners. A book of this sort, containing charts of games, and memoranda of moves, by experienced persons, would be invaluable to the young Draught-player. We shall reserve any further remarks on Draughts for our concluding observations, and now proceed at once to the tables and games.

The letters, N. C. F. T. at the head of each of the games, stand for *number, color, from, to.*

GAME 1, in which White loses by the twelfth move.

N	C	F	T	N	C	F	T
1	B	11	15	28	W	30	25
2	W	22	18	29	B	29	22
3	B	15	22	30	W	26	17
4	W	25	18	31	B	11	15
5	B	8	11	32	W	20	16
6	W	29	25	33	B	15	18
7	B	4	8	34	W	24	12
8	W	25	22	35	B	18	27
9	B	12	16	36	W	31	24
10	W	24	20	37	B	14	18
11	B	10	15	38	W	16	11
12	W	27	24	39	B	7	16
13	B	16	19	40	W	20	11
14	W	23	16	41	B	18	23
15	B	15	19	42	W	11	8
16	W	24	15	43	B	23	27
17	B	9	14	44	W	8	4
18	W	18	9	45	B	27	31
19	B	11	25	46	W	4	8
20	W	32	27	47	B	31	27
21	B	5	14	48	W	24	20
22	W	27	23	49	B	27	23
23	B	6	10	50	W	8	11
24	W	16	12	51	B	23	18
25	B	8	11	52	W	11	8
26	W	28	24	53	B	18	15
27	B	25	29	&c.	W	loses.	

GAME 2, a drawn game.

N	C	F	T	N	C	F	T
1	B	11	15	28	W	30	25
2	W	22	18	29	B	6	9
3	B	15	22	30	W	13	6
4	W	25	18	31	B	1	10
5	B	8	11	32	W	22	13
6	W	29	25	33	B	14	18
7	B	4	8	34	W	23	14
8	W	25	22	35	B	16	30
9	B	12	16	36	W	25	21
10	W	24	20	37	B	10	17
11	B	10	15	38	W	21	14
12	W	21	17	39	B	30	25
13	B	7	10	40	W	14	9
14	W	27	24	41	B	11	15
15	B	8	12	42	W	9	6
16	W	17	13	43	B	2	9
17	B	9	4	44	W	13	18
18	W	18	9	45	B	15	15
19	B	5	14	46	W	6	2
20	W	24	19	47	B	7	10
21	B	15	24	48	W	2	6
22	W	28	19	49	B	10	14
23	B	14	17	50	W	6	9
24	W	32	27	51	B	25	21
25	B	10	14	52	W	31	26
26	W	27	24	53	B	14	17
27	B	3	7	&c.	W	drawn.	

GAME 3, which is lost by 30th move.

N	C	F	T	N	C	F	T
1	B	11	15	5	B	10	17
2	W	22	17	6	W	21	14
3	B	9	13	7	B	8	11
4	W	17	14	8	W	24	19

K

GAME 3, continued.

N	C	F	T	N	C	F	T
9	B	15	24	25	B	16	20
10	W	28	19	26	W	31	27
11	B	11	16	27	B	13	17
12	W	25	21	28	W	30	26
13	B	6	9	29	B	1	6
14	W	29	25	30	W	18	15
15	B	9	18	31	B	20	14
16	W	23	14	32	W	27	20
17	B	16	23	33	B	7	10
18	W	26	19	34	W	14	7
19	B	4	8	35	B	2	27
20	W	25	22	36	W	21	14
21	B	8	11	37	B	6	9
22	W	22	18	38	W	32	23
23	B	11	16	39	B	9	27
24	W	27	23	40	W	loses.	

GAME 4, which is lost by 12th move.

N	C	F	T	N	C	F	T
1	W	22	18	19	W	21	17
2	B	11	16	20	B	1	6
3	W	25	22	21	W	17	13
4	B	10	14	22	B	3	7
5	W	29	25	23	W	28	24
6	B	16	20	24	B	12	16
7	W	24	19	25	W	26	23
8	B	8	11	26	B	8	12
9	W	19	15	27	W	23	19
10	B	4	8	28	B	16	23
11	W	22	17	29	W	31	26
12	B	7	10	30	B	7	10
13	W	25	22	31	W	26	19
14	B	10	19	32	B	11	16
15	W	7	10	33	W	18	11
16	B	6	15	34	B	16	23
17	W	23	7	35	W	27	18
18	B	2	11	36	B	loses.	

CONCLUDING REMARKS.

Even those who have some knowledge of the game of Draughts will, we have no doubt, derive much benefit from a perusal of the foregoing pages, and become enabled to defeat those by whom they have previously been beaten. A person who has never acquired any insight into the game may, we flatter ourselves, from the care which we have taken in preparing the treatise, acquire considerable proficiency, by a proper attention to our rules and instructions.

The few remarks which we are about to make, as to one circumstance in Draughts, could not, we conceive, be so aptly introduced anywhere else as here; we allude to the importance of having the move upon an antagonist. The value of this will, no doubt, have frequently occurred to the reader, in the course of the preceding games; but there are situations, when it is not only useless, but detrimental. To have the move when your men are in a proper position, upon an open board, will often, in a short time, give you the power of forcing your adversary into such a situation as will render his defeat certain; but, having the move, when your men are huddled in confusion together, and you are unprepared to point an attack from any quarter, that is to say, when you are strong in number, but powerless in position, will, not unfrequently, cause you to lose the game.

In order to know whether any one of your men have the move over one of your adversary's, you must carefully notice their respective positions, and, if your opponent have a black square on your right angle under his man, you have the move upon him. This is a general rule, and will apply to any number of pieces. To illustrate it with an instance: if white have a man on 22, it being his turn to play, and black's man be on 11, white has the move. A modern writer on this subject, gives another method of ascertaining whether a party, whose turn it is to play, has the move; namely, by counting the squares and the men; and if the squares be odd, and the men even, or the men odd, and the squares even, then the party whose turn it is to play has possession of the move: thus, if there be a black man on 19, on 26 a white king, on 28 a black king, and on 32 a white man, and white have to play, he has the move, and may certainly win the game, if he act judiciously; the opposite party's men being even, and the white squares, between them and his own, odd; there are three white squares from the black king on 28 to the white king on 26, (viz. 24, 27, and 31,) and between the black man on 19 and the white man on 32, two white squares, 23 and 27, making together, five. White begins by moving his man to 27, the black king goes to 32, the white man proceeds to 24, and is taken by the black man on 19; the white king now goes to 23; the black king must next step to 27, having no other move, (his man being on 28,) and is taken by the white king, who thus gets into 32, and wins the game, as black cannot move his man.

Persons who know but little of this game are sometimes found talking lightly of it, as a trifle undeserving of attention; to such speakers we quote the following passage from Dr. Johnson's dedication of Payne's Book on Draughts:—" Triflers may think or make anything a trifle; but since it is the great characteristic of a wise man to see events in their causes, to obviate consequences, and ascertain contingencies, your lordship will think nothing a trifle by which the mind is inured to caution, foresight, and circumspection."

In conclusion, we beg to assure our young readers, that, simple as it may appear, they will never be able to attain any proficiency in this game, without some study, and much caution. Every move should be well considered before it is taken; for, although it does not require one tenth of the attention necessary to the acquirement of chess, yet it is totally impossible for our young friends to derive much amusement at the game, if they are not as intent on the purpose of their moves, as the CARRIER PIGEON in taking his letter to the end of his journey.

LEGERDEMAIN.

Leaving, at length, the top and taw,
We magic learned from sage Breslaw,
Flockton, Katterfelto, Jonas,
Gyngell, Moon, Prudhoe, and Comas ;
As conjurors at once to prove us,
We vomit fire like Mount Vesuvius.

CIRCUMSTANCES of importance, after a man has arrived at the age of
maturity, frequently make a much weaker impression on his memory than
the trifling occurrences of his youthful days. The latter engrave all their
little histories on the " tablet of the brain," and retain all their original distinctness, years and years after those which have subsequently taken place
are past away and forgotten,—or, at least, until they have left but a dim and
fast-fading record in the " chamber of the mind." We cannot, if our
life depended on it, remember where we first saw the greatest author of the
day,—nor when, within three or four years, we first shook the " great
captain of the age" by the hand ; but the memory of that moment, which
revealed to our delighted young gaze the mountebank in all his glory of
grimace, is as fresh within us, nay, more so, than if it were only a fruition of
the last past hour. The recollection of an event, one of the most weighty
and influential, perhaps, of our whole life, which took place some ten years
ago, or thereabout, has almost departed from us ; we cannot, mentally, and
without a blunder, con it over fact by fact in regular order, as we often do
the first exhibition of Legerdemain that we ever witnessed ;—we see only
disjointed portions of it huddled confusedly together—the shadow of the
event, vague and indistinct as the morning vapor, flits occasionally before

our mind's eye, but the substance itself is almost buried in oblivion;—while every feature of that seeming magician, who swallowed fire—kept it alive and brilliant below the surface of water,—enacted other feats of apparent dominion over the elements,—caused dumb figures to give proper answers to all sorts of questions,—padlocked an urchin's cheek,—and in a hundred ways cheated our eyes, before we had well worn out our second suit of boy's clothes,—is as well remembered, as though we had never ceased to look upon him. He has long since been dead—his body is no more; but in an instant we can conjure up his image, as he stood before us, smiling contentedly, while bathing his hands in molten lead! The very order of the wonders he performed has not yet escaped us, and we doubt not, but that should we live to be gray-headed, we shall ever be able to tell the color of his eyes, —the precise position of a mole which he had on his face,—the first, second, third, fourth, and so on, up to the twentieth feat which he exhibited. He was an itinerant quack doctor's Jack Pudding,—a mountebank, as we afterwards ascertained; but, at that time, we had not the least idea of who or what he could be. It was evident, to our unpractised eye, that he was not a mere mortal; for, no man, as we thought, innocent as we were, could by any possibility conjure a shilling, which we held fast in our hand, into one of our little school-fellows' pockets, or make a haberdasher's shop of his mouth, and draw from it dozens upon dozens of yards of ribbons of all colors, and at the option of those around him; we could not conceive that human flesh could withstand red-hot iron, or that any power short of witchcraft could remove a thing from before our eyes, which were all the time earnestly fixed on it, without our seeing its motion. What virtue was there, we reasoned thus, in "Hiccus doctius!" when uttered by the lips of another? But no sooner did he pronounce those mysterious words, than money danced about as if it possessed life. Would "Crinkum Bovis, Domine Jovis!" restore a chicken to life after its head was cut off, were the phrase to come from any but him? It was clearly impossible. What could he be then? Certainly not a mere mortal; and if not—what was he? Here we were as much involved and puzzled in conjecture, as a grave philosopher upon some learned and abstruse problem. The feat which mystified us most was this:— He apparently devoured a piece of raw meat, and then actually, as it seemed to us, swallowed a quantity of fire, as he said, to dress it—thus making his stomach its own cook, and his inside, a kitchen!

Remembering, as we do, the delight we felt at this, our first glance at Legerdemain, and the pleasure which we afterwards derived on sundry occasions during the youthful period of our life, from similar, but still more astonishing and scientific exhibitions, as well as the gratification it frequently afforded us, when a boy, to play off certain feats of conjuring, which we had learned from a highly-talented professor; and knowing, as we well do, that the youthful mind is, as ours once was, fond of this sort of recreations, we shall bestow even more than our usual pains in making this article as rich and complete as can be consistent with the nature of our work. We think that it would be by no means rash in us to pledge ourselves, that there is no superior treatise on Legerdemain to be obtained; it is true, that there are a few more bulky ones, but they contain so much useless matter, and accounts of tricks which it is impossible to perform at all, or, at any rate, by the rude, antiquated instructions which they afford, that one half of them is useless. The following pages will, we trust, be found to contain everything that is valuable in this art, unencumbered with dross. We have brought a tolerable share of knowledge on this matter, to the preparation of "Feats of Legerdemain;" we have also gleaned the cream of several old and scarce works, and translated many choice recreations from foreign publications on this subject. Several friendly contributions have been afforded to us; and what is of the greatest value, we have been favored with the assistance of some eminent and highly popular professors of the art; so that, we are enabled to present to our young readers a collection of conjuring tricks, which is at once copious and select. Our object has been, not only to facilitate the acquisition of such a variety of amusing feats, as will render him, who is enabled to exhibit them, a parlor magician, but also to instruct our young readers in the mode of performing several master-pieces of Legerdemain, which require considerable agility, and expensive apparatus, so that they may understand the means of effecting the apparent wonders displayed by the public professors of the art. In addition to the Feats of Legerdemain, we have devoted several of our pages to descriptions of various Automata and Androides, which have been exhibited to the public. The Marionnettes, or figures, whose motions are governed by strings, are too simple for a lengthened notice: it is true, that, among the ancients, they were deemed of importance sufficient to be exhibited in their public shows,—but they are now mere toys, of which every lad knows the construction; for there are few who have not at one time or other possessed, played with, and dissected a pasteboard harlequin, or a bleeding nun. An improvement has lately been made on these juvenile Marionettes, which, while we are on this subject, is perhaps deserving of notice. The limbs, body, and head of a comic figure, are drawn and colored on a piece of paper, cut out, and gummed separately to a piece of card of similar dimensions; they are then united by bits of thread, which, acting as hinges, suffer them to play loosely, and in various directions, when the body is moved. A piece of dark twine is fastened, by its middle, to the back of the body; the ends are tied, by a boy, just below his two knees; he sits, on a low stool, in a dark place, with a light on the ground, a little in front of him—the spectators standing at some distance from the light. By moving his knees quickly to and from each other, a variety of grotesque motions is given to the Marionnette, which dances, apparently, without assistance.

We doubt not but that this part of the work will be a favorite amusement with our readers, and that it will afford much innocent amusement during the long evenings of winter, around the comfortable parlor fire, to many a little social circle. Such is our end and intent; and we assure those who amuse themselves, whether alone or in society, with these Feats of Legerdemain, that they are indulging only in what is often instructive, generally agreeable, and always innocent.

We must detain our readers from the practical instructions, to make a few more observations, which are necessary, as well on our own behalf as for their benefit. We wish it to be remembered, that in addition to the matter contained under this title, many excellent scientific recreations, which will be accounted capital conjuring tricks, are to be found in the preceding pages, among the Chemical, Arithmetical, and Optical Amusements, and elsewhere in the work; where they are more properly placed than they would be here; and to these we take leave to refer those who have an inclination to become "Magiciens de Societe."

THE POISED PENNY.

Place a smooth card on the tip of the middle finger of your left hand, and on it, nicely balanced, and with its centre exactly over your finger's point, a penny-piece. Then, by a smart fillip with the middle finger of your right hand, you may strike away the card from under the penny, leaving the latter poised on the tip of your finger. A very little practice will enable you to do this trick without ever failing. The card must be carefully struck, so as to drive it straight off the finger; if you fillip it upward, it will, of course, take the penny with it. (*Vide cut at head.*)

WATER BEWITCHED.

Pour some water into a plate, light a bit of loosely-crumpled paper, and throw it into a glass; then turn the glass upside down, with the burning paper in it, in the plate, and the water will gradually rise from the plate into the glass, until the latter becomes half full, so that the surface of the water it contains is much higher than that of what is left in the plate.

FIRE UNDER WATER.

Fasten a small bit of wood across the mouth of a glass, stick therein a piece of candle lighted, and, with a steady hand, convey the mouth to the surface of the water; then push it carefully down, and the candle will burn under the water; you may even bring the candle up again lighted. In the same manner, you may put a handkerchief, rolled tightly together, and it will not be wet.

The principal art in performing this trick, consists in the nicety of bringing the mouth of the glass exactly level with the surface of the water; for, if you put it in the least on one side, the water will rush in, and consequently put out the candle, or, in the other case, wet the handkerchief; so that a nice eye and steady hand are necessarily requisite for this performance.

THE SENTINEL EGG.

Lay a looking-glass upon an even table; take a fresh egg, and shake it for sometime, so that the yolk may be broken and mixed up with the white. You may then, with a steady hand, balance it on its point, and make it stand on the glass. This it would be impossible to do while the egg was in its natural state.

THE BRIDGE OF KNIVES.

To erect the bridge of knives, you must first place three glasses, or small cups at the corners of a supposed triangle, and about the length of

one of the knives you use distant from each other, upon a table, the floor, or any even surface. Then take three knives, and arrange them upon the glasses in the manner represented by the cut. The blade of No. 1 (as you may perceive by inspecting the engraving) goes over that of No. 2, and the blade of No. 2 passes across that of No. 3, which rests on that of No. 1. The knives being placed in this position, their blades will support each other.

EATABLE CANDLE-ENDS.

Peel some large apples that are rather of a yellow tint; cut several pieces out of them in the shape of a candle-end, round, of course, at the bottom, and square at the top; in fact, as much as possible, like a candle that has burnt down within an inch or so. Then, cut some slips out of the insides of sweet almonds, fashion them as much in the shape of spermaceti wicks as you can, stick them into your mock candles, light them for an instant, so as to make their tops black, blow them out again, and they are ready for use. When you produce them, light them, (the almond will readily take fire, and flame for a few moments,) put them into your mouth, chew and swallow them one after another. This may well be called the juggler's dessert.

THE LITTLE FLOATING BEACON.

Fasten a piece of lead to the end of a candle which has been half burnt; place it very gently in the water, so that it may find its proper equilibrium; then light it, and it will burn to the end without sinking.

THE RINGS AND RIBBONS.

Take two pieces of ribbon, precisely alike in length, breadth, and color; double each of them, separately, so that their ends meet; then tie them together very neatly, with a bit of silk of their own color, by the middle, or crease made in doubling them. This must all be done beforehand. When you are going to exhibit this trick, pass some rings on the doubled ribbons, and give the two ends of one ribbon to one person to hold, and the two ends of the other to another. Do not let them pull hard, or the silk will break, and your trick be discovered by the rings falling on the ground, on account of the separation of the ribbons. Request the two persons to approach each other, and take one end from each of them, and without their perceiving it, return to each of them the end which the other had previously held. By now giving the rings, which appeared strung on the ribbon, a slight pull, you may break the silk, and they will fall into your hand.

THE THUMB-STRING.

This is a very simple trick, but by performing it quickly, you may surprise and puzzle a spectator very considerably. Wind a piece of string round your thumb, thus :—Let one end of it (*a*) drop between the thumb and fore-finger of your left hand; then wind the other part, which you retain in your right hand, two or three times round your thumb; next, make a little loop (*b*) with the same end, which hold between your finger and thumb. Now let go the end, (*c*) and take hold of the end, (*a*) which you must have left about six or eight inches long, and you may make a spectator fancy you pass it through the loop, and take hold of it again, when so passed through, in the twinkling of an eye. To increase the surprise, you may make the loop as small as possible. This apparent piece of manual dexterity is performed by passing that end of the string marked *a*, as quickly as possible round the top of the thumb, so as to come between the fore-finger and thumb : it will thus get into the loop, and you will seem to have passed the end through it.

WINE UPON WATER.

Half fill a glass with water, throw a bit of the crumb of a loaf into it, about the size of a nut, pour some wine lightly on the bread, and you will see the water at the bottom of the glass, and the wine floating at the top of it.

THE CONJUROR'S JOKE.

Take a ball in each hand, and stretch your hands as far as you can, one from the other; then state that you will contrive to make both the balls come into either hand, without bringing the hands near each other. If any one dispute your power of doing this, you have no more to do, than to lay one ball down upon the table, turn yourself, and take it up with your other hand. Thus both the balls will be in one of your hands, without their approaching each other.

THE PERILOUS GOBLET.

To fill a glass with water, so that no one may touch it without spilling all the water. Fill a common wine-glass or goblet with water, and place upon it a bit of paper, so as to cover the water and edge of the glass; put the palm of your hand on the paper, and taking hold of the glass with the other, suddenly invert it on a very smooth table, and gently draw out the paper; the water will remain suspended in the glass, and it will be impossible to move the glass, without spilling all the water.

THE ENCHANTED COCK.

Bring a cock into a room with both your hands close to his wings, and hold them tight; put him on a table, and point his beak down as straight as possible; then let any one draw a line, with a piece of chalk, directly from its beak, and all the noise you can possibly make will not disturb him, for some time, from the seeming lethargy, which that position you have laid him in has effected.

TO LIGHT A CANDLE BY SMOKE.

When a candle is burnt so long as to leave a tolerably large wick, blow it out; a dense smoke, which is composed of hydrogen and carbon, will immediately arise. Then, if another candle, or lighted taper, be applied to the utmost verge of this smoke, a very strange phenomenon will take place; the flame of the lighted candle will be conveyed to that just blown out, as if it were borne on a cloud, or, rather, it will seem like a mimic flash of lightning proceeding at a slow rate.

THE WONDERFUL RE-ILLUMINATION.

After having exhibited the trick of lighting a candle by smoke, privately put a bit of paper between your fingers, and retire to one corner of the room with a single candle, and pass the hand, in which you hold the paper, several times slowly over the candle, until the paper takes fire; then immediately blow the candle out, and presently, pass your hand over the snuff, and relight it with the paper. You may then crumple the paper, at the same time extinguishing the flame, by squeezing it suddenly, without burning yourself. If this trick be performed dexterously, it is a very good one. It is not necessary for the performance of this trick that all the other lights in the room should be extinguished; in fact, the trick is more liable to a discovery in a dark room, than in one where the candles are burning, on account of the light thrown out by the paper while it is burning, previous to the re-illumination.

TO SUSPEND A RING BY A BURNT THREAD.

The thread having been previously soaked two or three times in common salt and water, tie it to a ring, not larger than a wedding ring. When you apply the flame of a candle to it, though the thread burn to ashes, it will yet sustain the ring.

THE ANIMATED SIXPENCE.

To make a sixpence leap out of a pot. This is done by means of a long black horse-hair, fastened to the rim of a sixpence, by a small hole driven through it. This feat should be done by night, with a candle placed between the spectators and the operator, their eyes being thereby hindered from discerning the deception.

THE FASCINATED BIRD.

Take any bird, and lay it on a table; then wave a small feather over its eyes, and it will appear as dead, but taking the feather away, it will revive again. Let it lay hold of the stem part of the feather, and it will twist and turn like a parrot; you may likewise roll it about, on the table, just as you please.

TO LIFT A BOTTLE WITH A STRAW.

Take a straw, and having bent the thicker end of it in a sharp angle, as the figure subjoined, put this curved end into a bottle, so that the bent  part may rest against its side; you may then take the other end and lift up the bottle by it, without breaking the straw, and this will be the more readily accomplished as the angular part of the straw approaches nearer to that which comes out of the bottle. It is necessary, in order to succeed in this feat to be particularly careful in choosing a stout straw, which is neither broken nor bruised; if it have been previously bent or damaged, it is unfit for the purpose of performing this trick, as it will be too weak in the part so bent, or damaged, to support the bottle.

THE MOVING PYRAMID.

Roll up a piece of paper, or other light substance, and privately put into it any small insect, such as a lady-bird, or beetle; then, as the creature will naturally endeavour to free itself from captivity, it will move its covering towards the edge of the table, and when it comes there, will immediately return, for fear of falling; and thus, by moving backward and forward, will excite much diversion to those who are ignorant of the cause.

THE PAPER FURNACE.

Enclose a bullet in paper, as smoothly as possible, and suspend it above the flame of a lamp or candle; you will soon see it begin to melt and fall, drop by drop, through a hole which it will make in the paper; but the paper, except the hole mentioned, will not be burnt. The art of performing this trick consists in using a smooth round bullet, and enclosing it in the paper with but few folds or uneven places.

THE BOTTLE EJECTMENT.

Fill a small white glass bottle, with a very narrow neck, full of wine; place it in a glass vase, which must previously have sufficient water in it to rise above the mouth of the bottle. Immediately, you will perceive the wine rise, in the form of a little column, toward the surface of the water, and the water will, in the meantime, begin to take the place of the wine at the bottom of the bottle. The cause of this is, that the water is heavier than the wine, which it displaces, and forces to rise toward the surface.

THE BALANCED STICK.

Procure a piece of wood about the length of your hand, half an inch thick, and twice as broad; within a short distance of one end of this piece,

thrust in the points of the blades of two penknives of equal weight, in such a manner, that one of them may incline to one side, the second to the other, as represented by the cut in the margin. If its other extremity be placed on the tip of the finger, the stick will keep itself upright without falling; and if it be made to incline, it will raise itself again and recover its former situation. This is a very pretty performance, and, if properly managed, cannot fail to excite some surprise in the minds of those who behold it for the first time, as the knives, instead of appearing to balance the stick, which they in fact do, will rather appear to increase the difficulty of the feat.

STORM AND CALM.

Pour water into a glass until it is nearly three parts full; then almost fill it up with oil; but, be sure to leave a little space between the oil and the top of the glass. Tie a bit of string round the glass, and fasten the two ends of another piece of string to it, one on each side, so that, when you take hold of the middle of it to lift up the glass, it may be about a foot from your hand. Now swing the glass to and fro, and the oil will be smooth and unruffled, while the surface of the water beneath it will be violently agitated.

THE TRAVELLING EGG.

Take a goose's egg, and, after opening and cleansing it, put a bat into the shell; glue it fast on the top, and the bat will cause the egg to move about in a manner that will excite much astonishment.

THE DOUBLED COIN.

Half fill a glass of water, and put a shilling or a sixpence into it; cover the glass with a plate, upon which, place one hand, while you hold the glass with the other; turn the glass upside down, so that none of the water may escape; place it on a table, and you will see the coin, at the bottom, larger than it is in reality, and another will appear, of the natural size, a little above it.

THE TOPER'S TRIPOD.

A trick similar to the Bridge of Knives may be performed by three tobacco-pipes, in the following manner:—Procure three common tobacco-

pipes; place the hollow part of the bowl of one of them on the table, as No. 1, and let its stem be supported by another, placed at No. 2; then put the other pipe across Nos. 1 and 2, (as No. 3,) so that its bowl end may support the stem of No. 2, and its own stem rest on the bowl end of No. 3. This little tripod, although constructed of such brittle materials, will, if carefully put together, support a jug of foaming October. When used to show that it will support a weight, the three bowls should be brought considerably closer together than as represented in the marginal cut, so that the bottom of the jug may rest upon all three of the stems.

THE KNOTTED THREAD.

Considerable amusement, not unmixed with wonder, may be occasioned among a party of ladies, by a clever performance of this trick. It is most frequently performed by a female, but the effect of it is considerably increased when it is displayed by a boy. A piece of calico, muslin, or linen, is taken in the left hand, a needle is threaded in the presence of the spectators, and the usual, or even a double or treble knot made at the extremity of one of the ends of it. The operator commences his work by drawing the needle and the thread in it quite through the linen, notwithstanding the knot, and continues to make several stitches in like manner successively.

The mode of performing this seeming wonder, is as follows: a bit of thread, about a quarter of a yard long, is turned once round the top of the middle finger of the right hand, upon which a thimble is then placed to keep it secure. This must be done privately and the thread kept concealed, while a needle is threaded with a bit of thread of a similar length. The thread in the needle must have one of its ends drawn up nearly close, and be concealed between the fore-finger and thumb; the other should hang down nearly as long as, and by the side of the thread, which is fastened under the thimble, so that these two may appear to be the two ends of the thread. The end of the piece that is fastened under the thimble is then knotted, and the performer begins to sew, by moving his hand quickly after he has taken up the stitch. It will appear as though he actually passed the knotted thread through the cloth.

THE BOTTLE IMPS.

Get three little hollow figures of glass, an inch and a half high, representing

imps, or Harlequin, Columbine, and Pantaloon, which may be obtained at the glass-blowers, with a small hole in each of their legs. Immerge them into water contained in a glass bottle, which should be about fifteen inches high, and covered with a bladder tied fast over the top. A small quantity of air must be left between the bladder and the surface of the water. When you think fit to command the figures to go down, press your hand hard upon the top, and they will immediately sink; when you would have them rise to the top, take your hand away, and they will float up. By these means, you may make them dance in the middle of the glass at your pleasure.

THE BIRD IN THE BOX.

Get a box made with a false lid, on which glue some bird-seed; privately put a bird into it, under the false lid; then show it, and it will seem to be full of seed. Put on the true lid, and say,—" I will command all the seed out of this box, and order a living bird to appear." Then, take off the covers together, and the bird will be seen.

THE MULTIPLYING MIRROR.

This feat must be performed with a looking-glass made on purpose; the manner of making it is this :—First, make a hoop, or fillet of wood or horn, about the size of a half-crown piece in circumference, and about a quarter of an inch in thickness. In the middle, fasten a bottom of wood or brass, and bore in it several small holes, about the size of peas ; then open one side of this bottom, set in a piece of crystal-glass, and fasten it in the hoop close to the bottom. Take a quantity of quicksilver, and put as much into the hoop as will cover the bottom; then let into it another piece of crystal-glass, fitted to it; cement the sides, that the quicksilver may not run out, and the apparatus is complete. One side will reflect the beholder's face as a common looking-glass; in the other it will be multiplied according to the number of holes in the wood or brass.

THE BOGLE BODKIN.

Take a hollow bodkin, (or, if you prefer it, a dagger,) so that the blade may slip into the handle as soon as the point is held upward. Seem to thrust it into your forehead, (or, if a dagger, into your bosom,) then, after showing some appearance of pain, pull away your hand suddenly, holding the point downward, and it will fall out, and appear not to have been thrust into the haft; but, immediately afterward, throw the bodkin, or dagger, into your lap or pocket, and pull out another plain one like it, which will completely deceive the spectators.

THE PRANCING DRAGOON.

Cut out the figure of a Dragoon, mounted, in wood; let the horse be in a prancing position: put the hind-legs on the edge of a table, and it will, of course, fall off; but you can prevent it from so doing, by adding to its weight. For this purpose, you must have a little hole made in the centre of its belly, into which run one end of a piece of wire, so bent backward, that the other end of it, to which a weight is fixed, may be under the table. The Dragoon will not only stand safe, but you may put him in motion, and he will prance up and down, without there being the least danger of his falling. The wire should be considerably longer in proportion to the size of the horse than is represented in the engraving in the margin, if you wish the figure to come much below the edge of the table when prancing. If it be no longer than that shown in the cut, the horse's fore-legs can only descend to a distance equal to that between the weight at the end of the wire, and the

L

bottom of the table on which the figure is set. In fact, the Dragoon may be made to descend lower, and rise higher, in proportion to the length of the wire, if it be properly curved and fixed in the figure.

THE MYSTERIOUS BOTTLE.

Pierce a few holes, with a glazier's diamond, in a common black bottle; place it in a vase or jug of water, so that the neck only is above the surface. Then, with a funnel, fill the bottle, and cork it well, while it is in the jug or vase. Take it out, and notwithstanding the holes in the bottom, it will not leak; wipe it dry, and give it to some person to uncork. The moment the cork is drawn, to the party's astonishment, the water will begin to run out of the bottom of the bottle.

THE HALF-CROWN UPHELD.

Privately cut the rim of the edge which is raised to protect the face of a half-crown, so that a little bit of the silver may stick up; take the coin in your right hand, and by pressing it with your thumb against a door or wainscot, the bit that sticks up will enter the wood, and thus support the half-crown.

THE BOWING BEAU.

Make a figure, resembling a man, of any substance, exceedingly light, such as the pith of the alder tree, which is soft, and can easily be cut into any form: then provide for it an hemispherical base, of some very heavy substance, such as the half of a leaden bullet, made very smooth on the convex part. Cement the figure to the plane part of the hemisphere; and, in whatever position it is placed, when left to itself, it will rise upright. In this manner were constructed those small figures, called Prussians, sold at Paris: they were formed into battalions, and being made to fall down, by drawing a rod over them, they immediately started up again as soon as it was removed. We think, that the figure of a beau, or master of the ceremonies, is much more appropriate for this trick, than that of a soldier; as the latter seldom bows, while, by the former, the most profound inclinations are often performed. By moving it once downward a succession of bows may be produced.

THE WONDERFUL WAFERS.

On each side of a table-knife, place, in the presence of your company, three wafers. Take the knife by the handle, and turn it over two or three times, to show that the wafers are all on. Desire some person to take off one wafer from one side of the blade; turn the knife two or three times again, and there will appear only two wafers on each side; remove another wafer, turn the knife as before, and there will appear only one wafer on each side; take the third wafer away, turn the knife as before twice or thrice, and there will appear to be no wafer on either side. After a momentary pause, turn the knife again two or three times, and three wafers will appear on each side.

The secret of this capital trick consists in using wafers of the same size and color, and turning the knife, so that the same side is constantly presented to the view, and the wafers are taken off that side, one by one. The three wafers will thus remain untouched on the other side, so that when you have first made it appear that there are no wafers on either side, you may, apparently, show three on each, by the same means. The way to turn the knife is as follows; when you lift it up, turn it in your hand, with your finger and thumb, completely round, until the side that was uppermost when you lifted it, comes uppermost again. This is done in an instant, and is not perceptible, if adroitly managed.

THE COUNTER CHANGED.

Take two papers, three inches square each, divided into two folds, of three equal parts on each side, so as each folded paper remain one inch square; then glue the back part of the two together, as they are folded, and not as they are opened, so that both papers seem to be but one, and which side soever you open, it may appear to be the same; if you have a sixpence in one hand, and a counter in the other, show one, and you may, by turning the paper, seem to change it.

THE CUT LACE JOINED.

Conceal a piece of lace in your hand; then produce another piece of the same pattern; double the latter, and put the fold between your fore-finger and thumb, with the piece which you have previously concealed, doubled in the same manner; pull out a little of the latter, so as to make a loop, and desire one of the company to cut it asunder. If you have conveyed the concealed piece of lace so dexterously as to be undetected, with the other between your thumb and fore-finger, the spectators will, naturally enough, think you have really cut the latter; which you may seem to make whole again, while repeating some conjuring words, and putting away the two ends of the piece that is actually cut.

THE WIZARD'S CHARIOT.

This trick will call your mechanical abilities into play. First, get a piece of board, planed quite smooth; fasten a cross-piece under it, to support it in 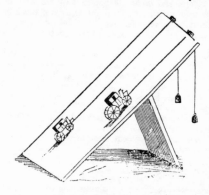 the position indicated by the cut. At the upper edge of the slanted piece, fix two little pulleys, the use of which may, at a glance, be seen by the engraving. Next, construct two little coaches, carts, or classical triumphal chariots; let the wheels of one of them be considerably larger than those of the other; they must, however, be precisely the same weight, or, if not, you must load one with shot to make it equal, in this respect, to the other. Do your work so neatly, that the wheels of each may run equally well on their respective axles. Next provide two lumps of lead, which must tally with each other to a scruple, and be sufficiently heavy to pull the chariots up the plane. Fix a piece of thread to the front of each of the chariots; pass these threads through the pulleys, and fasten one of your weights to each of them. The threads, be it remarked, should be long enough only to reach from the chariots, when placed at the foot of the inclined board, through the pulleys to the leads; and the board should be so inclined, that the distance from the pulleys to the ground be precisely the same as that of the chariots to the pulleys. Your apparatus being thus ready, weigh the chariots together, and afterwards the leads in the presence of the spectators, that they may be satisfied they are equal, and let them inspect your apparatus, to see that all is fair: then start your chariots, and, notwithstanding the equality of their weights, and the equality of those of the leads, one of them will considerably outstrip the other; the chariot with the highest wheels will always be the winner of the race. This mechanical truth is unknown to many, and may, if properly managed, produce much surprise.

THE SIMPLE DECEPTION.

Stick a little wax upon your thumb, take a by-stander by the fingers, show him a sixpence, and tell him you will put the same into his hand; then wring it down hard with your waxed thumb, and, using many words, look him in the face; suddenly take away your thumb, and the coin will adhere to it; then close his hand it will seem to him that the sixpence remains; now tell him to open his hand, and, if you perform the feat cleverly, to his great astonishment, he will find nothing in it.

PHILOSOPHY CHEATED.

This feat is really an excellent one, and has astonished crowds of spectators in London, and different parts of the United Kingdom. It was one of the favorites of a late popular professor, and is now first promulgated. Before you perform it in public, you must practice it, until you are quite perfect, in private, for it would be a pity to spoil its effect by making a blunder in it. Begin by stating very seriously, what is a well-known fact, that if a bucket full of water be hurled round his head by a man, who is sufficiently strong, none of the water will fall out. If this be at all discredited, be prepared not only to support your assertion, but to carry the point still further, by placing a tumbler full of any liquid in the inside of a broad hoop, which you hold in your hand by a small piece of string fixed to it, and twirling it round at your side. If you do this with velocity, although the tumbler, in the circles made by the hoop, is frequently quite bottom upward, it will neither fall from the hoop, nor will any of the water be spilt. To do this, however, requires even more practice than the trick which it prefaces; as, although there is no difficulty in it while the hoop is in rapid motion, yet there is some danger until you are rendered expert by practice, of the tumbler's falling, when you begin to put the hoop in motion, and when you wish to stop it. If, therefore, you are not perfectly capable of doing it, state the fact only, which some or other of your auditors will most probably support, as it is pretty generally known. You now go on to say, that the air, under the water in the glass, when it is topsy-turvy, keeps it in: and that, upon the same principle, if you can turn your hand, upon which you place a piece of thin wood, (about one inch broad, and six inches long,) sufficiently quick, although the back be uppermost, the air will actually keep the wood up against the palm of your hand, without any support.

This they will be readily inclined to believe; the more philosophical the

party is, the more easy may you lead them to credit your assertion. They will, however, doubt your being possessed of sufficient manual dexterity to perform it quick enough.

We must now tell you how it is to be done:—Lay the piece of wood across the palm of your left hand, which keep wide open, with the thumb and all the fingers far apart, lest you be suspected of supporting the wood with them. Next, take your left wrist in your right hand, and grasp it tightly, for the purpose, as you state, of giving the hand more steadiness. Now, suddenly turn the back of your left hand uppermost, and, as your wrist moves in your right hand, stretch out the fore-finger of your right hand, and as soon as the wood comes undermost, support it with such fore-finger. You may now shake

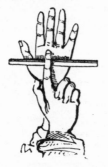

the hand, and, after a moment or two, suffer the wood to drop. It is two to one but the spectators will admit it to be produced by the action of the air, as you had previously stated, and try to do it themselves; but, of course, they must, unless you have performed the feat so awkwardly as to be discovered, fail in its performance. If you have no objection to reveal the secret, you can do it again, and, while they are gravely philosophizing upon it, suddenly lift up your hand, (*vide cut*,) and expose the trick. This will, doubtless, create much amusement. Observe that in doing this feat, you must keep your fingers so low, that no one can see the palm of your left hand; and move your finger so carefully, that its action may not be detected; and if it be not, you may rest satisfied that its absence from round the wrist of the left hand will not be discovered, some of the fingers being naturally supposed to be under the coat; so that, if the spectators only see two or even one, they will imagine the others are beneath the cuff. There is one other observation necessary before we conclude; it is this, when you have turned your hand over, do not keep the stick too long upheld, lest the spectators should take hold of your hands, and discover the trick; before their astonishment has ceased, adroitly remove your fore-finger, and suffer the stick to fall to the ground.

THE LOCKED JAW.

A lock is made for the purpose, similar to the cut; that side of its bow

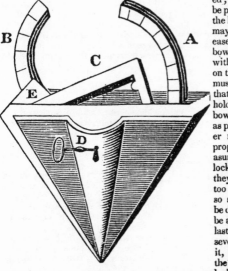

marked A, must be fixed; the other, B, must be pinned to the body of the lock, at E; so that it may play to and fro with ease. This side of the bow should have a leg, with two notches filed on the inner side, which must be so contrived, that one may lock or hold the two sides of the bow as close together as possible, and the other notch hold them a proportionable distance asunder, so that when locked upon the cheek, they may neither pinch too hard nor yet hold it so slightly that it may be drawn off. Let there be a key, D, to it; and, lastly, let the bow have several notches filed in it, so that the place of the partition, when the lock is shut, may not be suspected. You must get a person to hold a shilling between his teeth; then take another, and, with your left hand, offer to set it edge-wise between a second person's teeth, pretending that your intent is to turn both into which of their mouths they please. This will afford you a fair opportunity of putting on your lock.

THE RESTORED THREAD.

Take two pieces of thread, one foot in length each; roll one of them round, like a small pea, which put between your left fore-finger and thumb. Now, hold the other out at length, between the fore-finger and thumb of each hand; then let some one cut the same asunder in the middle; when that is done, put the tops of your two thumbs together, so that you may, with less suspicion, receive the thread which you hold in your right hand into your left, without opening your left finger and thumb. Then, holding these two pieces as you did before, let them be cut asunder in the middle also, and conveyed again as before, until they be very short; then roll all the ends together, and keep that ball of thread before the other in the left hand, and with a knife, thrust the same into a candle, where you may hold it until it be burnt to ashes; pull back the knife with your right hand, and leave the ashes, with the other ball, between your fore-finger and thumb of your left hand, and with the two thumbs and fore-fingers together, rub the ashes, and at length, draw out that thread which has been all this time between your fore-finger and thumb.

THE LONG PUDDING.

The following is a famous feat among those mountebanks who travel the country with quack doctors. This pudding must be made of twelve or thirteen little tin hoops, so as to fall one through another, and little holes should

be made at the biggest end, so that it may not hurt your mouth: hold it privately in your left hand, with the whole end uppermost, and, with your right hand, take a ball out of your pocket, and say, "if there be any old lady that is out of conceit with herself, because her neighbours deem her not so young as she would be thought, let her come to me, for this ball is a certain remedy; then seem to put the ball into your left hand, but let it slip into your lap, and clap your pudding into your mouth, which will be thought to be the ball that you showed them; then decline your head, open your mouth, and the pudding will slip down at its full length; with your right hand, you may strike it into your mouth again: after having done this three or four times, you may discharge it into your hand, and put it into your pocket without any suspicion, by making three or four wry faces after it, as though it had been too large for your throat.

THE EGG-BOX.

The egg-box is made in the shape of two bee-hives, placed together, as A: the inner shell B, is covered with half the shell of a real egg; the upper shell C, is of the same shape, but larger, being, in fact, the lid or upper part of the box, of which D is the lower. Place C, which is the outward shell, upon B, and both upon D, which arrangement puts all in readiness for the performance of the trick. Now call for an egg, and bid all the bystanders look at it, to see that it is a real one. Then take off the

upper part, B C, with your fore-finger and thumb, and placing the egg in the box, say, "Ladies and gentlemen, you see it fairly in the box;" and, uncovering it again, say, "You shall see me fairly take it out;" putting it into your pocket in their sight. Now open your box again, and say, "There's nothing;" close your hand about the middle of the box, and taking C off without B, say, "There is the egg again;" which will appear to the spectators to be the same that you put in your pocket; then, put C on again, and taking C, together with the inner shell, B, off again, say, "It is gone again;" and such will appear to be the fact.

THE OBEDIENT WATCH.

Borrow a watch from any person in company, and request the whole to stand round you. Hold the watch up to the ear of the first in the circle, and command it to go; then demand his testimony to the fact. Remove it to the ear of the next, and enjoin it to stop; make the same request to that person, and so on throughout the entire party.

Explanation. You must take care, in borrowing the watch, that it be a good one, and goes well. Conceal in your hand a piece of loadstone, which, so soon as you apply it to the watch, will occasion a suspension of the movements, which a subsequent shaking and withdrawing of the magnet will restore. For this purpose, keep the magnet in one hand, and shift the watch alternately from one hand to the other.

THE FLIGHT OF THE RING.

You may cause a ring to shift from one hand to another, and make it go on any finger required on the other hand, while somebody holds both your arms, in order to prevent communication between them, by attending to these instructions :—Desire some lady in company to lend you a gold ring, recommending her, at the same time, to make a mark on it, that she may know it again. Have a gold ring of your own, which fasten by a small piece of catgut-string to a watch-barrel, and sew it to the left sleeve of your coat. Take the ring that is given you in your right hand ; then putting, with dexterity, the other ring fastened to the watch-barrel, near the entrance of your sleeve, draw it privately to the fingers' ends of your left hand. During this operation, hide the ring that has been lent to you between the fingers of your right hand, and fasten it dexterously on a little hook, sewed for the purpose, on your waistcoat, and hidden by your coat. After that, show your ring, which hold in your left hand ; then ask the company on which finger of the other hand they wish it to pass. During this interval, and as soon as the answer has been given, put the before-mentioned finger on the little hook, in order to slip the ring on it ; at that moment let go the other ring, by opening your fingers. The spring which is in the watch-barrel, being confined no longer, will contract, and make the ring slip under the sleeve, without anybody perceiving it, not even those who hold your arms ; as their attention will be occupied to prevent your hands from communicating. After this operation, show the assembly that the ring is come on the other hand ; and make them remark that it is the same that had been lent to you, or that the mark is right. Much dexterity must be made use of to succeed in this entertaining trick, that the deception may not be suspected.

THE DEMI-AMPUTATION.

Provide yourself with two knives, a true and false one, (*vide cut,*) and  when you show this feat, put the true knife into your pocket, and, taking out the false one, place it on your wrist undiscovered ; then exhibit it, and you will appear to have nearly severed your arm.

THE MUTILATED HANDKERCHIEF RESTORED.

This feat, strange as it appears, is very simple ; the performer must have a confederate who has two handkerchiefs of the same quality, and with the same mark, one of which he throws upon the table, to perform the feat with. The performer takes care to put this handkerchief uppermost in making a bundle, though he affects to mix them together promiscuously. The person, whom he desires to draw one of the handkerchiefs, naturally takes that which comes first to hand. The performer then desires to shake them again to embellish the operation; but in so doing, takes care to bring the right handkerchief uppermost, and carefully fixes upon some simpleton to draw; and if he find the person is not likely to take the first that comes to hand, he prevents him from drawing by fixing upon another, under pretence of his having a more sagacious look. When the handkerchief is torn, and carefully folded up, it is put under a glass upon a table placed near a partition. On that part of the table on which the handkerchief is deposited, is a little trap, which opens and lets it fall into a drawer. The confederate, concealed behind the curtain, passes his hand under the table, opens the trap, and substitutes the second handkerchief for the first. He then shuts the trap, which so exactly fits the hole it closes, as to deceive the eyes of the most incredulous. If the performer be not possessed of such a table, he must have a second handkerchief in his pocket, and change it by slight of hand.

THE DOUBLE FUNNEL.

Get two funnels soldered one within the other, so as to appear like one; pour a little wine into the smaller end of the outside funnel, turn it up, and keep the wine in by placing your thumb at the bottom of the funnel; this must be done privately. Then pour some more wine into the broad part of the machine, drink it off completely; turn the broad end of the funnel downward, to show that all is gone; and instantly turning yourself about, pronounce some mystic terms; then withdraw your finger from the narrow end, so as to let the wine between the funnels run out.

THE FIRE AND WINE BOTTLE.

Get a tin bottle made with a tube nearly as big as its neck, passing from the bottom of the neck to the bottom of the bottle, in which there must be a hole of a size to correspond with it. Between the tube and the neck of the bottle, let there be sufficient space to allow you to pour in some wine which will remain in the bottle outside the tube. Begin the trick by pouring a glass of wine out of the bottle; then place it on the table, over a concealed hole, through which the confederate will thrust a burning fusee into the tube, so that, at your command, fire is emitted from the mouth of the bottle. As soon as the fire is extinguished, or withdrawn, you can take up the bottle again, and pour out more wine.

THE GLOBE BOX.

This trick is not inferior to the best that is shown with boxes. It is done with a box made of four pieces, and a ball as big as may conveniently be

contained therein; the ball serves, as the egg does in the egg-box, only to deceive the hand and eye of the spectators. This ball, made of wood, or ivory, is thrown out of the box upon the table, for every one to see that it is substantial; then put the ball into the box, which close up with all the pieces one within another; remove the upper shell with your fore-finger and thumb, and there will appear another of a different color, red, blue, yellow, or any other color you may fancy; this will seem to be another ball, though, in fact, it is no more than a shell of wood, ingeniously turned, and fitted to the box, as you may perceive by the cuts in the margin. L is the outer shell of the globe, taken off the figure M, the top of which represents the ball; N, is an inner shell; O, the cover of the same; P, another inner shell; Q, the cover of the same; R, a third shell; S, that which covers it. These globes may be made with more or less varieties, according to the desire of the practitioner.

THE HATCHED BIRD.

Separate an egg in the middle, as neatly as possible; empty it, and then, with a fine piece of paper and a little glue, join the two halves together, having first put a live canary bird inside it, which will continue unhurt in it for sometime, provided you make a small pin-hole in the shell to supply the bird with air : have, also, a whole egg in readiness. Present the two eggs for one to be chosen ; put the egg, which contains the bird, next to the person who is to choose, and, for this purpose, be sure to select a lady : she naturally chooses the nearest to her, because, having no idea of the trick to be performed, there is no apparent reason to take the further one : at any rate, if the wrong one be taken, you do not fail in the trick, for you break the egg, and say—" You see that this egg is fair and fresh, madam ; so you would have found the other, if you had chosen it. Now, do you choose to find in it a mouse, or a canary-bird ? " She naturally declares for the bird ; nevertheless, if she ask for the mouse, there are means to escape : you ask the same question of several ladies, and gather the majority of votes, which, in all probability, will be in favor of the bird, which you then produce.

THE PENETRATIVE SHILLING.

Provide a round tin box, of the size of a large snuff-box, and likewise eight other boxes, which will go easily into each other, and let the least of them be of a size to hold a shilling. Each of these boxes should shut with a hinge, and to the least of them there must be a small lock, fastened with a spring, but which cannot be opened without a key ; and observe, that all these boxes must shut so freely, that they may all be closed at once. Place these boxes in each other, with their tops open, in your pocket : then ask a person for a shilling, and desire him to mark it, that it may not be changed : take this piece in one hand, and in the other have another of the same appearance, and, putting your hand in your pocket, you slip the piece that is marked into the least box, and, shutting them all at once, you take them out : then, showing the piece you have in your hand, and which the company suppose to be the same that was marked, you pretend to make it pass through the box, but dexterously convey it away. You then present the box, for the spectators do not know yet that there are more than one, to any person in company, who, when he opens it, finds another, and another, till he come to the last, but that he cannot open without the key, which you then give him ; and, retiring to a distant part of the room, you tell him to take out the shilling himself and see if it be the one marked. This trick may be made more surprising by putting the key into the snuff-box of one of the company ; which you may do by asking for a pinch of snuff ; the key, being very small, will lie concealed among the snuff : when the person, who opens the boxes, asks for the key, tell him that one of his friends has it in his snuff-box.

THE MONEY BOX.

A piece of money, or a ring, is put into a box, in the presence of a person who holds it ; the operator stands at a distance, and bids him shake the box gently, and the piece is heard to rattle inside ; he is desired again to shake it, and then it is not heard to rattle; the third time, it is again heard, but the fourth time it is gone, and is found in the shoe of one of the company.

The box must be made on purpose, in such a manner that, in shaking it gently up and down, the piece within is heard; on the contrary, shaking it hard, horizontally, a little spring, which falls on the piece, prevents it from being heard, which makes you imagine it is not within. He who performs the trick, then touches the box, under pretence of showing how to shake it, and, although it is locked, he easily gets out the piece by means of a secret opening, availing himself of that minute to put in a false piece, and to leave the box with the same person, whom he causes to believe that the piece is or is not within, according to the manner the box is shaken : at length, the original piece is found in the shoe of one of the company, either by means of the person being in confederacy, and having a similar piece, or by sending another to slip it on the floor : in this last case, it is found on the floor, and the person fixed on is persuaded that it fell from his shoe as he was taking it off.

THE SALAMANDER.

An experiment to ascertain the degree of heat it is possible for a man to bear, was made in the month of July, 1828, at the New Tivoli, at Paris, in the presence of a company of about two hundred persons, amongst whom were many professors, *savans*, and physiologists, who had been especially invited to attend, by the physician Robertson, director of that establishment. The man on whom this experiment was made was a Spaniard of Andalusia, named Martenez, aged forty-three. A cylindrical oven, constructed in the shape of a dome, had been heated, for four hours, by a very powerful fire. At ten minutes past eight, the Spaniard, having on large pantaloons of red flannel, a thick cloak, also of flannel, and a large felt, after the fashion of a straw hat, went into the oven, where he remained, seated on a foot-stool, during fourteen minutes, exposed to a heat of from forty-five to fifty degrees of a metallic thermometer, the gradation of which did not go higher than fifty. He sang a Spanish song while a fowl was roasted by his side. At his coming out of the oven, the physicians found that his pulse beat one hundred and thirty-four pulsations a minute, though it was but seventy-two at his going in. The oven being heated anew for a second experiment, the Spaniard re-entered and seated himself in the same attitude, at three-quarters past eight, eat the fowl and drank a bottle of wine to the health of the spectators. At coming out his pulse was a hundred and seventy-six, and indicated a heat of one hundred and ten degrees of Reaumur. Finally, for the third and last experiment, which almost immediately followed the second, he was stretched on a plank, surrounded with lighted candles, and thus put into the oven, the mouth of which was this time closed : he was there nearly five minutes, when all the spectators cried out " Enough, enough !" and anxiously hastened to take him out. A noxious and suffocating vapor of tallow filled the inside of the oven, and all the candles were extinguished and melted. The Spaniard, whose pulse was two hundred at coming out of this gulf of heat, immediately threw himself into a cold bath, and, in two or three minutes after, was on his feet, safe and sound.

About the year 1809, one Lionetto, also a Spaniard, astonished not only the ignorant, but chemists and other men of science, in France, Germany, Italy, and England, by his insensibility to the power of fire. He handled, with impunity, red hot iron and molten lead, drank boiling oil, and performed other feats equally miraculous. While he was at Naples, he attracted the notice of Professor Sementeni, who narrowly watched all his operations, and endeavoured to discover his secret. He observed, in the first place, that when Lionetto applied a piece of red hot iron to his hair, dense fumes immediately rose from it; that when he touched his foot with the iron, similar vapors ascended, which affected both the organs of sight and smell. He also saw him place a rod of iron, nearly red hot, between his teeth, without burning himself; drink the third of a table-spoonful of boiling oil; and taking up molten lead with his fingers, place it on his tongue without apparent inconvenience.

Anxious to discover the means used by Lionetto to render himself capable of thus enduring the application of heat, Sementeni performed several experiments upon himself, and made many important discoveries. He found, that by friction with sulphuric acid diluted with water, the skin might be made insensible to the action of the heat of red-hot iron: a solution of alum, evaporated until it became spongy, appeared to be more effectual in these frictions. After having rubbed the parts, which were thus rendered, in some degree, incombustible, with hard soap, he discovered, on the application of hot iron, that their insensibility was increased. He then determined on again rubbing the parts with soap, and after this, found that the hot iron not only occasioned no pain, but that it actually did not burn the hair. Being thus far satisfied, the Professor applied hard soap to his tongue, until it became insensible to the heat of the iron; and after having placed an ointment, composed of soap mixed with a solution of alum, upon it, boiling oil did not burn it: while the oil remained on the tongue a slight hissing was heard, similar to that of hot iron when thrust into water; the oil soon cooled, and might then be swallowed without danger.

These are stated to be the results of the experiments performed by Professor Sementeni, and they tend to explain the astonishing performances of Lionetto. It is evident that he prepared his tongue and his skin in a similar manner, previously to his exhibitions. With regard to his passing the hot plate of iron over his hair, it seems pretty evident that the latter was first saturated with a solution similar to that of the alum or sulphuric acid. His swallowing the boiling oil ceases to become a phenomenon, when it is observed that, in order to show its high temperature, he threw pieces of lead into it, which, in the process of melting, absorbed a quantity of the caloric, or heat, of the oil; and that the small quantity of the latter which he poured upon his tongue, already prepared to receive it in the manner we have stated, cooled before he swallowed it. It is clear that he might put the molten lead upon his tongue with impunity, and suffer even less inconvenience from it, if possible, than from the oil, by the greater heat of which it had been melted. It is, however, probable, that instead of lead, Lionetto used a more fusible mixture; such, for instance, as that which will presently be found described under the title of "The Magic Spoon."

Several scientific men have successfully repeated the experiments of Professor Sementeni; and it is now no longer considered miraculous to behold a man applying hot iron to his skin without suffering from its powers. But we beg to caution our young readers very seriously against making any similar experiments upon themselves: they are only fit for men of science and profound chemical knowledge, and the least inaccuracy or omission would be productive of serious consequences. The foregoing account of the performances of the Fire-eaters and their secrets, we insert for the information of our young friends only, without holding them up as experiments calculated for their capacities or fit for their performance. If, in the course of this work, we should think fit to relate the mode of constructing wings to fly from St. Paul's to the monument, or even across the Hellespont, it by no means follows that the boys of England, for whose instruction and amusement we are, at this moment, "wasting the midnight oil," should make the attempt. The French author to whom we are indebted for the foregoing particulars,—Monsieur Julia Fontenelle, President de la Société Linneenne et des Sciences Physiques et Chimiques de Paris; Membre honoraire de la Société Royale de Varsovie; de l'Académie Royale de Medecine, et de celle des Sciences de Barcelonne; de la Société Royale Academique de Sciences de Paris, et cætera—(we like to give a clever man his titles in full)—states that, when the Spaniard, Lionetto, undertook the experiments which we have above described, he was under apprehensions of having something to do with the Inquisition, in consequence of his exploits.

TO MELT TWO METALLIC MIXTURES BY FRICTION.

Melt in one vessel, one part of mercury and two parts of bismuth; and in another, one part of mercury and four of lead; when cold, they will be quite solid: by rubbing them against each other, they will soon melt, as though each were rubbed separately against red hot iron.

THE HANDKERCHIEF HEARTH.

Cover the metal case of a watch with part of a handkerchief, single only; bring the ends to that side where the glass is, and hold the handkerchief by them there, so as to stretch it tightly over the metal. You may then place a red hot coal, or piece of lighted paper, upon that part of the handkerchief which is so strained over the metal, without burning it; the caloric merely passing through the handkerchief to fix in the metal.

THE INCOMBUSTIBLE THREAD.

Wind some linen thread tightly round a smooth pebble, secure the end, and if you expose it to the flame of a lamp or candle it will not burn. The caloric traverses, without fixing in it, and only attacks the stone which it encases.

Asbestos, a species of stone thread, can be held in the flame of a lamp, without being wound round a pebble, and will be equally incombustible.

SIMPLE AMALGAMATION AND SEPARATION.

Place a globule of mercury, about the size of a pea, on a piece of paper, by the side of a globule of potassium, about half the size of the mercury; fold up the paper so as to bring them into contact with each other; some caloric will be immediately disengaged, and the amalgamation will be complete in a few seconds. If it be then thrown into water, the mercury will be disengaged and fall to the bottom; the potassium, on the contrary, will decompose the water, absorb the oxygen, and the hydrogen being set at liberty, will discharge itself with some noise. The potassium will be converted into deutoxide of potassium, or potass, and dissolve in the water.

HIDEOUS METAMORPHOSIS.

Take a few nut-galls, bruise them to a very fine powder, which strew nicely upon a towel; then put a little brown copperas into a basin of water; this will soon dissolve, and leave the water perfectly transparent. After any person has washed in this water, and wiped with the towel on which the galls have been strewed, his hands and face will immediately become black; but, in a few days, by washing with soap, they will again become clean. This trick is too mischievous for performance.

TO MAKE A WET STONE PRODUCE FIRE.

Take quick-lime, salt-petre, tutia-Alexandrina and calamine, (lapis calaminaris,) of each, equal parts; live sulphur and camphor, of each, two parts: beat and sift them through a fine sieve; then put the powder into a fine linen cloth, tie it close, put it into a crucible, cover it with another crucible, mouth to mouth; bind and lute them well together; then set them in the sun to dry. When dry, the powder will be yellow. Then put the crucible into a potter's furnace, and when cold, take it out again, and you will find the powder altered into the substance of a stone.

When you have occasion to light a fire or candle, wet part of the stone with a little water, and it will instantly flame; when lighted, blow it out again, as you would a candle.

M

THE SUB-AQUEOUS VOLCANO.

Take one ounce of saltpetre; three ounces of powder; of sulphurvivum, three ounces; beat, sift, and mix them well together; fill a pasteboard, or paper mould, with the composition, and it will burn under the water till quite spent. Few persons will believe that this can be done before they have seen it tried.

THE CHEMICAL SAMSON.

To melt a rod of iron with a common fire. Heat a rod of iron, as thick as your finger, in a fire, urged by a pair of bellows, until it is white hot; draw it from the fire, and apply to the hot part a roll of brimstone, held by a pair of tongs; a profusion of most brilliant sparks will be thrown out, and the iron drop like melting sealing-wax. It is necessary to hold it over the hearth, to avoid mischief. If the heated part be a few inches from the end of the bar, a piece of it will be cut off.

THE MAGIC SPOON.

Put four ounces of bismuth into a crucible, and when in a state of complete fusion, throw in two ounces and a half of lead, and one ounce and a half of tin; these metals will combine, and form an alloy fusible in boiling water. Mould the alloy into bars, and take them to a silversmith to be made into tea-spoons. Place one of them in a saucer, at a tea-table, and the person who uses it will not be a little astonished to find it melt away as soon as he puts it into the hot tea.

METAL MELTED ON PAPER OVER A CANDLE.

An alloy, which may be kept in a state of fusion by placing it upon a piece of paper and holding it over a candle, may be made by melting together equal parts of bismuth, lead, and zinc.

THE WONDERFUL DYE.

Dissolve indigo in diluted sulphuric acid, and add to it an equal quantity of solution of carbonate of potass. If a piece of white cloth be dipped in this mixture, it will be changed to blue; yellow cloth, in the same mixture, may be changed to green; red to purple; and blue litmus paper be turned to red.

METALLIC TRANSMUTATION.

Dip a piece of polished iron, the blade of a knife, for instance, into a solution either of nitrate or sulphate of copper, and it will assume the appearance of a piece of pure copper; this is occasioned by the sulphuric acid seizing on the iron, and letting fall the copper.

THE FADED ROSE RESTORED.

Take a rose that is quite faded, and throw some sulphur on a chafing-dish of hot coals, then hold the rose over the fumes of the sulphur, and it will become quite white; in this state dip it into water, put it into a box or drawer for three or four hours, and when taken out, it will be quite red again.

THE PROTEAN LIQUID.

To make a red liquor, which, when poured into different glasses, will become yellow, blue, black, and violet. This phenomenon may be produced by the following process :—Infuse a few shavings of log-wood in common water, and when the liquor is red, pour it into a bottle; then take three drinking glasses; rinse one of them with strong vinegar, throw into the second a small quantity of pounded alum, which will not be observed if the glass has been newly washed, and leave the third without any preparation. If the red liquor in the bottle be poured into the first glass, it will assume a straw color, somewhat similar to that of Madeira wine; if into the second, it will pass gradually from bluish gray to black, provided it be stirred with a bit of iron, which has been privately immersed in good vinegar: in the third glass, the red liquor will assume a violet tint.

INCOMBUSTIBLE PAPER.

Dip a sheet of paper in strong alum-water, and when dry, repeat the process; or, it will be better still, if you dip and dry it a third time. After this, you may put it in the flame of a candle, and it will not burn.

THE MIMIC CONFLAGRATION.

Take half an ounce of sal-ammoniac, one ounce of camphor, and two ounces of aqua-vitæ; put them into an iron pot, narrowing towards the top, and set fire to it. The effect will be immediate; a mimic conflagration will take place, which will be alarming, but not dangerous.

PORTRAITS VISIBLE AND INVISIBLE.

These are performed with French chalk, a natural production of the earth, (sold in most oil-shops,) of a greasy, but extraordinary nature. It is made use of to draw portraits upon looking-glasses; which may be made visible and invisible, alternately, by breathing on and wiping off, and they will continue for many months fit for exhibition. The lines will appear very distinct where the glass is strongly breathed on, and disappear entirely when it is wiped dry again.

PERPETUAL MOTION.

Put very small filings of iron into aqua-fortis, and let them remain until the aqua-fortis is completely saturated with the iron, which will happen in

M 2

about two hours; pour off the solution, and put it into a phial an inch wide, with a large mouth, with a lump of lapis calaminaris; then stop it close, and the calamine stone will keep in perpetual motion.

THE DANCING EGG.

Boil an egg hard, and peel off a small piece of the shell at one end; then thrust in a quill filled with quicksilver, and sealed at each end. As long as the egg remains warm, it will not cease to dance about.

THE EGG IN THE PHIAL.

You may make an egg enter a phial without breaking, by steeping it in strong vinegar, for some time; the vinegar will so soften the shell, that it will bend and extend lengthways without breaking; when put in cold water, it will resume its former figure and hardness.

THE BLUE BOTTLE.

Expose an ounce of volatile alkali to the air, in a glass, for about a quarter of an hour; then put it into a flask, with twenty-four grains of the sulphate of copper, and the liquid will, by degrees, assume a beautiful blue color; pour it carefully into another flask, so as to separate the liquid from the copper. If you examine it a few days afterward, you will find that the blue color has totally disappeared; but, if you take out the cork for a minute, and replace it, you may see the blue re-appear on the surface of the liquid, and descend gradually, until the whole of it is of the same hue as it was when you laid it aside. In a few days, it will again become colorless, and you can restore the blue by the same simple means. The experiment may be performed a great number of times with the same liquid. Care must be taken in making your preparation, that the volatile alkali be not suffered to remain long enough in the first flask, to dissolve too much of the sulphate of copper; for, if it receive too great a degree of color, the blue will not disappear, when the liquid is deprived of air.

THE CANDLE OF ICE.

Cover a small portion of the upper end of a tallow candle with paper, and give the remainder of it a coat of fine coal and powdered sulphur, mixed together; dip it in water, and expose it to the air during a hard frost, and a slight coat of ice will form round it, which may be, subsequently, rendered thicker, in proportion to the number of immersions and exposures to the air which it receives. When it arrives at a sufficient consistency, take off the paper, light the upper end of the candle, and it will burn freely.

TO DIP THE HAND IN WATER WITHOUT WETTING IT.

Powder the surface of a bowl of water with lycopodium; you may then put your hand into it, and take out a piece of money, that had been previously placed at the bottom of the bowl, without wetting your skin; the lycopodium so attaching itself to the latter, as to keep it entirely from coming in direct contact with the water. After performing the experiment, a slight shake of the hand will rid it of the powder.

TO REMOVE AND AFTERWARDS RESTORE THE COLOR OF A RIBBON.

Dip a rose-colored ribbon into nitric acid, diluted with eight or ten parts of water, and as soon as the color disappears, which it will do in a short time, take out the ribbon, and put it into a very weak alkaline solution; the alkali will quickly neutralize the acid; and the color will then re-appear.

THE PAPER ORACLE.

Some amusement may be obtained among young people, by writing, with common ink, a variety of questions, on different bits of paper, and adding a pertinent reply to each, written with nitro-muriate of gold. The collection is suffered to dry, and put aside until an opportunity offers for using them. When produced, the answers will be invisible; you desire different persons to select such questions as they may fancy, and take them home with them; you then promise, that if they are placed near the fire, during the night, answers will appear written beneath the questions in the morning; and such will be the fact, if the papers be put in any dry, warm situation.

THE SIBYL'S CAVE.

Write several questions and answers, as directed in the preceding article: for the answers, instead of nitro-muriate of gold, you may use the juice of a citron, or an onion. Let any of the questions be chosen by a party, and placed in a box, which may be called "The Sibyl's Cave." This box must be furnished with a piece of hot iron, beneath a false bottom of tin; when the paper is put in it, the heat will cause the answer to appear; you then take it out, show it to the person who made choice of the question, and, as soon as it is read, put it aside; the answer will vanish, when the paper becomes cold again.

TO SEPARATE OIL FROM WATER.

Most of our young readers are, doubtless, aware, that oil is lighter than water, and floats upon its surface. If a vessel of any convenient description, be half filled with water, and a portion of oil be then poured on it, the oil may be easily separated from the water, by one end of a wick of cotton being placed in it, the other end of which is carried into another vessel : the oil, obedient to the laws of capillarity, will rise gradually into the cotton, and fall, drop by drop, from the other extremity of it, into the vase or cup, which is placed to receive it. We are told, that the process is much quicker, if the cotton be previously dipped in oil.

TO MAKE A COLORLESS LIQUID BECOME BLUE, LILAC, PEACH-COLORED, AND RED WITHOUT TOUCHING IT.

Put a drachm of powdered nitrate of cobalt into a phial, containing an ounce of the solution of caustic potass : a decomposition of the salt, and precipitation of a blue oxide of cobalt, takes place. Cork the phial, and the liquid will now assume a blue color, from which it will pass to a lilac, afterward to a peach tint, and, finally, to a light red.

THE FOUR ELEMENTS.

Procure a glass tube, about the thickness of a man's finger, and securely seal one end of it. Mark it, all round, with four equal divisions. Introduce mercury, sufficient to fill the space below the first mark ; a solution of sub-carbonate of potass for the second division ; white brandy, to which a blue tint is imparted, for the third ; and turpentine, colored red, for the fourth. After these preparations are completed, close up and seal the mouth of the tube, and you may then give a fanciful exhibition of chaos and the four elements. Shake the tube, and you will mix all the contents together, and this mixture will represent chaos ; in a short time, if the tube be not removed, all the ingredients will separate, and each go to its allotted division, placing itself according to its specific gravity, in comparison with the others : the contents of the upper division, which is red, will represent fire ; the next, which has a blue tint, air ; the third, which is colorless, water ; and the lower one, earth.

THE MINERAL CHAMELEON.

We are indebted to Sheele for a composition, known by the above title, which is prepared by mixing together, and exposing to a strong heat, in an open crucible, for little more than a quarter of an hour, three parts of nitrate of potass, and one of deutoxide of manganese, both in a finely powdered state. The compound thus obtained, possesses the following singular properties :—If a few grains of this preparation be put into a glass, and cold water be then poured on it, the liquor will first turn green, and then pass rapidly to purple, and finally, by beautiful gradations, to red. If hot water be used, instead of cold, the liquid will assume a beautiful violet color. The colors will be more or less intense, in proportion to the quantity of the oxide used, for a more or less quantity of water ; ten grains, in a very little water, will produce a beautiful green color, which will pass with rapidity to a dark purple, and, subsequently, to red. If a small portion of the Chameleon Mineral be used for four ounces of water, the color will be a deep green; by the addition of more water, it will turn rosy, and become colorless in a few hours, giving in the process a yellowish precipitate. When the liquid changes slowly, it is easy to discover other hues, which it takes in the following order—green, blue, violet, indigo, purple and red.

It appears that the phenomena produced by the Chameleon Mineral, have attracted the attention of several men of science, and it seems, from the result of their experiments, that in those preparations of the Chameleon Mineral, in which there is a greater proportion of potass than manganese, the green requires more time to change into the other colors, and the greater the proportion of manganese, the more intense is the first color, and the quicker does the liquid acquire the other tints. The effect of hot water in this experiment, is much more powerful than that of cold.

PHOSPHORIC FISH, METEORS, &c.

Phosphorus was discovered by the alchymist Brandt, who sold the secret to Krafft, with whom Kunkel associated himself for its purchase. He was, however, deceived by Krafft, who never communicated the secret to him. Kunkel immediately commenced a series of experiments, and in 1674, discovered the mode of making it.

Phosphorus, in a state of purity, is solid, demi-transparent, and of a consistence similar to wax; the solar light gives it a red color; it will unite with almost all metallic substances. When it is taken in the hand, it should never be held for more than a few seconds, for the heat thus applied, is sufficient to inflame it, if continued; and a burn from phosphorus is more painful than any other kind of burn. A basin of cold water ought always to be at hand, to dip the phosphorus in occasionally; and when it is cut to pieces, it must be cut in water. Phosphorus can only be preserved by keeping it in places where neither light nor heat has access. It is obtained from druggists in rolls, about the thickness of a quill; these are put into a phial filled with cold water; which has been boiled to expel air from it, and the phial is enclosed in an opaque case. It does not exist in nature in a state of purity, but as a salt; it is extracted from bones.

The light produced in the night time, by writing with a stick of phosphorus on a wall, owes its existence to a slight coat which the stick leaves behind it on the parts over which it has passed; this, being combustible, burns slowly, in absorbing the oxygen of the air.

It has been well-known, from time almost immemorial, that animal or vegetable substances, in a state of putrefaction, often become luminous. The glow-worm has, doubtless, been seen by many of our readers, bearing its brilliant midnight lamp; several insects, and some fishes also, possess a luminous property.   In 1642, an old woman presented the Prince of Condé with some meat, bought by her the preceding day in the market of Montpelier, and which illuminated her room during the night.   We have seen a sole emit most brilliant and beautiful flashes of light on a dark night.

A great number of experiments have been performed by scientific men, to ascertain the cause of the luminous aspect of the sea ; it is attributed to those putrid substances, which are found in the waters.   The following experiment, which has reference to this subject, is rather curious :—A little fresh whiting was placed in a vase containing water.   It produced no light, even after having been agitated ; that part of the fish only that was above the water, and not the water itself, grew luminous during the night.   On lifting up the fish, by means of a stick, which was passed beneath it, and rested against the opposite side of the vase, the water appeared luminous behind it ; on being much agitated, it became entirely luminous, and continued so for some time after it was left undisturbed.   The strongest emission of light takes place after the fish has been about twenty hours in the water ; after three days, the water loses this property.   About four drachms of the substance of a fresh herring were put into a solution of two drachms of sulphate of magnesia, in two ounces of water.   On the succeeding evening, the whole of the liquor, upon shaking the phial, became beautifully luminous, and it continued luminous till the fourth day.

There is a fish mentioned by Pliny, the naturalist, which renders such objects luminous as are touched by it.   It differs from its fellow tenants of the waters, which become phosphorescent only when in a state of putrefaction ; whereas, the fresher the pholas is, the more luminous does it appear.   Brandy extinguishes its light ; when it becomes dry, a little pure or salt water will revivify its lustre.   When putrid, it loses its brilliancy, which it does not recover until putrefaction has gone its full length, when, by agitating it in water, the latter becomes luminous.   Solutions of hydrochlorate of soda and nitrate of potass, augment the brilliancy of the water ; acids and wine extinguish it.   The water may be rendered still brighter by pouring it on recently calcined sulphate of lime, on quartz, sugar, &c.

The phosphoric meteors, commonly called Will-o'-wisps, which are seen in marshes, near rivers, in churchyards, and in low and humid places, in different forms, are to be attributed to the combustion of some hydrogen gas, principally phosphoric hydrogen gas, which, as is well known, has the property of inflaming itself on coming into contact with oxygen gas or air.   These meteors are more frequently seen in winter than in summer ; in rainy weather their light is more intense than when it is dry.

PHOSPHORIC WOOD.

Rotten wood often becomes luminous ; many circumstances induce us to ascribe its light to slow combustion ; a fact in favor of this idea is, that if phosphorescent wood be placed in a pneumatic machine, and the air be pumped out of it, the light disappears, and if the air be restored, the wood again becomes luminous. The same experiments performed with a fish that emitted light, produced the same results. The light of fish differs from that of rotten wood in this respect,—namely, that water, alcohol, and several saline solutions, destroy the light of the latter ; while water does not diminish the brilliancy of the former, no more than it does that of the glow-worm. If luminous wood be introduced to a tube of glass, and plunged into a freezing mixture, the light will be extinguished.

Rods of wood may be rendered phosphorescent, by steeping them in a solution of chlorate of lime, and then burning one of their ends in the flame of a lamp or candle ; after the combustion has taken place, if the stick be withdrawn, a little white matter will be found at the extremity, which will shed a brilliant light. The harder kinds of wood are most proper for this experiment. The white remains of the combustion, it is said, are pure lime ; and that a similar luminous property might be given to the wood, by plunging it into lime-water, or a solution of sulphate of magnesia.

PHOSPHORIC PLANTS.

Persons working in mines sometimes meet with phosphorescent plants ; the light is perceptible at the points of the plants, especially when they are broken. This phosphorescence disappears in an atmosphere of hydrogen gas, of chlora, or oxide of carbon.

The daughter of the celebrated Linnæus discovered that the *tropeolum majus* is sometimes phosphorescent in the evening.

PHOSPHORIC OYSTER SHELLS.

Place some very thick oyster shells upon, and cover them with, some burning coals ; in half an hour take them carefully out of the fire, and it will be only necessary to expose them to the light for a few minutes to be convinced that they have become phosphorescent. In fact, if put in a dark place, they shed a light accompanied by the greater part of the prismatic colors. If the calcination be made in a closed crucible, the colors will be less brilliant. If the crucible be of lead, the parts that have come into contact with it will yield a reddish light ; if a few bits of steel be strewed about the crucible, the phosphorescence will be more lively ; but if some flat pieces of coal be used instead of steel, the colors will be more beautiful, particularly the blue, red, and green. It seems that scientific men either do not know positively, or are not agreed as to the cause of the phosphorescence of certain bodies ; according to some, it is owing to an accumulation of solar light ; while others say that it ought to be attributed to a light inherent in the phosphoric substance.

TO RENDER MILK LUMINOUS.

Milk may be rendered luminous by immersing a pholas in it. One of these fishes is sufficient to communicate light to seven ounces of milk, which, as it becomes luminous, appears also to be turned transparent. Beccaria felt convinced that air was necessary for the production of this light; for, having filled a tube with milk made luminous in the foregoing manner, he could only disengage the light from it by suffering the admission of air to the tube. The juice of this fish, reduced into a paste with meal, throws out considerable light when plunged into hot water. If preserved in honey, the fish will retain its luminous property for more than a year; and, in fact, by plunging it into hot water, it will shed as much light as if it were quite fresh.

IGNITION BY COMPRESSION.

By compressing a bit of phosphorus between two pieces of wood, it will inflame. The same effect may be produced by the friction of one piece of phosphorus against another.

THE MASK OF FLAME.

Take six parts of oil of olives and one of phosphorus, suffer them to digest well together, and preserve the solution, which, in the dark, will become luminous. An experiment that is considered amusing may be performed by closing the eyes and lightly passing a sponge, dipped in this solution, over the face and hands, which will then, in the dark, appear covered with a light bluish flame. This trick, we are told, is not at all dangerous.

THE MINIATURE RIVER ON FIRE.

Let fall a few drops of phosphorized ether on a lump of loaf sugar, place the sugar in a glass of warm water, and a very beautiful appearance will be instantly exhibited; the effect will be increased, if the surface of the water, by blowing gently with the breath, be made to undulate.

PHOSPHORESCENT SPAR.

Coarsely powder some fluor spar, and sprinkle it, in a dark room, on a fire-shovel made hot, (but not to redness,) and it will emit a beautiful phosphorescent light for some time.

IGNITION BY PERCUSSION.

Put into the middle of some dry cotton, a piece of phosphorus the size of a large pin's head, previously dried on blotting paper; strike it with a hammer and it will inflame.

THE PHOSPHORIC STEAM BATH.

Lay a small piece of phosphorus upon a bit of glass, place the glass upon the surface of hot water in a basin, and the phosphorus will inflame.

TO BURN BROWN PAPER BY PHOSPHORUS AND FRICTION.

Wrap a grain of phosphorus, dried on blotting paper, in a piece of brown paper, rub it with some hard body, and it will set fire to the paper.

THE ILLUMINATOR AND EXTINGUISHER.

Make two little figures of wood or clay, or any other materials you please, with a little hole in the mouth of each. Put in the mouth of one, a few grains of bruised gunpowder, and a little bit of phosphorus in the other. Then take a lighted wax candle, and present it to the mouth of the figure with the gunpowder, which, taking fire, will put the candle out; then present your candle, having the snuff quite hot, to the other figure, and it will light again immediately.

TO LIGHT A CANDLE BY A GLASS OF WATER.

Take a little piece of phosphorus, of the size of a pin's head, and with a piece of tallow, stick it on the edge of a drinking-glass. Then take a lighted candle, and having blown it out, apply it to the glass, when it will immediately be lighted. You may likewise write, with a bit of phosphorus, on paper, some words, which will appear awful, when the candle is withdrawn from the room.

AUTOMATA.

Our object being to acquaint our young readers with the mode of performing many pieces of astonishing deception, as well as to instruct them how to do several pleasant tricks of a more simple nature, the most celebrated Automata occur to us as being subjects which ought to occupy a conspicuous station in our Feats of Legerdemain.

THE CHESS PLAYER.

The construction of machines capable of imitating the mechanical action of the human body shows exquisite skill. This, however, has been done; M. De Kempelen, a gentleman of Presburg, in Hungary, constructed an Androides capable of playing at chess. Every one, who is in the least acquainted with this game, must know that it is so far from being mechanically performed, as to require a greater exertion of the judgment and rational faculties than is sufficient to accomplish matters of greater importance. That such a machine really was made, the public had ocular demonstration. The inventor came over to Britain in 1785, and exhibited his automaton to public inspection for more than a year. On his death, it was purchased by M. Maelzel, who paid this country a visit in 1827, when the invention created as much wonder as ever, notwithstanding the vast progress made in mechanical science.

The room where it was exhibited had an inner apartment, within which appeared the figure of a Turk, as large as life, dressed after the Turkish fashion, sitting behind a chest of three feet and a half in length, two feet in breadth, and two feet and a half in height, to which it was attached by the wooden seat on which it sat. The chest was placed upon four castors, which, together with the figure, might be moved to any part of the room.

On the plain surface formed by the top of the chest, in the centre, was raised an immovable chess-board, of handsome dimensions, upon which the figure had its eyes fixed, its right arm and hand being extended on the chest, and its left arm somewhat raised, as if in the attitude of holding a Turkish pipe, which was originally placed in its right hand.

The exhibitor proceeded by wheeling the chest to the entrance of the apartment within which it stood, in front of the spectators. He then opened certain doors contrived in the chest, two in the front and two in the back, at the same time pulling out a long shallow drawer, made to contain the Chessmen, a cushion for the arm of the figure to rest upon, and some counters; two lesser drawers and a green cloth screen, contrived in the body of the figure and its lower parts, were likewise opened, and the Turkish robe which covered them was raised; so that the construction, both of the figure and chest, intentionally was displayed, and the exhibitor introduced a lighted candle into the body of the chest and figure, by which the interior of each was, in a great measure, rendered transparent.

The chest was divided by a partition into two equal chambers; that to the right of the figure was the narrowest, and occupied scarcely one third of the body of the chest; it was filled with little wheels, levers, cylinders, and other machinery used in clock-work: that to the left contained two wheels, some small barrels with springs, and two quarters of a circle, placed horizontally. The body and lower parts of the figure contained certain tubes, which appeared to be conductors to the machinery. After a sufficient time, during which each spectator satisfied his scruples and curiosity, the exhibitor closed the doors, made some arrangement in the body of the figure, wound up the works with a key inserted into a small opening in the body of the chest, and placed the cushion under the left arm of the figure, which then rested upon it.

In playing a game, the automaton made choice of the white men; it likewise gave the first move. It played with the left hand instead of the right,—

the right hand being constantly fixed on the chest. This slight incongruity proceeded from inadvertence of the inventor, who did not discover his mistake until the machinery was too far completed to remedy the defect. At the commencement of a game, the automaton made a motion of the head, as if taking a view of the board; the same motion occurred at the close of the game. In making a move it slowly raised its left arm from the cushion placed under it, and directed it toward the square of the piece to be moved. The arm then returned to its position on the cushion. Its hand and fingers opened on touching the piece, which it took up and conveyed to any proposed square. The motions were performed with perfect correctness, and the anxiety with which the arm acted, especially in the delicate operation of castling, seemed to be the result of spontaneous feeling; bending at the shoulder, elbow, and knuckles, and cautiously avoiding to touch any other piece than that which had been moved.

On giving check to the king, it moved its head as a signal. When a false move was made by its antagonist, which frequently occurred through curiosity to observe in what manner the automaton would act,—as for instance, if a knight had been moved like a castle,—the automaton smote impatiently on the chest with its right hand, replaced the knight in its former square, and would not permit its antagonist to recover his move, but proceeded immediately to move one of its own pieces, thus appearing to punish him for his inattention.

It was considered of importance that the person matched against the automaton should be attentive in moving a piece exactly in the centre of a square; otherwise, the figure, in attempting to lay hold of the piece, might even sustain some injury in the delicate mechanism of the fingers. If its antagonist hesitated for a considerable time to move a piece, it tapped smartly on the chest with its right hand, as if testifying impatience at the delay.

During the time the automaton was in motion, a low sound of clock work was heard, as if running down, which ceased soon after the arm was reclined on the cushion. The works were wound up at intervals of ten or twelve moves by the exhibitor, who was usually employed pacing up and down the room; approaching the chest, however, from time to time, on its right side. It was understood that the automaton could not play, unless M. De Kempelen, or his substitute, was near to direct its moves; but it is very certain that the whole mystery lay in the chest, and that there could be no connexion with the floor, as the inventor advertised his willingness to exhibit at private houses.

To avoid the obstructions frequently occasioned by the inattention of strange antagonists, in moving the pieces required exactly to the centre of squares, a new arrangement was subsequently made, by which the adversary did not play at the same board with the automaton, but had a chess-board to himself, on which he copied the automaton's moves, and made his own; while a person who attended at the automaton's board, copied, with due precision, for the automaton, the adversary's moves.

In concluding our account of this extraordinary machine, we must observe that it has been asserted, without contradiction, that, although it beat numerous skilful chess players, in different countries, its moves were directed by a boy concealed within the machinery; so that, in fact, whoever the boy could beat at the game, was sure to be conquered by the automaton. This will show that it is in the power of youth to attain such a mastery over chess, as to render them capable of competing with capital players of a mature age.

THE FLUTE PLAYER.

The celebrated Vauconson invented an Automaton Flute-player, of which there is a minute description in the Memoirs of the Royal Academy of Sciences at Paris, by which it appears that the figure was about five feet and a half high, and was placed upon a square pedestal, which concealed a portion of the machinery. The air entered the body by three separate pipes, into which it was conveyed by nine pairs of bellows, which expanded and contracted in regular succession, by means of a steel axis turned by clock-work. These bellows performed their functions without any noise, which might have discovered the means of conveying the air into the machine. The three tubes that received the air from the bellows passed into three small reservoirs in the trunk of the figure, where they united, and ascending towards the throat, formed the cavity of the mouth, which terminated in two small lips. Within this cavity was a small movable tongue, which, by its motion, at proper intervals, admitted the air or intercepted it in its passage to the flute. The fingers, lips, and tongue, derived their appropriate movements from a steel cylinder, also turned by clock-work. It was divided into fifteen equal parts, which, by means of pegs pressing upon the ends of fifteen different levers, caused the other extremities to ascend. Seven of these levers directed the fingers, having wires and chains fixed to their ascending extremities, which being attached to the fingers, caused them to ascend in proportion as the other extremity was pressed down by the motion of the cylinder, and *vice versa;* thus the ascent or descent of one end of a lever produced a similar ascent or descent in the corresponding fingers, by which one of the holes of the flute was occasionally opened or stopped, as it might have been by a living performer. Three of the levers served to regulate the ingress of the air, being so contrived as to open and shut the three reservoirs above mentioned, by means of valves, so that more or less strength might be given, and a higher or lower note produced. The lips were directed by four levers, one of which opened them to give the air a freer passage; the other contracted them; the third drew them backward;

and the fourth pushed them forward : the lips were projected upon that part of the flute which received the air, and by the different motions already mentioned, properly modified the tune. The remaining lever was employed in the direction of the tongue, which it easily moved, so as to open or shut the mouth of the flute. The just succession of the several motions performed by the various parts of the machine, was regulated by the following simple contrivance :—the extremity of the axis of the cylinder terminated, on the right side, by an endless screw, consisting of twelve threads, each placed at the distance of an eighth of an inch from the other. Above the screw was fixed a piece of copper, and in it a steel pivot, which falling in between the threads of the screw, obliged the cylinder to follow those threads ; and thus, instead of turning directly round, it was continually pushed on one side. Hence, if a lever were moved by a peg placed on the cylinder, in any one revolution, it could not be moved by the same peg in the succeeding revolution because the peg would be an eighth of an inch beyond it, by the lateral motion of the cylinder. Thus, by an artificial disposition of these pegs in different parts of the cylinder, the statue was made, by the successive elevation of the proper levers, to exhibit all the different motions of a flute-player.

THE INVISIBLE GIRL.

The operators have a communication, from the exhibition room to another where the confederate is concealed, by tin pipes, which end in a clear horn trumpet, inserted in an isolated glass chest or barrel, attached to the ceiling by colored ribbons, twined round a small gilt chain. In the inside of these pipes, at right angles, are placed small mirrors, which reflect and contract every object in the exhibition room, so that the confederate, who answers the questions put, can not only hear all that is said, but see even the objects that are held in the hands of the visiters, such as watches, money, miniatures, letters in a book, and every other thing that is uncovered. The following curious dialogue took place between a traveller from this country, and the Invisible Girl, at Siccard's Diversion Room, in Paris :—"What age are you ? Fourteen years of age. Where were you born ? At Marseilles. What is your name ? Francoise. Are you pretty ? No. Are you good ? Yes, though sometimes ill-natured. What is your position ? I am reclining. Do not all the questions that are put to you disgust you ? Never ; but I am sometimes very much vexed. How is it that you see everything that is presented to you ; that you hear everything that is said to you ; and that no person can discover you ? That is a secret of those to whom I belong," &c. It is a matter of much complication, and cannot be performed without a good confederate and considerable scientific knowledge. We trust, however, we have said sufficient to render the Invisible Girl no wonder.

THE MAHOMETAN MAGICIAN.

The following description of the mechanical conjuring figure, so called, as well as that of " The wise little Turk," will, doubtless, remind our readers of the Automaton Chess-player.

The Mahometan Magician is a figure of sixteen or eighteen inches high, and holds a little hammer in its hand. When exhibited, it is first taken off the table on which it stands, and shown to the company, to convince them that it is perfectly detached, and stands by itself: the exhibitor then having replaced it on the table, asks if he will compliment his master? The little Turk, by turning his head, expresses " No," He then asks if he will pay his respects to the company? He bows his head to express "Yes." A pack of cards is then presented to the spectators, who draw out one by chance; without seeing the card, or approaching the automaton, his master orders him to strike the number of strokes, necessary to describe the card, with his hammer, on a bell :—the little Turk instantly obeys. He is then asked if the card drawn be a heart, a diamond, club, or spade? And, as the suits are mentioned, he moves his head, to give approbation or disapprobation, and an answer conformably to truth. He then tells the number thrown on dice ; and also, before-hand, the number which a second throw will produce. One of the company having hid a little figure in a box, divided into several compartments, he tells in which of them, and at what number, the little figure is to be found ; and, to give a humorous termination to this trick, when he is asked which of the company is the most amorous he points out some old gentleman with spectacles.

The table on which the little Turk is placed, is covered with a green cloth, concealing three levers, which are put in motion by the aid of three brass wires, passing through the feet of the table, and conducted behind the partition : the person who is hid, and acts as the confederate, draws these brass wires as he has occasion to act on the cranks concealed in the pedestal of the automaton, which cranks terminate in the base. By these means, the different motions are communicated to the machine the moment they are required, in the same manner as a repeating watch is made to strike by pushing the button of the case. The performer then holds in his hand a pack of cards, arranged in such a manner that he understands their sequence ; that the spectators may not suspect this arrangement of the cards, he apparently mixes them, but, in reality, he only cuts them, which does not change the combination of the game ; when he has had a card drawn, he cuts them the last time in the place where the card has been chosen, by which means, he passes to the bottom the card which was immediately over the one drawn : then, looking adroitly at the bottom, he knows, without seeing, the card which the spectator had drawn by chance. He then interrogates the little Turk by a question, which is so composed, that either the words, syllables, or vowels, communicate to the confederate the color and denomination of the card. By a similar stratagem, knowledge is conveyed to the confederate of the first number thrown on dice; the automaton can then very easily tell what number will come up on the second throw of the dice, because fresh dice are introduced, and such are substituted as have the same numbers on all their faces. As the person, to whom the dice are given, might, by looking at them, perceive the imposition, to escape detection, peculiar care is taken not only to recommend to him to hold the dice carefully hidden in his hand until he throws them, but also to prevent them being too long exposed to the sight; loaded dice might also be employed, which are so contrived, that the centre of gravity operates invariably. As the person who has already thrown the dice may wish to throw again, either accidentally or through suspicion, and as the return of the same points might occasion the honesty of the dice to be suspected, all these inconveniences are removed by getting rid of them as soon as possible.

The box where the little figure has been concealed has a bottom of soft leather, by which means, in handling beneath the compartment where the little figure is, may be discovered by the hand of the operator; and the figure is constructed of such dimensions as to press on the bottom of the box when it is shut.

THE CANARY.

A Canary bird is shown, perched on a bottle, which sings any air required. He also sings equally well when changed to different bottles, and on different tables: the breath from his bill blows out a candle, and lights it afterward. The machinery and manner of working we shall now proceed to describe.

Behind the curtain which covers part of the partition are placed two hollow cones of metal. These cones, which are unequal in size, serve as a speaking trumpet to the confederate, and act as echoes, which conduct the voice to different parts, as two mirrors, of different concavities, operate in the reflection of objects at different distances. The confederate, imitating the notes of a bird, executes the required air. The confederate employs the two different echoes to convey the voice to different points, according to the position of the table and the bottle on which the bird is perched. The bird has in its body a little double bellows, and between its legs, a little moving peg, which puts the bellows in motion; this peg, entering the neck of the bottle, leans on a piece of wood which cannot be seen, as the bottle is opaque. This piece of wood, being placed vertically on the movable bottom of the bottle, easily moves the bellows, and is readily moved by the levers which are under the cloth, when the confederate draws the brass wire which is hidden in the feet of the table: by the same means, the bellows are moved to blow out the candle, and it apparently proves to the spectators

N

that the notes are really formed in the throat of the bird, because the air comes through the bill. When the operator takes the bird in his hand he puts the bellows in motion with his thumb, and the wind in the same manner extinguishes the candle, and he persuades the company that the bird sings without the aid of any machinery hidden in the table; the candle being only a moment extinguished, and the wick still warm, is lighted instantly, by the air through the bill of the bird, which, for that purpose, has been furnished with a little flour of brimstone, and operates as a match.

Besides the curious Automata we have already described, various others have been produced by ingenious persons of different countries. Albertus Magnus is said to have devoted thirty years of his life to the construction of a head that not only moved, but spoke: Thomas Aquinas was, it is related, so terrified at its powers, under the impression that it was the work of magic, that he broke it to pieces. A locksmith of Nuremberg, in the sixteenth century, constructed figures that beat drums, while others played on lutes: and the emperor Charles the Fifth amused himself, in his retirement, by making similar Automata, or rather, Androides, for so such figures are called by the learned. The celebrated John Muller, it is reported, made a wooden eagle, in 1470, which, on the emperor Maximilian's approach to Nuremberg, flew to meet him. Vauconson made an Automatic duck, and, as Labat tells us, General de Gennes, (who, in 1688, defended St. Christopher against the English,) an Automatic peacock; both of these were of a size and plumage perfectly natural: they eat, drank, walked about, and uttered the same sounds as the birds themselves. The machinery, in both cases, was similar to that of a watch. However astonishing these more complicated pieces of machinery may have been to our forefathers, in modern times, enlightened persons regard Vauconson and his Flute-player, and De Kempelen and his Turk, with much less wonder than that with which the rustics of the present day gaze upon the Jack-pudding Jugglers, who amuse them on a Cart-stage.

TRICKS WITH CARDS.

The King of Conjurors at Cards
His glib discourse oft interlards
    With crabbed Greek, and Latin lame :—
By sleight of hand, performing feats,
    Which even magic put to shame.
But when he works his master-cheats,
This mighty King is forced to crave
The aid of some confederate Knave.

AMONG the most amusing feats of Legerdemain are the tricks with cards, of which, in the ensuing pages, we present our reader with an excellent series. Whatever may be the objections, and whether they be well founded or not, against card-playing among youth, it is neither our duty nor inclination here to discuss ; it must be admitted, by every liberal mind, that for the mere purpose of performing a few amusing feats of dexterity, to wile away a winter evening, and relax the mind, for a time, from scholastic studies, the introduction of a pack of cards is unexceptionable.

Cards have been, for many centuries, in use, having, as it is generally believed, been invented about the year 1390, to amuse Charles the Sixth, king of France, of whose wisdom, it must be confessed, historians do not speak very highly. Upon this circumstance the ingenious Mr. Malkin has observed, that the universal adoption of an amusement which was invented for a fool, is no very favorable specimen of the wisdom of mankind. The

Honorable Daines Barrington, however, in his "Observations on the Antiquity of Card-playing in England," asserts, that they came originally from Spain; while other authors attribute their invention to a more classic and ancient era, and give the honor, if it be any, of their first production to the Romans. Having given this slight sketch of the history of cards, we shall proceed to furnish the necessary instructions for the performance of the following feats.

FORCING.

Forcing is making a person take such a card as you think fit, while he supposes he is taking one at hazard, or according to his own inclination. It is almost impossible to describe how this is done; we must, however, attempt it. First, ascertain what the card you intend to force is; this must be done privately, or while you are playing with the cards; then place it, to all appearance, carelessly in the pack, but still keep your eye, or the little finger of your left hand, in which you hold the pack, upon it. Now, request a person to take a card from the pack; open them nimbly from your left to your right hand, spreading them backward and forward, so as to puzzle the person in making his choice: the moment you see him putting out his hand to take a card, spread on the cards till you come to the one you wish to force; let its corner be most invitingly put forward in front of the other cards, and let it make its appearance only the moment his fingers reach the pack. This mode of operation seems so fair, that unless he knows the secret of forcing, you may put what card you please into his hand, while he thinks he is making a choice himself. Having thus forced your card, you may tell him to look at it, give him the pack to shuffle as much as he pleases, for, in fact, do what he will, you, of course, can always tell what it was. A method of doing this cleverly is the first thing to be acquired; for without it, few of the master-feats can be performed.

TO TELL A CARD THOUGHT OF BLINDFOLD.

Take twenty-one cards, and lay them down in three rows, with their faces upward; (i. e.) when you have laid out three, begin again at the left hand, and lay one card upon the first, and so on to the right hand; then begin on the left hand again, and so go on until you have laid out the twenty-one cards in three heaps, at the same time requesting any one to think of a card. When you have laid them out, ask him which heap his card is in: then lay that heap in the middle between the other two. This done, lay them out again in three heaps as before, and again request him to notice where his noted card goes, and put that heap in the middle, as before. Then taking up the cards with their backs toward you, take off the uppermost card, and reckon it one; take off another, which reckon two; and thus proceed till you come to the eleventh, which will invariably prove to be the card thought of,

You must never lay out your cards less than three times, but as often above that number as you please. This trick may be done without your seeing the cards at all, if you handle and count them carefully. To diversify the trick, you may use a different number of cards, but the number chosen must be divisible by three, and the middle card, after they have been thrice dealt as directed, will always be the one thought of; for instance, if done with fifteen cards, it must be the eighth, and so on; when the number is even, it must be the exact half; as, if it be twenty-four, the card thought of will be the twelfth, &c.

THE SHUFFLED SEVEN.

Desire a person to remember a card and its place in the pack; then, in a dexterous manner, convey a certain number of the cards from the top to the bottom, and subtract them, in your mind, from the number of the pack: for example, the pack consists of fifty-two cards, and you have conveyed seven to the bottom; tell the person the card he has thought of will be the forty-fifth, reckoning from the number of the card, the place of which he has to name: thus, if he say it is the ninth, you go on counting nine, ten, eleven, &c. and the card he thought of will be exactly the forty-fifth, as you announced.

THE PIQUET PACK

Desire some person to choose three cards out of a piquet pack, observing that the ace is to be counted eleven points, the court cards ten, and the other cards according to the counts they mark. When he has made his choice, desire him to lay on the table his three cards, separately, and to put upon each parcel as many cards as are wanted to make up fifteen points; that is to say, if the first card should be nine, he must place six cards; if the second a ten, five cards; and if the third a knave, five cards upon it, this will make nineteen cards employed; consequently, there will remain thirteen cards in the pack, which you are to ask for, and while pretending to examine, count them, in order to be certain of the number left; add sixteen to the remaining number and you will have twenty-nine, the number of points that the three chosen cards contain.

THE DOUBLE DOZEN.

Present a pack of cards to one of the company, desire him to shuffle them well, and to get them shuffled by whomsoever he pleases; then make several persons cut them: after which, you will propose to one of the company to take the pack and think of a card, and remember it, and like-wise its order in the pack, by counting one, two, three, four, &c. till he comes, inclusively, to the card thought of; offer to go into another room, or to be blindfolded, while he is doing this. Now declare in what order the card shall be in the pack : say, for instance, the twenty-fourth; and, by attending to the following instructions, it will prove to be so : suppose the person, who thinks of the card, stops at thirteen, and that the thirteenth card was the queen of hearts; the number you have stated it shall be in the pack, being twenty-four : you return to the room, in case you had left it, or desire the handkerchief to be removed, if you have been blindfolded; and, without asking any question of the person who has thought of the card, ask only for the pack, and apply it to your nose, as if to smell it; then passing it behind your back, or under the table, take, from the bottom of the pack, twenty-three cards; that is to say, one less than the number you have stated the card thought of shall be; place these twenty-three cards on the top. This being done, return the pack to the person who had thought of the card, requesting him to reckon the cards from the top of the pack, beginning by the number of the card he thought of. His card being the thirteenth, he will be compelled to count fourteen, and you are to stop him when he comes to twenty-three, reminding him that the number you have mentioned is twenty-four, and that, consequently, the twenty-fourth card, which he is going to take up, will be the card thought of; and so it will most certainly be.

THE NOTED CARD NAMED.

Take any number of cards, ten or twelve for instance, bear in mind how many there are, and holding them with their backs toward you, open four or five of the uppermost, and, as you hold them out to view, let any one note a card, and tell you whether it be the first, second, or third, from the top. Now shut up your cards in your hands, and place the rest of the pack upon them; knock their ends and sides upon the table, so that it will seem impossible to find the noted card; yet it may be easily done,—thus : subtract the number of cards you held in your hand from fifty-two, the whole number in the pack, and to the remainder add the number of the noted card, which will give you the number of the noted card from the top.

GATHERING OF THE CLANS.

Have in readiness a pack, all the cards of which are well arranged in successive order : that is to say, if it consist of fifty-two cards, every thirteen must be regularly arranged, without a duplicate of any one of them. After they have been cut (but do not suffer them to be shuffled,) as many times as a person may choose, form them into thirteen heaps of four cards each, with the colored faces downward, and put them carefully together again. When this is done, the four kings, the four queens, the four knaves, and so on, must necessarily be together.

THE MAGIC TWELVE.

Let any one take the pack of cards, shuffle, take off the upper card, and, having noticed it, lay it on the table, with its face downward, and put so many cards upon it as will make up twelve with the number of spots on the noted card. For instance: if the card which the person drew was a king, queen, knave, or ten, bid him lay that card with its face downward, calling it ten; upon that card let him lay another, calling it eleven, and upon that, another, calling it twelve; then bid him take off the next uppermost card: suppose it be a nine, let him lay it down on another part of the table, calling it nine; upon it let him lay another, calling it ten; upon the latter another, calling it eleven; and upon that another, calling it twelve: then let him go to the next uppermost card, and so proceed to lay out in heaps, as before, till he has gone through the whole pack. If there be any cards at the last, that is, if there be not enough to make up the last noted card the number twelve, bid him give them to you; then, in order to tell him the number of all the spots contained in all the bottom cards of the heaps, do thus—from the number of heaps subtract four, multiply the remainder by fifteen, and, to the product, add the number of remaining cards, which he gave you; but if there were but four heaps, then those remaining cards alone will show the number of spots on the four bottom cards. You need not see the cards laid out, nor know the number of cards in each heap, it being sufficient to know the number of heaps, and the number of remaining cards, if there be any, and therefore you may perform this feat as well standing in another room, as if you were present

TO TURN A CARD INTO A BIRD.

Take a card in your hand, and show it fairly to the company, bidding them seriously observe it;—having a live bird in your sleeve—turning your hand suddenly, draw the card into your sleeve with your thumb and little finger, and, giving a shake, the bird will come out of your sleeve into your hand; you may then produce it and let it fly.

TO MAKE A CARD JUMP OUT OF THE PACK.

Let any person draw a card, and afterward put it into the pack, but take care that you know where to find it at pleasure. This you may do by having *forced* it. Then put a piece of wax under the thumb-nail of your right hand, and fasten a hair by it to your thumb, and the other end of the hair by the same means, to the card chosen; spread the pack upon the table, and, making use of any words you think fit, make it jump from the pack about the table.

THE CONFEDERATE WATER-DROP.

Put on your hat, and privately drop a little water, about the size of a crown-piece, upon the table at which you sit; rest your elbows upon the table, so that the cuffs of your sleeves may meet, and your hands stick up to the brim of your hat; in this posture your arms will hide the drop of water from the company; then let any one shuffle the cards, put them into your hands, and set a candle before you, for this trick is only done by candlelight: —then, holding the cards in your left hand, above the brim of your hat, close up to your head, so that the light of the candle may shine upon them, and holding your head down, you will see in the drop of water, as in a looking-glass, all the cards in your hands. Draw the finger of your right hand along each card, as if you were feeling it before you name and lay it down. Thus you may lay down all the cards in the pack, and name them, one by one, without once turning your eyes toward them.

THE FOUR ACCOMPLICES.

Let a person draw four cards from the pack, and tell him to think of one of them. When he returns you the four cards, dexterously place two of them under the pack, and two on the top. Under those at the bottom you place four cards of any sort, and then, taking eight or ten from the bottom cards, you spread them on the table, and ask the person if the card he fixed on be among them. If he say no, you are sure it is one of the two cards on the top. You then pass those two cards to the bottom, and drawing off the lowest of them, you ask if that be not his card. If he again say no, you take that card up, and bid him draw his card from the bottom of the pack. If the person say his card is among those you first drew from the bottom, you must dexterously take up the four cards that you put under them, and placing those on the top, let the other two be the bottom cards of the pack, which draw in the manner before described.

THE NERVE TRICK.

Force a card, and when the person who has taken it puts it in the pack, let him shuffle the cards; then look at them again yourself, find the card, and place it at the bottom; cut them in half; give the party that half which contains his card at the bottom, and desire him to hold it between his finger and thumb just at the corner; bid him pinch them as tight as he can; then strike them sharply, and they will all fall to the ground, except the bottom one, which is the card he has chosen. This is a very curious trick, and, if well done, is really astonishing. It is a great improvement of this trick to put the chosen card at the top of the pack, and turn the cards face upward, so that when you strike, the choosing party's card will remain in his hand, actually staring him in the face.

THE CHOSEN CARD REVEALED BY A PINCH OF SNUFF.

Force a card, suppose, for instance, the five of clubs, having previously written the words, or drawn the spots, on a clean sheet of paper, with a tallow candle : then hand the pack to the person on whom the card is forced, bid him place it where, and shuffle the pack how, he pleases ; ask for a pinch of snuff, strew it over the sheet of paper, blow the loose grains off, and the remainder will stick to those places which the tallow has touched ; thus telling the person what card he has chosen. The paper, be it observed, if done lightly with the candle, will not appear to have any marks on it. For this trick we are indebted to a celebrated performer of Legerdemain, and it is really a most excellent one.

THE DRAWN CARD NAILED TO THE WALL.

Drive a flat-headed and sharp-pointed nail through a card,—force a similar one on any person present,—receive it into the pack,—dexterously drop it, and pick up, unseen, the nailed card ; place the latter at the bottom of the pack, which take in your right hand, and throw it, with the bottom forward, against a wainscot or door ; the nailed card will be fixed, and the rest, of course, fall to the ground. Take care to place your nail so that the front of the card, when fixed to the door, may be exposed : to effect this, you must also remember to put the back of the card outward, placing it face to face with the others, when you put it at the bottom of the pack.

UPS AND DOWNS.

This is one of the most simple ways, but by no means the less excellent, of ascertaining what card a person chooses. When you are playing with the pack, drop out the diamonds, from the ace to the ten, and contrive, without being perceived, to get all the other cards with their heads in the same direction ; then request a person to choose a card ; do not force one, but let him choose whichever he pleases : while he has it in his hand, and is looking at it, carelessly turn the pack in your hand, so that the position of the cards may be reversed ; then bid him put the card he has chosen into the centre of the pack ; shuffle and cut them, and you may to a certainty know the card chosen, by its head being upside down, or in a different direction from the rest of the pack.

THE CARD UNDER THE HAT.

When you have discovered a drawn card by the last or any other trick, contrive to get the card to the top of the pack, which place on a table under a hat ; put your hand beneath it, take off the top card, and, after seeming to search among the cards for some time, draw it out.

THE TURN-OVER.

When you have found a card chosen, which you have previously forced, or any card that has been drawn, and which you have discovered by the means before described, in order to finish your trick cleverly, convey the card, privately, in the top of the pack; get all the other cards even with each other, but let the edge of your top card project a little over the rest; hold them between your finger and thumb, about two feet from the table, let them drop, and the top card (which must be, as we have said, the one drawn,) will fall with its face uppermost, and all the rest with their faces toward the table.

THE REGAL ALLIANCE.

Take four kings, and place between the third and fourth any two common cards whatever, which must be neatly concealed; then show the four kings, and place the six cards at the bottom of the pack; take one of the kings, and lay it on the top, and put one of the common cards into the pack nearly about the middle; do the same with the other, then show that there is one king at the bottom; desire any one to cut the pack, and as three of the kings were left at the bottom, the four will, therefore, be found together in the middle of the pack.

THE ODD SCORE.

Take a pack of cards, and let any gentleman draw one; then let him put it in the pack again, but contrive so as you may be sure to find it at pleasure, which you will be enabled with ease to do, by some of the preceding tricks; then shuffle the cards, and let another gentleman draw a card, but be sure you let him draw no other than the one before drawn, which you must force upon him; go on in this way until twenty persons have each drawn the same card; shuffle the cards together, and show your forced card, which will, of course, be every man's card who has drawn.

THE CARD IN THE EGG.

To do this wonderful feat you must have two sticks exactly resembling each other in appearance: one of these sticks must be made so as to conceal a card in the middle of it; for this purpose it must be hollow from end to end, and have a spring to throw the card into the egg at pleasure. The operation is this:—peel a card, roll it up, put it into the false stick, and there let it lie until you have occasion to make use of it. Take a pack of cards, and let any person draw one; but be sure to let it be a similar card to the one which you have in the hollow stick. This must be done by forcing. The person who has chosen it will put it into the pack again, and, while you are shuffling, let it fall into your lap. Then, calling for some eggs, desire the person who drew the card, or any other person in the company, to choose any one of the eggs. When they have done so, ask the person if there be anything in it? He will answer there is not. Take the egg in your left hand, and the hollow stick in your right;—break the egg with the stick, let the spring go, and the card will be driven into the egg. You may then show it the spectators, but be sure to conceal the hollow stick, and produce the solid one, which place upon the table for examination.

THE PAINTED PACK.

Take a pack of cards, and paint the backs of one half of the pack with

what figures you think fit, as men, women, birds, flowers, &c. Also paint the faces of the other half of the cards in the same manner; thus you will have a complete pack of odd pictures, and may, by showing the faces, of that part of the pack whose backs only have been painted, and then, by a momentary shuffle, apparently transforming them into a set of grotesque figures, produce much amusement. There is another manner of making the pack; it is as follows :—Take a dozen cards, or more, and draw a line from the right-hand upper corner to the left-hand lower corner of the face of each of them; they will thus be all equally divided. Then paint part of some odd figure on the right division of each card, leaving the left untouched. By a little dexterity, you may now seem to transform a set of common cards into a painted pack.

TO CONVEY A CARD INTO A CHERRY-STONE,

Burn a hole through the shell of a nut or cherry-stone, and also through the kernel, with a hot bodkin, or bore it with an awl, and with a needle, pick out the kernel, so that the hole in it may be as wide as the hole of the shell ; then write the name of a card on a piece of fine paper, roll it up hard, put it into the nut or cherry-stone, stop the hole up with some bees' wax, and rub it over with a little dust, and it will not be perceived; then while some by-stander draws a card, observe, "It is no matter what card you draw;" and, if you use the cards well, you will offer him, and he will receive, a similar card to that you have rolled up in the nut. Give him the nut and a pair of crackers, and he will find the name of the card he drew rolled up in its kernel.

THE CARD IN THE MIRROR.

Provide a circular mirror, the frame of which must be, at least, as wide as a card. The glass in the centre must be made to move in two grooves, and so much of the silvering must be scraped off as is equal to the size of a common card. Observe that the glass be likewise wider than the card. Then paste over the part where the quicksilver is rubbed off, a card that exactly fits the space. The mirror must be placed against a partition, through which two strings pass to an assistant in the adjoining room, who can easily move the glass in the grooves, and consequently, make the card appear or disappear at pleasure. Matters being thus prepared, contrive to make a person draw the same sort of card with that fixed to the mirror, and place it in the middle of the pack; then make the pass, and bring it to the bottom; direct the person to look for his card in the mirror, when the confederate, behind the partition, is to draw it slowly forward, and it will appear as if placed between the glass and quicksilver. While the glass is being drawn forward, you slide off the card from the bottom of the pack, and convey it away. The card fixed to the mirror may easily be changed each time the experiment is performed. This recreation may also be made with a print that has a glass before it, and a frame of sufficient width, by making a slit in the frame, through which the card is to pass; but the effect will not be so striking as in the mirror.

THE MOUSE IN THE PACK.

Have a pack of cards fastened together at the edges, but open in the middle like a box, a whole card being glued on as a cover, and many loose ones placed above it, which require to be dexterously shuffled, so that the entire may seem a real pack of cards. The bottom must likewise be a whole card, glued to the box on one side only, yielding immediately to exterior pressure, and serving as a door by which you convey the mouse into the box. Being thus prepared, and holding the bottom tight with your hand, require one of the company to place his open hands together, and tell him you mean to produce something very marvellous from this pack of cards; place the cards then in his hands, and while you engage his attention in conversation, take the box in the middle, throw the pack aside, and the mouse will remain in the hands of the person who held the cards.

THE MARCHING CARD.

One of the company is desired to draw a card, which is afterward mixed with the pack, and commanded to appear on the wall : it accordingly obeys, advancing as it is ordered, and describes an inclined line from the right to the left : it disappears at the top of the room, and appears an instant afterward, moving in a horizontal direction :—to do this, first force a card; after having shuffled the pack, withdraw the forced card, privately, and show the company the pack again, that they may see it is no longer there: when you order it to appear on the wall, a confederate adroitly draws a thread, at the end of which is previously fastened a similar card, which comes from behind a glass; it is fastened by very minute loops of silk to another thread fully stretched, along which it runs, and performs its route as directed.

THE BURIED HEART.

A curious deception may be practised, by cutting out neatly, and thinly shaving, the back of a club, which is then to be pasted slightly over an ace of hearts. After showing a person the card, let him hold one end of it, and you hold the other, and, while you amuse him with discourse, slide off the club ; then, laying the card on the table, bid him cover it with his hands, knock under the table, and command the club to turn into the ace of hearts.

CONFEDERATE SIGNALS.

This amusement is to be performed by confederacy ; you previously agree with your confederate on certain signs, by which he is to denote the suite, and the particular card of each suite, as thus : if he touch the first button of his coat it signifies an ace, if the second, a king, &c. and then again if he take out his handkerchief, it denotes the suite to be hearts ; if he take snuff, diamonds, &c. These preliminaries being settled, you give the pack to a person who is your confederate, and tell him to separate any one card from the rest while you are absent, and draw his finger once over it. He is then to return you the pack, and while you are shuffling the cards, you carefully note the signals made by your confederate ; then turning the cards over one by one, you fix on the card he touched.

THE CARD IN THE POCKET-BOOK.

A confederate is previously to know the card you have taken from the pack, and put into your pocket-book; you then present the pack to him, and desire him to fix on a card, (which we will suppose to be the queen of diamonds) and place the pack on the table; you then ask him the name of the card, and when he says the queen of diamonds, you ask him if he is not mistaken, and if he be sure that the card is in the pack? When he replies in the affirmative, you say, " It might be there when you looked over the cards, but I believe it is now in my pocket; then desire a third person to put his hand in your pocket, and take out your book, and when it is opened the card will appear.

The assistant in this, and, in fact, in all similar tricks, must be dexterous; he ought to understand what you wish him to do by the slightest hint,—a cough, a motion of the finger, or conjuring stick—or he will never answer for the confederate of a Conjuror.

PARADOXES AND PUZZLES.

Come hither all ye youthful Sages,
Come and peruse our sequent pages;
We care not whence the good wind blows you,
For sure we are that we shall poze you.

PARADOXES and Puzzles, although by many persons looked upon as mere trifles, have, in numerous instances, cost their inventors considerable time, and exhibit a great degree of ingenuity. We can readily imagine that some of the complicated puzzles in the ensuing pages may have been originally constructed by captives, to pass away the hours of a long and dreary imprisonment; thus does the misery of a few, frequently conduce to the amusement of many. We look upon a Paradox as a sort of superior riddle, and a tolerable Puzzle, in our opinion, takes precedence of a first-rate rebus. There is often considerable thought, calculation, patience, and management, required to solve some of these strange enigmas; and we have, ere now, followed the mazes of a Puzzle so ardently, as to be entirely absorbed in devising means to extricate ourself from its bewildering difficulties; and felt almost as much pleasure in eventually achieving a victory over it, as we have in conquering an adversary at some superior game of skill. It is, "in good sooth, a right dainty and pleasant pastime," to watch the stray wanderings of another person attempting to elucidate a Paradox, or perform a Puzzle, with which one is previously acquainted. It is laughable to see him elated with hope at the apparent speedy end of his trouble, when you know that, at that moment, he is actually farther from his object than he was when he began: and it is no less amusing to watch his increasing despair, as he conceives himself to be getting more and more involved, when you are well aware that he is within a single turn of a happy termination of his toils; but what a mirthful moment is that, when, there being only two ways to turn, the one right and the other wrong, as is usually the case, he takes the latter, and becomes more than ever

"Pozed, puzzled, and perplexed."

A Paradox or a Puzzle ought, perhaps, never to be explained; the party to whom it is proposed should rather be left in ignorance of its solution, unless he succeed in discovering it himself; if he fail after two or three efforts, and you disclose it, his vanity will be hurt, on account of his having been foiled by a question that, after its solution, appears so simple, or in some instances, he will call it silly and ridiculous; whereas, if he discover it without assistance, he will praise it for its excellence, and be pleased at his own cleverness.

We now proceed to open our budget :—Our first article is—

TROUBLE-WIT.

Take a sheet of stiff paper, fold it down the middle of the sheet, longways; then turn down the edge of each fold outward, the breadth a penny; measure it as it is folded, into three equal parts, with compasses, which make six divisions in the sheet; let each third part be turned outward, and the other, of course, will fall right; then pinch it a quarter of an inch deep, in plaits, like a ruff; so that, when the paper lies pinched in its form, it is in the fashion represented by A; when closed together, it will be like B; unclose it again, shuffle it with each hand, and it will resemble the shuffling of a pack of cards; close it, and turn each corner inward with your fore-finger and

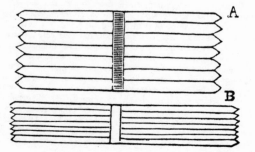

thumb, it will appear as a rosette for a lady's shoe, as C; stretch it forth,

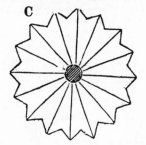

C

and it will resemble a cover for an Italian couch, as D; let go your fore-

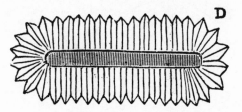

D

finger at the lower end, and it will resemble a wicket, E; close it again,

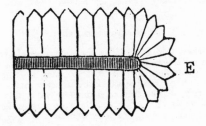

E

o

and pinch it at the bottom, spreading the top, and it will represent a fan, as F; pinch it half-way, and open the top, and it will appear in the form shown by G; hold it in that form, and with the thumb of your left hand, turn out the next fold, and it will be as H.

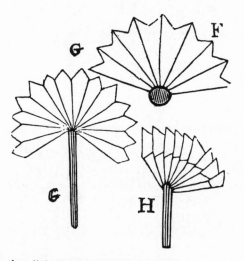

In fact, by a little ingenuity and practice, Trouble-wit may be made to assume an infinite variety of forms, and be productive of very considerable amusement.

THE SLIGHTED LADY.

We shall suppose there are 13 ladies in company, one of whom you wish to mortify; you, therefore, provide 12 nosegays, and, without showing any appearance of partiality, announce that you mean to let chance decide which of them is to go without one. For this purpose, make the 13 ladies stand up in a ring, allowing them to place themselves as they please; and distribute to them the 12 nosegays, counting them from 1 to 9, and making the ninth retire from the ring, and carry with her a nosegay. It will be found, that the eleventh, reckoning from the one by whom you began, will remain the last; and, consequently, will have no share in the distribution; you, of course, will begin counting with the one who stands second in the ring from the party to be excluded.

The following table will show the person, before her whom you wish to exclude, with whom you must begin to count 9; supposing, always, that the number of the nosegays is less by one than that of the persons.

For 13 persons, the 11th before.
12 . . . . . 2d.
11 . . . . . 5th.
10 . . . . . 7th.
9 . . . . . 8th.
8 . . . . . 8th.
7 . . . . . 7th.
6 . . . . . 5th.
5 . . . . . 3d.
4 . . . . . 3d.
3 . . . . . 2d.
2 . . . . . 1st.

THE WINE MERCHANT AND HIS CLERK.

A wine-merchant caused 32 casks of choice wine to be deposited in his cellar, giving orders to his clerk to arrange them, as in the annexed figure, so that each external row should contain nine. The clerk, however, took away 12 of them, at three different times; that is, four each time; yet, when the merchant went into the cellar, after each theft had been committed, the clerk always made him count nine in each row. How was this possible?

This problem may be easily solved by inspecting the following figures:—

2d Order.

3d Order.

4th Order.

PROFIT AND LOSS.

A man bought ninety-six apples at three a penny, and the same number at two a penny; he sold them again at the rate of five for two-pence. Query. Did he gain or lose?

Answer. He lost. The ninety-six apples, at three a penny, cost him 2s. 8d., and the ninety-six, at two a penny, 4s., making together, 6s. 8d. He had one hundred and ninety-two apples, and sold thirty-eight two-penny-worths; for which he received, of course, 6s. 4d. When he had done this, he had only two apples left: he, consequently, lost a fraction above 3½d.

THE GEOMETRICAL MONEY.

Draw on pasteboard the following rectangle, whose side, A C, is three inches, and A B, ten inches. Divide the longest side into ten equal parts,

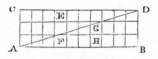

and the shortest side into three equal parts, and draw the perpendicular lines, as in the figure, which will divide it into thirty equal squares. From A to D draw the diagonal line, and cut the figure, by that line, into two equal triangles, and cut those triangles into two equal parts, in the direction of the lines, E F and G H. You will then have two triangles, and two four-sided irregular

figures, which you are to place together, in the manner they stood at first, and in each square you are to draw the figure of a piece of money; observing to make those in the squares through which the line, A D, passes, somewhat imperfect.

As the pieces stand together in the foregoing figure, you will count thirty pieces of money only; but if the two triangles and the two irregular figures be joined together, as in the two last annexed figures, there will be thirty-two pieces.

QUAINT QUERY.

What is the difference between six dozen dozen, and a half-a-dozen dozen?

Answer. 792:—Six dozen dozen being 864, and half-a-dozen dozen, 72.

THE SHEEP-FOLD.

A farmer had a pen made of 50 hurdles, capable of holding 100 sheep only : supposing he wanted to make it sufficiently large to hold double that number,—how many additional hurdles would he have occasion for ?

Answer. Two. There were 48 hurdles on each side of the pen ; a hurdle at the top, and another at the bottom ; so that, by moving one of the sides a little back, and placing an additional hurdle at the top and bottom, the size of the pen would be exactly doubled.

THE IMPOSSIBILITY MADE POSSIBLE.

Place three pieces of money on the table, and desire some person to take away the piece from the centre without touching it.

If the manner of executing it be not discovered, remove one of the end pieces to the other side, and thus you take away the piece from the centre without touching it.

THE CURIOUS CROSS.

Compose a cross, with thirteen sixpences, shillings, or any other coins, as No. 1, in which it will be perceived you may reckon nine in three different ways ; that is to say, in the entire perpendicular line, up the perpendicular line to the cross line, and including the cross line, first on the right, then on the left. These are the qualities of the cross. The puzzle is to take two of the pieces away, and still to leave the same qualities in the cross. This is done by taking away the two outside pieces of the cross line, and lifting the two which remain one piece higher. The figure will then be as No. 2.

No. 1.	No. 2.
o	o
o	o o o
o o o o o	o
o	o
o	o
o	o
o	o
o	o

SEVEN IN TWO.

Cut a piece of bread, or paper, in the form of a horse-shoe, (*vide* Fig. 1,) and desire some person, by two cuts, to divide it into seven pieces. The

manner of doing this is as follows :—Cut across from *a* to *b* ; this will divide the shoe into three pieces : then place the two ends by the side of the upper part, as Fig. 2, and cut across from *c* to *d*. The shoe will then be cut into seven pieces. There is a figure puzzle somewhat similar to this, by which five may be made seven in one cut. A piece of paper is cut out in the shape of a Roman numeral five (V) ; it is then, with a knife or scissors, cut across, and the two points placed on the right of the lower part ; thus it becomes seven, (VII.)

THE PARTIAL REPRIEVE.

To arrange 30 criminals in such a manner that, by counting them in succession, always beginning again at the first, and rejecting every ninth person, 15 of them may be saved :—Arrange the criminals according to the order of the vowels in the following Latin verse :

4 5 21 3 1 1 2 2 3 1 2 2 1
Populeam virgam mater regina ferebat.

Because *o* is the fourth in the order of the vowels, you must begin by four of those whom you wish to save; next to these place five of those whom you wish to punish; and so on alternately, according to the figures which stand over the vowels of the above verse.

FAMOUS FORTY-FIVE.

How can number 45 be divided into four such parts that, if to the first part you add two, from the second part you subtract two, to the third part you multiply by two, and the fourth part you divide by two, the sum of the addition, the remainder of the subtraction, the product of the multiplication, and the quotient of the division, be all equal?

Answer.

The 1st is 8, to which add 2, the sum is 10
The 2d is 12, subtract . . . 2, the remainder is 10
The 3d is 5, multiplied by 2, the product is 10
The 4th is 20, divided by 2, the quotient is 10

—
45

THE WOLF, THE GOAT, AND THE CABBAGES.

Suppose a man have a wolf, a goat, and a basket of cabbages, on the bank of a river, that he wishes to cross with them; and that his boat is only big enough to carry one of the three besides himself. He must, therefore, take them over one by one, in such a manner, that the wolf shall have no opportunity of devouring the goat, or the goat of devouring the cabbages. How is he to do this?

Answer. First, he takes over the goat; he then returns, and takes the wolf; he leaves the wolf on the other side, and brings back the goat; he now takes over the cabbages, and comes back once more, to fetch the goat. Thus, the wolf will never be left with the goat, nor the goat with the cabbages.

THE CHERRY CHEAT.

Cut two longitudinal slips out of a card, as *a b c d* (Fig. 1 ;) also, cut out an oval above these slips, as *e*. Take the part (*f*) between the two lon-

gitudinal apertures, with your finger and thumb, and draw it toward you, until the card be bent into a half-circle; pass part of *f* through the oval, *e*, and then, through the part of *f* so passed through *e*, introduce one of two cherries, whose stems grow together. Let the stems, and also *f*, pass back through the oval; put your card as much in the original position as possible again, and it will appear as Fig. 2. The puzzle is to get the cherries off without breaking their stems, or damaging the card. It is only to be done in the manner described for putting them on.

THE TRIPLE ACCOMMODATION.

To form a regular geometrical solid, which shall fill up a circle, a square, and a triangle. Take a round piece of wood; let its height be the same

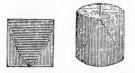

as its diameter; mark a line diametrically through its centre, at one end (Fig. 1 ;) then cut away the wood, right and left, from the line at the top, regularly, toward each edge, at the bottom. You will then have Fig. 2. Then, in a piece of card, or thin board, cut a circle of the same diameter, as the base of the figure you have formed, and a square, each side of which is the same as the diameter of the circle: also, a triangle, whose base and height are the same as the square; and the figure you have cut out will exactly fit all three. This may be performed, for the sake of expedition, with a cork, a piece of apple, or anything easy to cut, and a piece of stiff paper.

THE POOR-HOUSE PROBLEM.

There is a square piece of land, containing twenty-five acres, designed for the reception of twenty-four poor men and their governor, who are each to have a house situated in his own ground, with the governor's in the centre. How many people's land must the governor pass through before he gets to the outside of the whole?

Answer. Two; for the ground being a square, it will consist of five rows, each five acres.

EIGHTEEN WORDS IN TWENTY-THREE LETTERS.

What do the following letters signify in the French language, pronounced in the order in which they stand?

l n n e o p y l i a v q l i a t t l i e d c d

Answer. Hélène est née au pays grec, elle y a vécu, elle y a tété, elle y est décédée.

THE PUZZLING RINGS.

This perplexing invention is of great antiquity, and was treated on by Cardan, the mathematician, at the beginning of the sixteenth century. It consists of a flat piece of thin metal or bone, with ten holes in it; in each hole a wire is loosely fixed, beaten out into a head at one end, to prevent its slipping through, and the other fastened to a ring, also loose. Each wire has been passed through the ring of the next wire, previously to its own ring being fastened on; and through the whole of the rings, runs a wire loop or bow, which also contains, within its oblong space, all the wires to which the rings are fastened; the whole presenting so complicated an appearance, as to make the releasing the rings from the bow appear an impossibility. The construction of it would be found rather troublesome to the amateur, but it may be purchased at most of the toy-shops, very lightly and elegantly made. It also exists in various parts of the country, forged in iron, perhaps, by some ingenious village mechanic, and aptly named "The Tiring Irons." The following instructions will show the principle on which the puzzle is constructed, and will prove a key to its solution.

Take the loop in your left hand, holding it at the end B, and consider the rings as being numbered 1st to 10th. The 1st will be the extreme ring to the right, and the 10th the nearest to your left hand.

It will be seen that the difficulty arises from each ring passing round the wire of its right-hand neighbour. The extreme ring at the right hand, of course, being unconnected with any other wire than its own, may, at any time, be drawn off the end of the bow at A, raised up, dropped through the bow, and finally released. After you have done this, try to pass the 2d ring in the same way, and you will not succeed, as it is obstructed by the wire of the 1st ring; but if you bring the 1st ring on again, by reversing the process by which you took it off, *viz.* by putting it up through the bow, and on to the end of it, you will then find, that by taking the 1st and 2d rings together, they will both draw off, lift up, and drop through the bow. Having done this, try to pass the 3d ring off, and

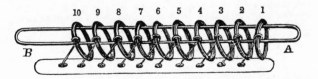

you will not be able; because it is fastened on one side to its own wire, which is within the bow, and on the other side, to the 2d ring, which is without the bow. Therefore, leaving the 3d ring for the present, try the 4th ring, which is now at the end all but one, and both of the wires which affect it being within the bow, you will draw it off without obstruction; and, in doing this, you will have to slip the 3d ring off, which will not drop through, for the reasons before given; so, having dropped the 4th ring through, you can only slip the 3d ring on again. You will now comprehend, that (with the exception of the 1st ring) the only ring, which can at any time be released, is that which happens to be 2d on the bow, at the right-hand end; because both the wires which affect it, being within the bow, there will be no impediment to its dropping through. You have now the 1st and 2d rings released, and the 4th also,—the 3d still fixed; to release which, we must make it last but one on the bow, and to effect which, pass the 1st and 2d rings together through the bow, and on to it; then release the 1st ring again by slipping it off, and dropping it through, and the 3d ring will stand as 2d on the bow, in its proper position for releasing, by drawing the 2d and 3d off together, dropping the 3d through, and slipping the 2d on again. Now to release the 2d, put the 1st up, through and on the bow; then slip the two together off, raise them up, and drop them through. The 6th will now stand 2d, consequently, in its proper place for releasing; therefore, draw it toward the end, A, slip the 5th off, then the 6th, and drop it through; after which replace the 5th, as you cannot release it until it stand in the position of a 2d ring; in order to effect this, you must bring the 1st and 2d rings together, through and on to the bow; then, in order to get the 3d on, slip the first off, and down through the bow; then bring the 3d up, through and on to the bow; then bring the 1st ring up and on again, and, releasing the 1st and 2d together, bring the 4th through, and on to the bow, replacing the 3d : then bring the 1st and 2d together on, drop the 1st off and through, then the 3d the same, replace the 1st on the bow, take off the 1st and 2d together, and the 5th will then stand 2d, as you desired; draw it toward the end, slip it off and through, replace the 4th, bring the 1st and 2d together up and on again, release the 1st, bring on the 3d, passing the 2d ring on to the bow again, replace the 1st in order to release the 1st and 2d together; then bring the 4th toward the end, slipping it off and through, replace the 3d, bring the 1st and 2d together up and on again, release the 1st, then the 3d, replacing the 2d, bring the 1st up and on, in order to release the 1st and 2d together, which having done, your 8th ring will then stand 2d, consequently you can release it, slipping the 7th on again. Then to release the 7th, you must begin by putting the 1st and 2d up and on together, and, going through the movements in the same succession as before, until you find you have only the 10th and 9th on the bow; then slip the 10th off and through the bow, and replace the 9th. This dropping of the 10th ring is the first effectual movement toward getting the rings off, as all the changes you have gone through, were only to enable you to get at the 10th ring. You will then find that you have only the 9th left on the bow, and you must not be discouraged on learning, that in order to get that ring off, all the others to the right hand must be put on again, beginning by putting the 1st and 2d together, and working as before, until you find that the 9th stands as 2d on the bow, at which time you can release it. You will then have only the 8th left on the bow; you must again put on all the rings to the right hand, beginning by putting up the 1st and 2d together, till you find the 8th standing as 2d on the bow, or in its proper position for releasing; and so you proceed, until you find all the rings finally released.

As you commence your operations with all the rings ready fixed on the bow, you will release the 10th ring in 170 moves: but as you then have only the 9th on, and as it is necessary to bring on again all the rings up to the 9th, in order to release the 9th, and which requires 15 moves more, you will consequently, release the 9th ring in 256 moves; and, for your encouragement, your labor will diminish, by one half, with each following ring which is finally released. The 8th comes off in 128 moves, the 7th in 64 moves, and so on, until you arrive at the 2d and 1st rings, which come off together, making 681 moves, which are necessary to take off all the rings. With the experience you will, by this time, have acquired, it is only necessary to say, that to replace the rings, you begin by putting up the 1st and 2d together, and follow precisely the same system as before.

THE CARD PUZZLE.

One of the best puzzles hitherto made, is represented in the annexed cut. A, is a piece of card; *b b,* a narrow slip divided from its bottom edge,

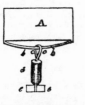

the whole breadth of the card, except just sufficient to hold it on at each side; *c c,* is another small slip of card, with two large square ends, *e e ; d,* is a bit of a tobacco-pipe, through which *c c* is passed, and which is kept on by the two ends, *e e.* The puzzle consists in getting the pipe off without breaking it, or injuring any other part of the puzzle. This, which appears to be impossible, is done in the most simple manner. On a moment's consideration, it will appear plainly, that there must be as much difficulty in getting the pipe in its present situation, as there can be in taking it away. The way to put the puzzle together, is as follows :—The slip, *c c, e e,* is cut out of a piece of card, in the shape delineated in Fig. 3. The card in the first figure, must then be gently bent at A, so as to allow of the slip at the bottom of it being also bent sufficiently to pass

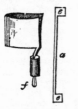

double through the pipe, as in Fig. 2. The detached slip with the square ends, (Fig. 3,) is then to be passed half way through the loop, *f,* at the bottom of the pipe; it is next to be doubled in the centre, at *a,* and pulled through the pipe, double, by means of the loop of the slip to the card. Upon unbending the card, the puzzle will be complete, and appear as represented in Fig. 1. In order to take the pipe off, the card must be doubled, as (Fig. 2,) the slip passed through it, until there is sufficient of the loop below the pipe to allow of one of the square ends of the slip (Fig. 3) being passed through it. Fig. 3 is then to be taken away, and the pipe slipped off. The card for this puzzle must be cut very neatly, the puzzle handled gently, and great care taken, that in doubling the card, to put on the pipe, no creases are made in it, as they would, in all probability, spoil your puzzle, by betraying, to an acute spectator, the mode of operation.

THE SQUARE HOLE AND ROUND STOPPER.

How can a mechanic file a square hole with a round file, and fill up an oval hole with a round stopper?

Answer. A piece of pliable metal being doubled, by applying a round file to the double edge, and filing a half square gap, on opening the metal, a square will appear. Again, if two corners and an edge, at the end of a miser's iron chest, be filed away with a round, or any other file, there will be an exact square hole left. And further, if a cylindrical body be cut obliquely, the plane of the section will be an oval; and, consequently, a round body, situated obliquely in an oval hole, will completely fill it.

THE HEART AND BALL PUZZLE.

To make this puzzle, it is only necessary to cut a thin piece of wood into the shape of a heart, to make six holes in it, as represented in the annexed cut, and provide a thin silken cord, which is to be doubled, and the two ends fastened into a small wooden ball. To play the ball on, pass the loop through the hole 6, from face to back, up to 2, through which bring it, and then through 3, 5, 4, and 1, in succession: then through 2 again, and down

the back to 6; bring it through 6 to the face, and pass it over the ball; then draw the loop back again through 6 and 2, and the puzzle (which is to take the ball and string off after being thus fixed) is set. To play the ball off, place the heart before you in the position described by the cut: slacken the string by drawing, at the back, the ball toward the hole 6; then loosen the rest of the string by pulling it toward you, and draw up the loop as far as you can: then pass the loop through hole 2, down the other side of the heart, to 6; through which bring it to the face, and pass it over the ball; then draw the loop back again

through the same hole, and the ball and the string will come off. Care should be taken to avoid twisting or entangling the string. The length of the string should be proportioned to the size of the heart; if you make the heart two inches and a half high, the string, when doubled, should be about nine inches long.

THE SCALE AND RING PUZZLE.

Provide a thin piece of wood of about two inches and a half square; make a round hole at each corner, sufficiently large to admit three or four times the thickness of the cord you will afterward use, and, in the middle of the board, make four smaller round holes, in the form of a square, and about half an inch between each. Then take four pieces of thin silken cord, each about six inches long, pass one through each of the four corner holes, tying a knot underneath at the end, or affixing a little ball or bead to prevent its drawing through; take another cord, which, when doubled, will be about seven inches long, and pass the two ends through the middle holes, *a a*, from the front to the back of the board, (one cord through each hole,) and again from back to front through the other holes, *b b*: tie the six ends together in a knot, so as to form a small scale, and proportioning the length of the cords, so that when you hold the scale suspended, the middle cord, besides passing through the four centre holes, will admit of being drawn up into a loop of about half an inch from the surface of the scale: provide a ring of metal, or bone, of about three quarters of an inch in diameter, and place it on the scale, bringing the loop through its middle: then draw-

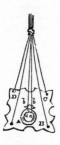

ing the loop a little through the scale toward you, pass it, double as it is, through the hole at the corner, A, over the knot underneath, and draw it back: then pass it in the same way through the hole at corner B, over the knot, and draw it back: then drawing up the loop a little more, pass it over the knot at top, and, afterward, through the holes C and D, in succession, like the others, and the ring will be fixed. The puzzle consists in releasing the ring; to effect which, you have only to reverse the former process, by passing the loop through the holes, D, C, B, and A, in the manner before described.

THE OYSTER WAGER.

Two men eat oysters together for a wager, who should eat most. One eat ninety-nine only, the other eat a hundred and *won*. How many did the winner eat? *Answer.* One hundred.

HODGE AND HIS HAY.

A truss of hay, weighing but half a hundred weight in a scale, weighed two hundred weight stuck upon the end of a fork, carried upon Hodge's shoulder: how could that be?

Answer. The fork was as the steel-yard; Hodge's shoulder as the fulcrum sustaining the burden between the two powers, acting at both ends of the fork.

THE SQUARES OF TRIANGLES.

Cut twenty triangles out of a square bit of wood, as marked in the engraving, mix them up together, and bid any person make an exact square

of them. The key to this puzzle may be acquired by remembering the black lines in the cut; by which it will be seen, that four triangles are to be placed at the corners, and a small square made in the centre; when this is done, the remainder is easy of execution. A piece of card will do instead of wood; it is much easier to cut out; but, on account of its warping, wood is to be preferred to it. Great care must be taken that all the edges are smooth and regular; for if any of them are notched, or wavy, so as to tally with each other, they may, of course, with little difficulty, be put together.

Many other Puzzles, similar to the Square of Triangles, may, with a little ingenuity, be constructed, in such a manner as to afford their young inventor the means of much amusement.

VARIETIES.

Bluff Æolus, who roars across the deep
And howls among the mountain pines to-day,—
To-morrow, on the harp or lyre, will breathe
Such melting music, as from Memnon's head,
When first Apollo's gleam fell on his brow,
Was heard to issue in the days of yore.

THE ÆOLIAN HARP

THE instrument consists of a long narrow box of very thin deal, about five or six inches deep, with a circle in the middle of the upper side, of an inch and a half in diameter, in which are to be drilled small holes. On this side, seven, ten, or more strings, of very fine gut, are stretched over bridges at each end, like the bridge of a fiddle, and screwed up, or relaxed with screw-pins. The strings must be all tuned to one and the same note, and the instrument be placed in some current of air, where the wind can pass over its strings with freedom. A window, of which the width is exactly equal to the length of the harp, with the sash just raised to give the air admission, is a proper situation. When the air blows upon these strings, with different degrees of force, it will excite different tones of sound ; sometimes, the blast brings out all the tones in full concert, and sometimes, it sinks them to the softest murmurs. See engraving at the head of this article.

TO MAKE FRUIT AND FLOWERS GROW IN WINTER.

Take up the trees, on which the fruit grows, by the roots, in the spring, just as they put forth their buds, taking care to preserve some of their own earth about the roots. Set them, standing upright, in a cellar, till the middle of September, and put them into vessels with an addition of earth; then bring them into a stove, taking care to moisten the earth around them every morning with rain water, in a quart of which, dissolve the size of a walnut of sal-ammoniac, and about the middle of March the fruit will appear.

TO CONVERT PAPER INTO FRAMES FOR PICTURES.

For this purpose, a convenient quantity of the best sort of white paper must be steeped for two or three days in water, till it becomes very soft; then, being reduced by the mortar and hot water into a thin pulp, it is to be laid upon a sieve to draw off its superfluous moisture; after which, it is to be put into warm water, wherein a considerable quantity of fresh glue, or common size, has been dissolved; it may then be placed in moulds, to acquire the desired figure, and when taken out, may be strengthened as occasion requires, with plaster or moistened chalk, and when dry, painted or overlaid.

TO TAKE THE IMPRESSION OF BUTTERFLIES ON PAPER.

Clip the wings of the butterflies; lay them upon clean paper in the form of the insect when flying. Spread some pure thick gum-water on another piece of paper, press it on the wings, and it will take them up; lay a piece of white paper over it, and rub it gently with your finger, or the smooth handle of a knife. The bodies are to be drawn in the space which you leave between the wings.

THE DEAF MADE TO HEAR.

Procure a stringed instrument, with a neck of some length, as a lute, a guitar, or the like; and, before you begin to play, you must, by signs, direct the deaf man to take hold, with his teeth, of the end of the neck of the instrument; then, if you strike the strings with the bow one after another, the sound will enter the deaf man's mouth, and be conveyed to the organ of hearing through the hole in the palate; and thus the deaf man will hear, with a great deal of pleasure, the sound of the instrument, as has been several times experienced; nay, those who are not deaf may make the experiment upon themselves, by stopping their ears, so as not to hear the instrument in the usual way, and then holding the end of the instrument in their teeth, while another touches the strings.

THE HYDROMETER.

The hydrometer is an instrument to measure the degrees of dryness or moisture of the atmosphere. There are various kinds of hydrometers; for whatever body either swells or shrinks by dryness or moisture, is capable of being formed into an hydrometer; such are woods of most kinds, particularly ash, deal, poplar, &c. The following is the most lasting and convenient mode of constructing an instrument of this description:—Take a very nice balance, and place in it a sponge, or other body which easily imbibes moisture, and let it be in equilibrio with a weight hung at the other end of the beam. If the air become moist, the sponge, becoming heavier, will preponderate; if dry, the sponge will be raised up. This balance may be contrived two ways, by either having the pin in the middle of the beam, with a slender tongue, a foot and a half long, pointing to the divisions of an arched plate, fitted to it; or the other extremity of the beam may be so long, as to describe a large arch on a board placed for the purpose.

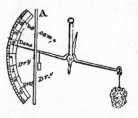

To prepare the sponge, it may be necessary to wash it in water, and, when dry, in water or vinegar, in which sal-ammoniac, or salt of tartar, has been dissolved, and let it dry again; then it is fit to be used. The instrument can be hung against a wall; and, in that case, a bit of steel, as at A, should be placed before the needle, to keep it straight.

THE AWN OF BARLEY HYDROMETER.

The awn of barley is furnished with stiff points, which, like the teeth of a saw, are all turned toward the lesser end of it; as it lies upon the ground, it extends itself in the moist night air, and pushes forward the barley-corn, which it adheres to in the day; it shortens as it dries; and as these points prevent it from receding, it draws up its pointed end; and thus, creeping like a worm, will travel many feet from the parent stem. That very ingenious mechanic philosopher, Mr. Edgeworth, once made, on this principle, a wooden automaton; its back consisted of soft fir-wood, about an inch square, and four feet long, made of pieces cut the cross-way in respect to the fibres of the wood, and glued together; it had two feet before, and two behind, which supported the back horizontally; but were placed with their extremities, which were armed with sharp points of iron, bending backward. Hence, in moist weather the back lengthened, and the two foremost feet were

P

pushed forward; in dry weather, the hinder feet were drawn after, as the obliquity of the points of the feet prevented it from receding.

SUBSTITUTE FOR A COPYING MACHINE.

Write with common ink, in which lump sugar has been dissolved—four scruples, or one and a half drachm of sugar to one ounce of ink. Moisten copying paper, by passing a soft wet brush over it; then press it gently between soft cap paper, so as to absorb the superabundant moisture. Put this moistened paper upon the writing, and both between some smooth soft paper, placing the whole within the folds of a carpet, when by pressure, a correct copy will be obtained.

TO PRESERVE ROSES TILL CHRISTMAS.

When roses are budding and blooming is the time to lay by a treat for Christmas. Select from your rose-trees such buds as are just ready to blow; tie a piece of thin thread round the stalk of each; do not handle the bud or the stalk; cut it from the tree with the stalk two or three inches in length; melt sealing-wax, and quickly apply it to the end of the stalk; the wax should be only so warm as to be ductile; form a piece of paper into a cone-like shape, wherein place the rose; screw it up so as to exclude the air; do so by each; put them into a box, and the box into a drawer; all which is intended to keep them free from air. On Christmas-day, or on any other day in winter, take them out, cut off the ends of the stalks, place them in a flower-pot or bottle, with lukewarm water, or, if in a heated room, the water may be cold; in two or three hours, they will blow, retaining all their fragrance as in the meridian of summer.

MAGNIFICENT CRYSTALS.

A solution of the salt to be crystallized is to be slowly evaporated to such a consistency that it shall crystallize upon cooling, which may be known by letting a drop of it fall on a plate of glass. When it is in this state, set it by; and pour into a flat-bottomed vessel the liquid part of the solution, when cold, from off the mass of crystals which will be formed at the bottom of it. After a few days, solitary crystals will be formed, which will gradually increase in size. Pick out the most regular of these, put them into another flat-bottomed vessel, and pour over them a fresh solution of the salt evaporated, till it crystallize on cooling. After this, alter the position of every crystal, once a day, with a glass rod, so that all the faces of it may be alternately exposed to the liquid, as the face on which the crystal rests never receives any increment. By this process, the crystals will gradually increase in size. When they are so large, that their forms can be easily distinguished, take the best of them, and put each into a vessel separately;

add a fresh solution of the salt, as before directed, and turn every crystal several times a-day. By this treatment, you may obtain them almost of any size desired. It is necessary to pour off the liquid from the crystals, and add fresh liquid in its place, very frequently; as the solution, after depositing a certain portion of its salts, becomes weakened, and then attacks the crystals, rounding off their angles, in the first place, as an attentive observer may perceive, and infallibly destroying them, unless renewed. By a little dexterity, a regular crystal of alum may be thus obtained.

CRYSTALLIZATION UPON CINDERS.

Saturate water, kept boiling with alum; then set the solution in a cool place, suspending in it by a hair or fine silk thread, a cinder; as the solution cools, a beautiful crystallization will take place upon the cinder, which will resemble a specimen of mineralogical spar.

TO PRODUCE VARIOUS FLOWERS FROM ONE STEM.

Scoop the pith from a small twig of elder; split it lengthways, and fill each of the parts with seeds that produce flowers of different colors. Surround them with earth, and then tying the two bits of wood, plant the whole in a pot filled with earth. The stems of the different flowers will thus be so incorporated, as to exhibit to the eye only one stem, throwing out branches covered with flowers analogous to the seed which produced them. By selecting the seeds of plants which germinate at the same period, and which are nearly similar in regard to the texture of their stems, an intelligent person may obtain artificial plants exceedingly curious.

HARLEQUIN INKS.

Inks, of various colors, may be made in the modes following: they are very beautiful, and frequently of considerable utility. For red ink, boil an ounce of fine chips of Brazil-wood, in half a pint of water, for a quarter of an hour; add to the decoction, three drachms of gum-arabic, and as much alum as it will dissolve. For blue, diffuse Prussian blue or indigo through strong gum-water. For scarlet, dissolve vermilion in gum-water. Inks of other colors may be made from a decoction of the materials used in dying, mixed with a little alum and gum-arabic.

TO BRONZE PLASTER BUSTS, &c.

Apply isinglass size, until no part of the surface become dry or spotted; then, with a brush, go over the whole, observing carefully to remove any of the size, while it is yet soft, that may lodge on the delicate or sharp places, and set the bust aside to dry. Then take a little very thin oil gold-size, and, with as much of it as will just damp the brush, go over the figure, allowing

P 2

no more of this size to remain, than what causes it to shine. Set it in a dry place, free from smoke; and after it has remained there forty-eight hours, the figure is prepared for bronzing. The bronze powder may be had at the color shops, of all metallic colors; it should be dabbed on with a little cotton wool. After having touched the extremities of the whole figure, let it stand another day; then, with a soft dry brush, rub off all the loose powder, and the figure will resemble the metal which it is intended to represent, and possess the quality of resisting the weather.

TO CUT GLASS.

Make a small notch, by means of a file, on the edge of a piece of glass; then, make the end of a tobacco-pipe, or of a rod of iron of the same size, red-hot in the fire; apply the hot iron, or pipe, to the notch, and draw it slowly along the surface of the glass in any direction you please; a crack will be made in the glass, and will follow the direction of the iron. Cylindrical glass vessels, such as flasks, may be cut in the middle, by wrapping round them a worsted thread dipped in spirit of turpentine, and setting it on fire when fastened on the glass.

THE ECLIPSE GLASS.

Take a burning glass, or a spectacle-glass that magnifies very much; hold it before a book or pasteboard, twice the distance of its focus, and you will see the round body of the sun, and the manner in which the moon passes between the glass and the sun, during the whole eclipse.

TO CALM AGITATED WATER.

Drop a small quantity of oil into water agitated by the wind; it will immediately spread itself with surprising swiftness upon the surface, and the oil, though scarcely more than a tea-spoonful, will produce an instant calm over a space several yards square. It should be done on the windward side of a pond or river, and you will observe it extend to the size of nearly half an acre, making it appear as smooth as a looking-glass. One remarkable circumstance in this experiment is, the sudden wide and forcible spreading of a drop of oil on the surface of the water; for, if a drop of oil be put upon a highly polished marble table, or a looking-glass, laid horizontally, the drop remains in its place, spreading very little; but when dropped on water, it spreads instantly many feet round, becoming so thin, as to produce the prismatic colors for a considerable space, and beyond them so much thinner, as to be invisible, except in its effect of smoothing the waves at a much greater distance. It seems as if a repulsion of its particles takes place as soon as it touches the water, and so strong as to act on other bodies swimming on the water, as straw, leaves, chips, &c. forcing them to recede every way from the drop, as from a centre, leaving a large clear space.

ENGRAVING ON EGG-SHELLS.

Design on the shells any figure or ornament you please, with melted tallow, or any other fat oily substance; then immerse the eggs in very strong vinegar, and let them remain until the acid has corroded that part of the shell which is not covered with the greasy matter, those parts will then appear in relief, exactly as you have drawn them.

LAUGHING GAS.

A few lines on the mode of preparing and administering nitrous oxide gas, or, as it is termed, Laughing Gas, will, we doubt not, prove acceptable and interesting. Although not fitted to support life, yet it may be respired for a short time, and the effects, produced by it upon the animal frame, are its most extraordinary properties. The manner of breathing it is this: the nitrous oxide gas, having been previously purified by standing over water, is put into a large bladder, or varnished silk bag, having a wide glass tube, or a stop-cock with a large bore, affixed to its neck. The bladder is then held by the tube in the right hand, the mouth of it being closed by applying the thumb, and the nostrils are closed with the left hand; the air contained in the lungs is expelled by a long respiration; and the tube of the bladder being instantly applied to the mouth, the gas is breathed from and into the bladder as long as possible, which, perhaps, will be about two or three minutes. The effects differ greatly, according to the constitutions of the persons by whom it is respired. In general, however, they are highly agreeable. Exquisite sensations of pleasure,—an irresistible propensity to laughter,—a rapid flow of vivid ideas,—singular thrilling in the toes, fingers and ears,—a strong incitement to muscular motions,—are the ordinary feelings produced by it. We have read of one gentleman, who, after breathing the gas some time, threw the bag from him, and kept breathing on laboriously with an open mouth, holding his nose with his fingers, without the power to remove them, though perfectly aware of his ludicrous situation; he had a violent inclination to jump over the chairs and tables, and seemed so light that he thought he was going to fly. What is exceedingly remarkable, is, that the intoxication thus produced, instead of being succeeded by the debility subsequent to intoxication by fermented liquors, does, on the contrary, generally render the person who takes it cheerful and high-spirited for the remainder of the day.

THE COMICAL CARDS.

The juvenile artist may treat his friends with an hour's merriment by this humorous little device, which is effected by drawing, on a number of cards, all of one size, a series of grotesque-looking faces, some male, others female, with droll head-dresses, night-caps, hats, wigs, and helmets, which he may select from any of the prints or caricatures that fall in his way; but the general compass of the face part should be within about the same space in all of them. Then divide each card into three pieces, cutting it across in a line just below the eye, and again, across the upper lip; the middle piece will be narrower than the upper or lower piece. A box should be provided with partitions in it, so as to keep all the parts in their respective classes. The cards should be cut straight, so that the pieces of each will fit all the others, and all the tops should be of the same width; all the middles of one width, but narrower than the tops, and all the bottoms about the same size as the tops.

An almost endless variety of changes may be obtained, by placing the forehead of one card in contact with the nose on a second, and the chin on a third. Thus, a laughable effect is produced by putting the red carbuncled nose of a City Alderman under the helmet of a Roman warrior, and finishing him below with the kerchiefed neck and shoulders of an old woman; or the cap, eyes, and nose of Moll Flaggon over the flowing wig and robes of a Judge on a court day.

THE RIDDLER.

A riddle is not solved, impatient sirs,
By peeping at its answers in a trice ;—
When Gordius, the plough-boy King of Phrygia,
Tied up his implements of husbandry
In the far-fam'd knot,—rash Alexander
Did not undo, by cutting it in twain.

RIDDLES are by no means of modern origin ; the Sphynx puzzled the brains of some of the heroes of antiquity, and even Alexander the Great, as it is written, made several essays to untie the knot (a practical riddle) with which Gordius, the Phrygian king, who had been raised from the plough to the throne, tied up his implements of husbandry in the temple, in so intricate a manner, that universal monarchy was promised to the man who could undo it : after having been repeatedly baffled, he, at length, drew his sword, considering that he was entitled to the fulfilment of the promise, by cutting the Gordian knot.

Charades, Rebusses, Conundrums, &c. are, with many persons, favorite occasional fire-side recreations. In the construction of several of them, considerable ingenuity is displayed ; they are not, in all cases, the production of mere witlings and holyday rhymesters; for more than one author of celebrity, doubtless, in some of those sportive moments when the mind relaxes from graver pursuits to toy and dally with comparative trifles, has contributed his mite toward the great fund of riddles now in circulation. One of the most clever and best-written among the following collection has been ascribed to the pen of the late Lord Byron :—we allude to the lines on the letter H (Enigma 1 page 241.) Conundrums, it must be admitted, are a set of

verbal distortions; but still, these distortions are often so droll as to excite
mirth.   Anagrams, or the letters of a name resolved into any apt phrase,
were, at one time, considered of great importance; many of them by no
means lack humor.   A work of thrice this bulk would scarcely contain all
the Enigmas, Charades, &c. now current: we have, therefore, endeavoured
to make a judicious selection from the mass.

CHARADES.

1.

My first is a part of the day,
   My second at feasts overflows;
In the cottage my whole is oft seen,
   To measure old Time as he goes.

2.

A cat does my first, and men drink at my second;
My whole is the drift of an argument reckon'd.

3.

My first gave us early support,
   My next is a virtuous lass;
To the fields if at eve you resort,
   My whole you will probably pass.

4.

My first, a native of the ground,
   In English countries much prevails;
My next's in every county found,
   My whole was never out of Wales.

5.

By candle-light, ladies, my first will appear,
   And the less light the larger it grows;
My second few like when applied to the ear,
   Though many my third to the nose.

6.

My first nor book nor volume nam'd,
   Contains more leaves than most;
My next, when certain crops are claim'd,
   Still stalks a numerous host:

My whole—a creeping flower so fair,—
    Regales the eye, and scents the air.

7.

My first is to ramble; my next to retreat:
My whole oft enrages in summer's fierce heat.

8.

My first do all nurses possess,
    And dandle my second upon it;
My whole is a part of the dress
    Attached to the cap or the bonnet.

9.

My first oft preys upon my second:
My whole a bitter shrub is reckon'd.

10.

My first in fruit is seldom rare;
My second all relations are:
My whole is only earthen-ware.

11.

My first dreads my second, for my second destroys my first; while many
delight in my whole.

12.

In every hedge my second is,
    As well as every tree;
And when poor school-boys act amiss,
    It often is their fee.
My first, likewise, is always *wicked*,
    Yet ne'er committed sin:
My total for my first is fitted,
    Compos'd of brass or tin.

13.

My first gives protection when robbers invade,
" Dear sir, this brown jug," of my second is made:
My total will show a pedestrian, whose name,
Unrivalled will stand in the annals of fame;
And also a brewer, whose mighty renown
Has been spread, by his beer, all over the town.

14.

Without my first, my second would be undone:
My whole's a village near Hyde Park and London

15.

My first's a prop, my second's a prop, and my whole's a prop.

16.

My first is in most shops;
In every window my second:
My whole is used for the bed,
And, in winter, a comfort is reckon'd.

17.

My whole is under my second, and surrounds my first.

18.

My first assuages the appetite of a horse, and agonizes the foot of a man; my second, if made of brick, is good; when of stone, better; and, as the seaman would say, when wooden, is best of all: my whole is famous for its—(but hold! we must make a charade upon a charade here)—take the principal produce of China, a part of the body that is often black, and as frequently gray or blue, and a useful domestic bird,—or, rather, the three letters which, in pronunciation, resemble these things,—and they will show for what my whole is famous.

19.

My first, if you do, you won't hit;
My next, if you do, you won't leave it:
My whole, if you do, you won't guess it.

20.

My first we oft lend to each other in turn,
To borrow it would be excessively droll;
My next, *near* my first you may often discern;
In my first, too, alas! you'll perhaps find my whole

21.

My first is appropriate; my second 'tis nine to one if you guess it; my whole elevates the sole above the earth.

22.

My first is always;
My second durable;
My whole without end.

23.

My first marks time; my second spends it; and my whole tells it.

24.

My first makes all nature appear with one face;
At my second is music and beauty and grace;
And if this charade is not easily said,
My whole you deserve to have thrown at your head.

25.

My first is a tree which with cedars will vie,
My second's the tenderest part of the eye.
My whole is a fruit which to none will give place,
For delicate flavour, and exquisite taste.

26

Of my first there is but one in the year :—of my second, but two in the world :—and my whole has every quality of a vegetable, except vegetation.

27.

Drink deep of my first : admit me to your second : and let me play upon my whole.

28.

My first troubles you in summer : my next is a most careful mother : my whole is no Christian.

29.

If you are able to do my first as well as my second can, you will soon be a good player at my whole.

30.

My first is an important part of the human frame; a constituent of all bodies, regular or irregular; it is sometimes *in* sometimes *out*, sometimes *this* and sometimes *that*, sometimes *one* and sometimes the *other*. My second is a common action,—sometimes induced by the hurry of business, sometimes by the mere love of pleasure; it offers economy the cheapest medicine, and taste the most picturesque scenery; it is what English ladies like best, and Turks like least; and it may well be said to be fashionable, for it is *the go* throughout the world. My whole is indispensable in every city,—yet valuable as it is, it is trampled on by all classes; all who use it are raised above the common track,—yet high and low, rich and poor, great and small, unite to destroy it.

31.

My first is nothing but a name;
My second is more small;
My whole is of so little fame,
It has no name at all.

32.

My first on foreign churches you may greet :
At home it's seldom found in church, or street ;
My second oft is used by household care,
To make old garments fit for folks to wear ;
My whole may well describe ill-humored folks,
Who knit their brows at puns, charades, and jokes.

CONUNDRUMS.

1. What does a seventy-four gun ship weigh, with all her crew on board, just before she sets sail?

2. Why is a short negro like a white man?

3. Why is the statute book like the Grecian army before Troy?

4. Why is your nose like V in civility?

5. Why is Virgil's greatest work like a baker?

6. What is most like a horse's shoe?

7. Who is that lady, whose visits nobody wishes, though her mother is welcomed by all parties?

8. What is that which few like to give away, and yet nobody wishes to keep?

9. What word is that in the English language, of one syllable, which, by taking away the two first letters, becomes a word of two syllables?

10. Which is the left side of a plum-pudding?

11. Why are children at the breast like soldiers on a campaign?

12. What thing is that which is lengthened by being cut at both ends?

13. Why is a horse in a stable like a tortured criminal?

14. What word of five syllables is that, from which, if you take one syllable away, no syllable remains?

15. What burns to keep a secret?

16. Why is a stormy, windy day, like a child with a cold in its head?

17. What word is that, to which, if you add a syllable, it will make it shorter?

18. Why should boiled peas of a bad color be sent to Knightsbridge?

19. Where did Noah strike the first nail in the ark?

20. Why is a tailor like a woodcock?

21. Why is a pack of cards like a garden?

22. Why do we all go to bed?

23. Why is a lottery-office-keeper like Lord Lyndhurst?

24. Why was Titian's fat daughter, Mary, like William Cobbett?

25. If you give a kiss and take a kiss, what does it make?
26. In which month do ladies talk least?
27. Why is a man who is making cent. per cent. by trade like Ireland?
28. Why is a town in Essex like a noisy dog?
29. Why is Paris like the letter F?
30. What town in Devonshire will denote a woman making a wry face?
31. Why is a man sailing up the Tigris, like one putting his father into a sack?
32. Why does the eye resemble a schoolmaster in the act of flogging?
33. Why is a room full of married folks like an empty room?
34. Why is an angry person like a loaf?
35. Why is a placeman like a cobler?
36. Why is a peach-stone like a regiment?
37. Why is a dwarf's whole suite like a pair of breeches?
38. Why is a dancing master like a cook?
39. Why is money like a whip?
40. Why is a man, who runs in debt, like a clock?
41. What question is that to which you must answer "Yes?"
42. If you throw a man out of a window, what does he first fall against?
43. Why is an island like the letter T?
44. When is a door not a door?
45. Why is a bee-hive like a spectator?
46. Why is a tale-bearer like a brick-layer?
47. Why is a Welshman, on St. David's day, like a foundering vessel?
48. What is that which a coach cannot move without, and yet is not of the least use to it?
49. Why is a man in love like a lobster?
50. When is a man over head and ears in debt?
51. What is smaller than a mite's mouth?
52. Why is the soul like a thing of no consequence?
53. Why is a handsome woman like bread?
54. What snuff is that, the more of which is taken, the fuller the box is?
55. Why is the wick of a candle like Athens?
56. Why is a fender like Westminster Abbey?
57. Why is Richmond like the letter R?
58. Why is a blind beggar often like a wig?
59. What fruit is that whose name answers to a busy-body?
60. Why is a cat on her hind legs like a waterfall?
61. Why is a poor man like a seamstress?
62. Why is that which never fails, like a strong knot?
63. Why are false wings like mushrooms?
64. Why is swearing like a ragged coat?

65. Why is sealing-wax like a soldier?

66. If I buy four books for a penny, and give one of them away, why am I like a telescope?

67. Why is a man led astray like one governed by a girl?

68. Why is a clergyman's horse like a king?

69. What is that which makes every one sick but those who swallow it?

70. What kin is that child to its own father who is not its father's own son?

71. What is that which is often brought to table, always cut, and never eaten?

72. Why is a dejected man like one thrown from a precipice?

73. Why is a Jew in a fever like a diamond?

74. Why are fixed stars like pens, ink, and paper?

75. Why is a jest like a fowl?

76. Why is a man in a garret committing murder like a good man?

77. What relation is your uncle's brother to you who is not your uncle?

78. Why should ladies wringing wet linen remind us of going to church?

79. What is that which lives in winter, dies in summer, and grows with its root upward?

80. Why is an avaricious man like one with a short memory?

81. Why is a man walking to a town like one endeavouring to prevent a blow?

82. Why is the sun like a man of fashion?

83. Which is the heaviest, a bargeman or a lighterman?

84. Why is a blacksmith's apron like a duenna?

85. Why is a lady embraced like a pocket-book?

86. What step must I take to remove the letter A from the alphabet?

87. Why are there three objections to a glass of spirits?

88. Why do cats see best in the dark?

89. A man would drink a glass of wine, and not let it go down his throat how could he do it?

90. Why is a man beating a boy for telling a falsehood, like another playing on a certain musical instrument?

91. Why is a cook like a barber?

92. Why is a man opening oysters like Captain Cook firing on the savages?

93. A farmer meeting Jack Ketch, asked him the difference between their occupations, which he gave in one word:—what is that word?

94. What is that which is always invisible, yet never out of sight?

95. Why is Alderman B's belly like the street he lives in?

96. Why is the devil riding on a mouse like one and the same thing?

97. Why is a pair of trowsers, too big every way, like two populous towns in France?

98. What word in the English language expresses the following question, "Are you a reserved man?"

99. Why is a waiter like a race-horse ?

100. Why is a dandy like a haunch of venison ?

101. Tom went out, and his dog with him, he went not before, behind, nor on one side of him :—then where did he go ?

102. Why is a madman like two men ?

103. What is a man like that is in the midst of a river and can't swim ?

104. Why is a lady curling her hair like a housebreaker ?

105. Why is a lady in her shift like Amsterdam ?

106. Why is a fish-hook like a badger ?

107. Why is a man in a fever like a burning candle ?

108. Why is your hat, when it is on your head, like a giblet-pie ?

109. A carpenter made a door, but it was too large ; he cut it, and cut it too little ; he cut it again, and made it just fit.

110. Why is a good story like a parish bell ?

111. Why is Chancery Lane like your eye ?

112. What most resembles a cat in a hole ?

113. If a man sham hanging himself, why does he resemble a conjuror ?

114. In what place did the cock crow, when all the world could hear him ?

115. Why does a brunette's face resemble a wet day ?

116. You are requested to ask the following question in one word :—"Are you the person ?"

117. Why is a man moping from morning till night like a favorite clown ?

118. What animal is that, who, in the morning, goes upon four legs ; in the afternoon, upon two ; and in the evening upon three ?

119. Why is a conundrum like a monkey ?

120. Why is Mr. McAdam like one of the seven wonders of the world ?

121. What smells most in a doctor's shop ?

122. What do we all do when we first get into bed ?

123. What is the weight of the moon ?

124. Why is St. Paul's like a bird's nest ?

125. Why do pioneers march at the head of regiments ?

126. What river is that which runs between two seas ?

127. What sea would make the best bed-room ?

128. What words are those which we often see in a pastry-cook's shop window, which a person afflicted with hydrophobia would use in describing his malady ?

129. When is the river Thames good for the eyes ?

130. Why has a glass-blower more command over the alphabet than any other man ?

131. What is that which you would say to a short boy, and which names a trade ?

132. Why is a speech delivered on the deck of a man-of-war like a lady's necklace?

133. Why is a lady in a sedan like the equator?

134. Why is a tallow-chandler the most vicious and unfortunate of men?

135. Why is Ireland likely to become very rich?

136. Why is a Chinese city like a man looking through a key hole?

137. Why is Liverpool like benevolence?

138. What two letters make a county in Massachusetts?

139. Why is the Prince of Wales like a cloudy day?

140. Did you ever see the elegy on a Turkey?

141. The figures representing my age, are what you ought to do in all things. How old am I?

142. What foreign letter makes the title of a noble lady?

143. Why is London like the letter E?

144. Why is a good tavern like a bad one?

145. Why is an angry man like a lady in full dress?

146. Why is a thread-bare coat and a person too soon awakened, similar to each other?

147. Why are deep sighs like long stockings?

148. What occupation is the sun?

149. Why are your eyes like stage-horses?

150. Why are your teeth like verbs?

151. Why is a tattler unlike a mirror?

152. Why is an andiron like a yard stick?

153. What word makes you sick, if you leave out one of its letters?

154. Why is A like a honeysuckle?

155. Why is gooseberry pie like counterfeit money?

156. What word of ten letters can be spelled with five?

157. What class of people have a name, which means " I can't improve?"

158. Why is a man who walks over Charlestown bridge, like one who says, " Yes?"

159. What plant is the name of a fop and a wild beast?

160. Why should red-haired men be chosen for soldiers?

161. What is higher and handsomer when the head is off?

162. Why is the letter D like a sailor?

163. If the alphabet were invited out to dine, what time would U, V, W, X, Y, and Z go?

164. Why is the letter G like the sun?

165. Why is Mr. Tuft's brewery like a Jewish tavern?

166. Why is a theological student like a merchant?

167. Why is a palm-tree like a chronologer?

168. Why is a man on horse-back like difficulties overcome?

169. Why is a person afflicted with the rheumatism, like a glass window?

170. Decline Ice cream.

171. From what motive does a fisherman blow his horn in the market?

172. How can you take one from nineteen, and leave twenty?

173. Which side of a pitcher is the handle?

174. Why is a furnace for powder like the letter S?

175. Spell Elder-blow tea, with four letters.

176. Why is a little green musk-melon like a horse?

177. Why is an industrious girl like a very aged woman?

178. Why are Protestants like flies?

179. Why was the Irish riot, at South Boston, like General Washington?

180. Why is a tailor like one who resides in the suburbs of a city?

181. Spell the Archipelago in three letters?

182. If the letter D were never used more, why would it be like a dead man?

183. Why is grass like a mouse?

184. Why do white sheep furnish more wool than black ones?

185. According to the laws of retaliation, what right have you to pick a painter's pocket?

186. What two species of falsehood are in the last novel by the author of Redwood?

187. Why has Mr. Timothy More, since he lost his hair, become like one of our southern cities?

188. Why is an avaricious man like one with a short memory?

189. A backgammon table contains the garden of Eden; does it not?

190. Describe a cat's clothing botanically?

191. Why are the eye-brows like mistakes?

192. Why should there be a marine law against whispering?

193. What kind of portrait can you spell with three letters?

194. What river in England is what naughty girls do?

195. Why is an Irishman turning over in the snow like a watchman?

196. How can a man live eighty years, and see only twenty birth days?

ENIGMAS.

1.

'Twas whispered in heaven, 'twas mutter'd in hell,
And echo caught faintly the sound as it fell;
On the confines of earth 'twas permitted to rest,
And the depths of the ocean its presence confess'd;
'Twill be found in the sphere, when 'tis riven asunder:
'Tis seen in the lightning, and heard in the thunder;

Q

'Twas allotted to man from his earliest breath,
It assists at his birth, and attends him in death;
Presides o'er his happiness, honor, and health,
Is the prop of his house, and the end of his wealth;
In the heap of the miser 'tis hoarded with care,
But is sure to be lost in his prodigal heir;
It begins every hope, every wish it must bound;
It prays with the hermit, with monarchs is crown'd;
Without it the soldier and seaman may roam,
But wo to the wretch that expels it from home;
In the whispers of conscience 'tis sure to be found,
Nor e'en in the whirlwind of passion is drown'd;
'Twill soften the heart, though deaf to the ear,
'Twill make it acutely and constantly hear;
But, in short, let it rest; like a beautiful flower,
(Oh! breathe on it softly,) it dies in an hour.

2.

In a garden there strayed
A beautiful maid,
As fair as the flowers in the morn;
The first hour of her life
She was made a wife,
And she died before she was born.

3.

Without a bridle or a saddle,
Across a thing I ride a-straddle,
And those I ride, by help of me,
Though almost blind, are made to see

4.

I've seen you where you never were,
And where you ne'er will be;
And yet within that very place,
You shall be seen by me.

5.

A shining wit pronounced, of late,
That every acting magistrate
Is water in a freezing state.

6.

Form'd long ago, yet made to-day,
Employ'd while others sleep;
What few would ever give away,
Or any wish to keep.

7.

A word of four syllables seek till you find,
That has in it the twenty-four letters combin'd.

8.

Form'd half beneath and half above the earth,
We, sisters, owe to art a second birth;
The smith's and carpenter's adopted daughters,
Made on the earth to travel o'er the waters.
Swifter we move, as tighter we are bound,
Yet neither touch the water, air, nor ground.
We serve the poor for use, the rich for whim,
Sink when it rains, and when it freezes, swim.

9.

I'm rough, I'm smooth, I'm wet, I'm dry;
My station low, my title high;
The king my lawful master is;
I'm us'd by all, though only his.

10.

There is a thing was three weeks old,
    When Adam was no more;
This thing it was but four weeks old,
    When Adam was fourscore.

11.

We are two brothers, born together, who seldom touch the earth, though
we often go to the ground; although we never eat fodder, buy, sell, or bar-
ter, we may be said to be interested in the *corn* laws.

12.

Never still for a month, but seen mostly at night.

13.

In spring, I am gay in my attire; in summer, I wear more clothing than
in spring; in winter, I am naked.

14.

In camps about the centre I appear:
In smiling meadows seen throughout the year;
The silent angler views me in the streams,
And all must trace me in their morning dreams;
First in each mob conspicuous I stand,
Proud of the lead, and ever in command;

Without my power no mercy can be shown,
Or soft compassion to their hearts be known;
Each sees me in himself, yet all agree
Their hearts and persons have no charm for me;
The chemist proves my virtue upon ore,
For, touch'd by me, he changes it to more.

15.

I am a character well known in England; and there are few, either high or low, rich or poor, but know my name and qualifications. As I confess myself a stranger to beauty and innocence, in the fair sex I can never appear. I avoid towns and cities, and commonly take my abode towards the extremity of a village. In respectable society I am never admitted, but in a gang of gypsies or beggars make a principal figure; and without me smuggling would be nothing. I cannot well show my face in day-time, but late in the evening, or middle of night I appear, and always in disguise. I am fond of gaming, though must own, whatever company I am in, never fail to end in cheating and plundering. It is the opinion of Burn and Blackstone, that I should always be put in jail: but, be that as it may, my fate is certainly not to be there at present. From the character I have given of myself, and the company I keep, you may suppose me some thief or pickpocket; but, as a proof that I am neither, I delight not in a crowd; and, as a further hint, I no sooner appear before one, than it is instantly gone.

16.

I am rough, smooth, hard, soft, long, short, round, flat, oval, square, or oblong. Am now honored with the grasp of a monarch, and now in the hand of him who executes the meanest office. I possess the art of pleasing in a very eminent degree. Am now the delight of the idle beau, and now assist the skilful artist. My station is ever varying: I am now thrown carelessly in a corner, now put into the mouth, now in the pocket, and now under the grate. I will only add, that every room is indebted to me for its chief ornament.

17.

I am no monarch, but am superior to all of them, except the Pope; I have no noble blood in my veins, yet the meanest of my family has precedence over the heads of others; I wear no sword, but in my evening walks often meet and beat those that do; indeed, I have fought more battles, and gained more victories, than all the conquerors and heroes recorded in history, from the beginning of the world. Sometimes my army has been defeated; yet, in that part of the action where I fought myself, the enemy has always submitted, when I carry off my prisoners under an armed band, dressed in the French uniform, and sometimes adorned with gold and precious stones, to an apartment where no eye was ever suffered to intrude. Perhaps you will think me a ghost, or at least a conjuror, if I tell you, that to-day I am in a thousand places at once, and to-morrow (as far as you know) I am nowhere; now I am in a room, soon after I am not there; again I appear, yet the doors and windows are all shut. With all this dignity, valor, and address, 'tis no wonder, if, like other military beaux, I am a great favorite with the ladies; as soon as they see me, they embrace me with delight, but are very cautious of keeping our connexion a profound secret; yet such is the capriciousness of the sex, that in a little time they discover it themselves, and part from me with as much pleasure as they met me. However, this separation is no disgrace; for they hope to have me again, and count me their highest honor; should I decline visiting them for a whole night, even the proudest heart would be discomposed; and the more violent and indiscreet would utter their displeasure in complaints to their neighbours: but this attachment is no wonder, for, like themselves, my countenance is sometimes a lively mixture of the lily and the rose; like them, too, I am changeable, and, in the space of a few minutes, grow black in the face; yet my consequence is not lessened, but sometimes increased; and, in a little time, I generally resume my former complexion.

It may be of some advantage to me with the ladies, that I sometimes resemble that part of their dress, of which they are most vain; and, at other times, that part, the obtaining of which is the end for which they dress, and the object of their wishes. Let these ladies look to their own bosoms to discover me, but in an open manner; for no trick opposed to me ever succeeded, and I believe none ever will.

18.

> He that in music takes delight,
> And he that sleeps secure by night,
> And he who sails too near the land,
> And he that's caught by law's strong hand;
> He who his time in taverns spends,
> And he that courts of law attends;
> He that explains heraldic signs,
> And he that works in silver mines,—
> Are all acquainted well with me:
> My name you surely now must see.

19.

In Sir Walter Scott's celebrated poem, called "Marmion," are the following lines:

> "Charge, Chester, charge! On, Stanley, on!
> Were the last words of Marmion."

These lines have occasioned the following enigma:

> Were I in noble Stanley's place,
> When Marmion urged him to the chase,
> The word you then might all descry,
> Would bring a tear to every eye.

20.

A lady in prison received an animal as a present from her niece, which signified to her " Make your escape;" in reply she sent back a fruit which imported " It is impossible to escape." What was the animal, and what was the fruit?

REBUSSES.

1.

> To three-fourths of a cross, add a circle complete;
> Then, let two semi-circles a perpendicular meet;
> Next add a triangle that stands on two feet;
> Then, two semi-circles, and a circle complete.

2.

> A hundred and fifty, if rightly applied,
> To a place where the living did once all reside,
> Or a consonant joined to a sweet singing bird,
> Will give you a name that you've oftentimes heard;
> Which 'mong your friends, at least, one person owns,
> It's the rival of Smith, and as common as Jones.

3.

A numeral, a pronoun, and a syllable that, in sound, resembles the neighing of a horse, will compound that, without which, even a palace would prove an uncomfortable habitation.

The following are Rebusses on the Names of London Performers.

4. What Roman Catholics reverence.
5. The head of a monastery.
6. One of the tallest productions of nature.
7. A color and a vowel.
8. A king of England and a consonant.
9. A word synonymous with sharp.
10. What we all stand upon, and a vowel.

11. A famous French dancer.

12. One-fourth of what a lover gives his mistress, a measure, and a vowel.

13. A measure, a vowel, and four-fifths of a weight used in Smithfield.

14. A numeral, the French for A, and the refuge of a wild beast.

15. The usual distinction of a Scotch name, and what we should always be to do a good action.

16. The fourth of a sovereign, and five-sevenths of an age of terror.

17. A female Christian name, and three-fourth of the reverse to soft.

18. A trade.

19. A word implying distance, and three-fourths of a small bird.

20. A preparer of eatables and a vowel.

21. An exclamation of the ghost in Hamlet, and a preposition

22. A vowel, and four-fifths of the safe-guards of a prison.

23. A consonant, and a portion of the earth.

24. A production of the pastry-cook.

25. Four-sixths of traffic, and a liquid made with pearl-ash.

26. A Hebrew measure.

27. A tool used to take off coach-wheels.

28. A famous river on the continent, and what we all wish to be.

29. What most young ladies try to obtain, preceded by a consonant.

30. An abbreviation for Harry, part of the earth, and a vowel.

31. An Irishman's nick-name, and the reverse to off.

32. Two thirds of a lively color, and the mother of mankind.

33. An English city : or, a box, and two-thirds of to do wrong.

34. What we rub our feet on, and what the woodman does when he cuts down a tree.

35. One of the points of the compass.

36. A fruit, and what your father is, and your mother is not.

37. The initials of his majesty, two-thirds of what the inhabitants of Bedlam are, and a Spanish title.

38. Four-fifths of the earth in a dead language, and the penultimate letter of the alphabet.

39. Part of a ship, and two-thirds of an eye.

40. What the ambitious wish to possess.

41. Part of a lock, and a vowel.

42. Half of a foreign country, and what shopkeepers buy for.

43. A measure, and the middle of a hare.

44. A city that was mistress of the world, and a rough consonant.

45.

Take a word that's composed of three letters alone,
The initial then change thirteen times, all but one;

Thirteen words will appear, though all ending the same,
As various in sense, as they can be in name.
First a place must be found, where brave tars oft retreat,
When the wind, in a storm, makes the waves o'er them beat;
The first letter exchange, as a song 'twill appear;
Then exchange it again, 'tis a part of the year;
Now it's lively and brisk, the next place to possess;
Then gives name to a pole, in its holyday dress;
Next the produce of earth, when for food 'tis prepared;
Then a chattering thing, to a magpie compared;
For brightness and glory, now see it far famed;
Whatsoe'er I allege, the next word will be named;
A denial, alas! too, it sometimes must be;
May it never be so, when the next's due to me;
A famed Scottish river, its assistance must lend;
Last, a road's to be found, bringing us to the end.

46.

Since, gentle reader, in this our RIDDLER, thou hast often seen represented various characters,—the grave and gay, the lively and severe,—lo! now we lead thee to a gallery, where poets and philosophers, high famed in classic page, stand ranged before thy admiring view. Full fifteen hundred years have now elapsed, since on the world these luminaries shone. Survey them closely; scan their history; avoid their faults, and emulate their virtues.

Behold that figure, reeling like a Bacchanal!—See how his swollen eyes and bloated cheeks bespeak the temper of his body. Hark!—he recites an ode: the honied strains drop from his pen, while reason holds possession of his mind!—How sweet, how elegant the poetry!—But, alas! his subject and his state too well agree. Ah! shame to see such talents so abused.

Next view the Samian Sage: observe his stature:—every joint and every limb denotes the strength that he possesses:—but could his mind be seen by mortal eye, 'twould seem still more gigantic. Observe his dress; how simple!—Humility his garb, and modesty his chief adornment! Although his friends would willingly have called him "the Wise Man,"— that title he refused; and chose the appellation of "the Friend of Wisdom." But, great as was this teacher, a little child, in this most happy and enlightened land, might teach him wisdom that he ne'er could reach.

But, lo! the Theban General appears, laden with spoils, his brows full crowned with laurel, and his garments red with the slaughter of the vanquished foe. What field has witnessed this great conquest, and who are the

sufferers? Leuctra beheld the fate of Sparta's sons, and streams of blood defiled her pleasant plains.

Behold Eunomus' son, the Sage of Lacedæmon. His lowering aspect and contracted brows seem indications of the sanguinary disposition of his mind. His laws forbade the use of gold and silver, and substituted iron :— so far 'twas good, to stop the progress of voluptuousness, and obviate temptations to dishonesty ;—but Nature shrinks, and Cruelty herself draws back with horror, when she beholds infants, unstained with any actual crimes, doomed by unbending policy to premature destruction.

Next view the Spartan Sculptor. The rumor of his skill had reached the ears of "Philip's warlike son :" the conqueror of the world forbade any other hand to carve his martial features on the stone. In the great Augustan age, his statues' worth was rated at their weight in gold.

But see the Poet of Salamis; whose natal day was ushered in with shouts of victory, and with songs of triumph :—when Xerxes and his numerous host sustained a dire defeat, and felt the punishment so justly due to pride and to ambition. No warrior he, yet did his magic verse obtain the freedom of those Greeks, who groaned beneath the Syracusan bondage.

Now, to complete this "motley group," see, tripping " on the light fantastic toe," a sprightly Damsel. Famed Lesbos gave her birth ; but she, more famed for beauty and for wit, has far excelled her sex in poetry. The happy verse in which her numbers flowed, still bears her name. But, alas ! her breast became the seat of every passion : and thence flowed the poison that tainted all her compositions :—else were that judgment just, that ranked her among the Muses.

Here, reader, pause ; and call to mind these names ; of each then take the initials, and in due order range them. Then will appear the Ephesian Artist ; whose excelling skill has far surpassed the united brilliancy and majesty of Rubens and of Raphael.

47.

Find the thing by Pandora entail'd on mankind,
When, on opening her box, only Hope staid behind :
Let this word stand entire, and before it prefix
Initials fifteen, but no letter e'er mix :
Thus by changing the head, as the principal part,
You may render it various as nature and art :
First I find it form part of a bird in the air ;
Then examine a fish, and as sure find it there ;
As an eminence now it will rear up its head ;
Then the last deed of man, as is commonly said ;

As a farmer's employment it next will appear;
And a thing to your door you will find very near;
What the doctors oft give, to relieve us from pain;
And a plant we now look for in gardens, in vain;
What I bid my friend do when I give him a toast;
And a place much frequented by knights of the Post;
A short name that's well known in a nursery song;
And what runs through a country for many miles long;
What's the aim of a sportsman, pursuing his game;
What we style a neat box, or a township's short name;
And then all your labor will nearly be over,
And a double head's all you have left to discover,
For one, being mute, a companion and friend,
Must forever stand by, its assistance to lend;
In revealing what's common to birds and a beast,
And whose use to us scribblers is none of the least.

48.

Reverse a snug apartment, and you'll find
A dreary marsh presented to your mind.

49.

Now to your enigmatic eyes,
Behold six worthies shall arise,
From their initials to compound
A modern poet, much renowned
   First in the list we enter thee,
Father of English poetry:
Next thee, of Scotia's bards the first;
Thy muse from darkest ages burst
Next thee, philosopher divine,
And poet,—all the praise is thine;
'Twas thine the sweetest notes to raise
From David's harp, in British lays:
Thee, Theban bard, whose rapid fire
Succeeding ages still admire;
While a vain modern, grasping fame,
Profanes thy venerable name:
Thee next, hypocrisy's great foe,
An agent in Rome's overthrow,
When Luther's zeal o'er Europe spread,
And shook the Antichristian head;
Batavia boasts thy worthy name,
" The priesthood's glory, and its shame :"

With thee, at last, the verse shall shine,
The prince of painters, styled "divine;"
A sovereign pontiff knew thy worth,
And old Urbino claims thy birth.

50.

Two letters, expressing profusion and waste,
Transposed, show a county to most people's taste.

51.

A modern bard of universal fame;
A classic river's oft-repeated name;
A naval hero dear to ev'ry heart;
A ruthless tyrant with a murd'rous dart;
An English author, famous for his style;
A poet who our leisure may beguile:
Th' initials join, an ancient bard you'll find,
Who to his verse has left his name behind.

The following are Rebusses on the Names of Birds.

52. A child's plaything.
53. What we all do at every meal
54. A disorder incident to man and horse.
55. Nothing, twice yourself, and fifty.
56. What we should always be ready to do to persons fighting, and the top of a house.
57. Equality and decay.
58. A celebrated English architect.
59. A tailor's implement.
60. A lever.
61. An instrument for raising weights.
62. Three-eights of a monthly publication, with a baked dish
63. A valuable species of corn, and a very necessary part of it
64. A cheated person.
65. A distant country.
66. Spoil half a score.
67. The defence of a bridge.
68. An instrument of diversion for men and boys.
69. A piece of wood, and a fashionable name for a street.
70. To cut off, and a vowel.
71. A piece of land, and a good thing which it produces.
72. What we say a person has got when he falls into the water.
73. An Animal which a Jew must not eat, a vowel, and a preposition.

74.

I am found in a jail; I belong to a fire;
And am seen in a gutter abounding in mire:
Put my last letter third, and then 'twill be found
I belong to a king, without changing my sound.

75

Ye rebus wits,
Now mind your hits;
For your's the task
My name to unmask:
A fruit we eat,
As sauce to meat;
And with fish too,
That wants a *gout*;
One letter, pray,
Take quite away;
A point of land
You'll understand,

Which sailors dread
Too near their lead,
But when embay'd,
Enjoy its shade:
One more letter
Then unfetter,
The thing that's left,
When thus bereft,
Is worn by all,
Both great and small,
From king and queen
To beggar mean.

ANAGRAMS.

1. Ten tea pots.
2. Sly Ware.
3. It's in charity.
4. Golden land.
5. Great helps.
6. Rare mad frolic.
7. Honor est a Nilo.
8. Hard case.
9. Claims Arthur's seat.
10. No, appear not at Elba.
11. No more stars.
12. O poison Pitt.
13. I hire parsons.
14. Got as a clue.
15. To love ruin.
16. Best in prayer.
17. Nay, I repent it.
18. Veto. Un corse la finira.
19. Comical trade.
20. Spare him not.
21. Real fun.
22. In Magic tale.
23. Evil fast.
24. Yes Milton.
25. 'Tis ye govern.
26. See a pug dog.
27. A just master.
28. Made in pint pots
29. A hot pen.
30. I call many sot.
31. A nice Pet.
32. The bar.
33. The law.
34. Truly he'll see war.
35. I send into Siam.
36. True, I am in.
37. Hire a prison.
38. There we sat.

LOGOGRIPHS.

1.

A creature was formerly seen in England, which has lately been expelled from it, and which has some very peculiar properties appertaining to it. It stands upon one leg,—on which, without any body, is seen a great square head. It has three eyes, of which the centre is by far the largest ; indeed, so much so, that it has before now contained two more. The head is of a very peculiar construction, but exactly suited to its design : whenever it is about to be used, it is separated in halves, and, when reconnected, is held up to the gaze of an insolent rabble. All the notice, however, which it generally attracts, results from its being the effectual means of exhibiting another to the gaze of a hostile crowd. Such is this when entire ; but when divided, and cut to pieces, a curious and careful observer may collect all that follows, by a selection and appropriate arrangement of its fragments.

A dose of medicine conveyed in a very agreeable manner, as, however nauseous its ingredients may have originally been, it is quite tasteless. Such a state of the physical powers as requires such a dose. A part of the face, of a color quite different from the rest, and the more handsome, the greater the difference. A public record on which many are very anxious to get their names entered ; or, to descend from great things to small, a substance that is devoured every morning for breakfast. A river which flows through a very delightful and agreeable part of Europe. What curious people are very fond of doing. What a candidate, for your vote at the next general election, if he should think it worth his while, will demand. A very poetical portion of the watery element, which murmurs and meanders in the description of many a poetaster. A quality of resinous substances. A female nickname. What is very necessary to be done occasionally in your shrubbery. An exclamation of surprise. A flower displaying more to admire than Solomon in all his glory. To tear. The expressed juice of olives,—and its adjective. A conjunction. And two initial letters, whose reiterated sounds have drowned the voices of strutting monarchs and ephemeral heroes.

2.

Ye who in mystic lines delight,
Unveil and bring me forth to light,
Nor deem me tiresome, if my song
Should, like myself, prove wondrous long.
It may perhaps excite your mirth,
That animals to me give birth ;
Yet vegetables oftener claim
The honor to produce the same :

One time as white as snow I'm seen,
Another, red, blue, yellow, green;
The friendly brown I also wear,
Or in a sable garb appear:
The rhetorician owns my power,
For though well dressed with many a flower,
His florid speech would gain no praise,
But, losing me, contempt would raise.
But now my name you surely know,
Dissected in the lines below.

That power to which we all must bend;
And what we call a valued friend;
A goddess of revengeful fame;
And Abram's near relation's name;
Two articles in common use;
And what we oft complain of news;
A weed which grew upon the plain,
Suffer'd till harvest to remain;
Two quadrupeds will next appear,
Which both conduce to sport and cheer;
A third, a noxious little creature;
And what adds charms to simple nature;
A fruit; a color; and a date
A firm support of Britain's state;
What high, yet low, we wish to be;
A term for one who goes to sea;
One thing another oft put over;
Two things by this you may discover,—
To make my hint somewhat more plain,
One keeps the other from the rain;
The vital spring of every wo;
And every pleasure that we know;
What's always done whene'er we walk;
And what we do when others talk;
With what we've done when they give o'er;
Two notes in music next explore;
What, join'd to *home*, is sent about,
As invitation to a rout;
What oft we see upon the plain;
Two little words denoting pain,
Or quick surprise, or laughter vain;
A sign of sorrow; mark of spirit;
What envy bears superior merit;

A fragrant shrub we oft infuse :
Two pronouns in most frequent use ;
A passion which the envious feel ;
A weapon pointed oft with steel ;
One of the properties of stone ;
A term for misanthrope well known ;
What oft in summer months we feel ;
What aids when secrets you reveal ;
What sinful deeds should ever be ;
What's daily done by you and me.
    If all these meanings you expound,
Just five and forty will be found.

3.

I was before the world begun,
Before God made the rising sun ;
Before He made the lesser lights
To drive the darkness from the nights
I'm at the bottom of the sea,
And I am in immensity ;
The daily motion of the earth
Dispels me, and to me gives birth ;
You cannot see me if you try,
Although I'm oft before your eye.
Such is my whole. But for one part
You'll find in taste I'm rather tart ;—
Now I become th' abode of men,—
And now for meaner things, a pen ;
I am a man who lives by drinking,—
Anon I keep a weight from sinking ;
To take me, folks go far and near,—
I am what children like to hear ;
I am a shining star on high,
And I'm its pathway through the sky ;
I take the strength from iron and steel,—
Am sometimes left behind a wheel ;
I am a term of due respect,—
Am used in English to connect ;
I'm made to represent a head,—
Am found on every loaf of bread.
Such are the many forms I take,
All these, and many more I make ;
Yet, after all, so strange am I,
Soon as you know me, then I die.

4.

The man of letters finds me in his books;
The angler by the side of babbling brooks;
The sportsman seeks me with his dog and gun;
In foreign lands the traveller thinks I'm won;
The spendthrift hopes to buy me with his gold;
And childhood has me when a tale is told;
The love of me decoys the giddy youth,
From useful studies, till he learns this truth,
" All those who seek me *only*, most I fly;"
Lastly, when you my hidden sense descry,
You'll own that for my sake you pondered long
The countless changes, that to me belong.
Such am I as a whole—but for *one* part,—
The youth invokes me when he feels love's dart;
The Swiss, when exiled from his native vales,
Hears me with anguish, and his fate bewails;
New zest I add to scandal's busy hour;
And adverse winds and tides confess my power ·
I am the dazzling source whence colors flow;
The sluggard's teacher; and your equal now;
Without me sails were useless; then a word
Expressing like; and now meek woman's lord;
To measure next; anon to add; to vex;
The gentle office of the weaker sex;
I'm flesh, not fish—I'm silent ever;
Sought by all ranks, on earth found never;
Your near relation, and the squirrel's food;
What you would keep when in a lazy mood;
Neptune's abode; the forest monarch's pride;
A term to the departed souls applied;
What you possess, but others oftener use:
Your coat must have me, spite of what you choose;
Now the soft clime of " the cedar and vine;"
And last, a short word importing new wine.
More could I tell, but I bid you adieu,
Lest by prating I cause my own loss to you.

SOLUTIONS.

CHARADES.

1 Hour-glass.
2 Pur-port.
3 Milk-maid.
4 Flint-shire.
5 Snuff-box.
6 Wood-bine.
7 Gad-fly.
8 Lap-pet.
9 Worm-wood.
10 Pip-kin
11 Fox-chase.
12 Candle-stick.
13 Bar-clay.
14 Hammer-smith.
15 Foot-stool.
16 Counter-pane.
17 Waist-coat.

18 Corn-wall, famous for its T I N. (tea-eye-hen.)
19 Mis-take.
20 Ear-wig.
21 Pat-ten.
22 Ever-lasting.
23 Watch-man.
24 Snow-ball.
25 Pine-apple.
26 May-pole.
27 Draught-board.
28 Heat-hen.
29 Leap-frog.
30 Side-Walk.
31 Name-less.
32 Cross-patch.

CONUNDRUMS.

1 She weighs anchor.
2 He's not at all (*tall black*) black.
3 It has many laws (*Menelaus*) in it
4 It's placed between two I's (*eyes*)
5 It is Æneid (*in-kneed.*)
6 A mare's.
7 Misfortune (*Miss-fortune.*)
8 A bed.
9 Plague—Ague.
10 That which is not eaten.
11 They are in arms.
12 A ditch.
13 He is tied to the rack.
14 Monosyllable—no syllable.
15 Sealing-wax.
16 It blows, it snows—(*it blows its nose.*)
17 Short—shorter.
18 It is the way to Turnham-Green —(*turn 'em green*)

19 On the head.
20 He has a long bill.
21 There are spades in it.
22 The bed will not come to us.
23 He is a chance-seller—(*Chancellor.*)
24 She was a great Polly Titian—(*politician.*)
25 A re-bus.
26 In February, because it is the shortest.
27 His capital is doubling (*Dublin.*)
28 It is Barking.
29 It is the capital of France.
30 Cockermouth (*cock her mouth.*)
31 He is going to Bag-dad.
32 It has a pupil under the lash.
33 There is not a single person in it.
34 He is crusty.
35 He sticks to the *last.*

R

36 It has a kernel—(*colonel.*)
37 They are small clothes.
38 He cuts *capers.*
39 It makes the mare to go.
40 He goes on *tick.*
41 What does Y, E, S spell?
42 Against his inclination.
43 It is in the midst of water—(*wa-t-er.*)
44 When it is a-jar—(*a jar.*)
45 It is a bee-holder—(*beholder.*)
46 He raises stories.
47 He carries a leak—(*leek.*)
48 Noise.
49 He has a lady in his head.
50 When he has a hat on that is not paid for.
51 His tongue.
52 It is immaterial.
53 She is often toasted.
54 The snuff of a candle.
55 It is in the midst of grease—(*Greece.*)
56 It contains the ashes of the grate—(*great.*)
57 It is next to Kew—(*Q.*)
58 He is cur-led—(*curled.*)
59 A medlar—(*meddler.*)
60 She is a cat erect—(*cataract.*)
61 He makes shifts.
62 It is a certainty—(*certain tie.*)
63 They are sham pinions—(*champignons.*)
64 It is a bad habit.
65 It often bears arms.
66 I make a farthing present—(*a far thing present.*)
67 He is misled—(*miss-led.*)
68 He is guided by a minister
69 Flattery.
70 His daughter.
71 A pack of cards.
72 He is down cast.
73 He is a Jew-ill—(*jewel.*)

74 They are stationary—(*stationery.*)
75 It contains a merry thought.
76 He is *above* committing a bad act.
77 Your father.
78 The belles are wringing (*ringing.*)
79 An icicle.
80 He is always forgetting—(*for getting.*)
81 He is going toward it—(*to ward it.*)
82 It turns night into day.
83 A bargeman.
84 It keeps off the sparks.
85 She is clasped.
86 By B heading it—(*beheading it*)
87 Because there are three scruples to a dram.
88 They eat *lights.*
89 By standing on his head and letting it go *up* his throat.
90 He is striking a liar—(*lyre.*)
91 He dresses hare—(*hair.*)
92 He's astonishing the natives.
93 Utility—(*you till, I tie.*)
94 The letter I, which is always invisible.
95 It's widened at the expense of the corporation.
96 He is sin-on-a-mouse—(*synonymous.*)
97 Because they are too long and too loose—(*Toulon and Toulouse.*)
98 R-u-shy(*are you shy? R U shy.*)
99 He often runs for a plate or a cup.
100 He's a bit of a buck.
101 On the other side.
102 He's one beside himself.
103 Like to be drowned.
104 She is turning locks.

105 She's in Holland.

106 It is often baited.

107 He's light-headed.

108 There's a goose's head in it.

109 He cut it too little, *i. e.* he did not cut enough of it.

110 It often tolled—(*told.*)

111 It is near the Temple.

112 A cat out of a hole.

113 He is a neck-romancer— (*necromancer.*)

114 In Noah's ark.

115 It is not fair.

116 R, U, E—(*Are you he?*)

117 He's grim all day (*Grimaldi.*)

118 Man : *viz.* In the morning of his life, on all fours ; in the afternoon, on two ; and in the evening, with a stick.

119 It is far-fetched and full of nonsense.

120 He is the colossus of roads— (*Rhodes.*)

121 The nose.

122 Make an impression.

123 Four quarters.

124 It was built by a Wren.

125 To *axe* the way.

126 The Thames, which flows between Chel*sea* and Batter*sea.*

127 Adriatic—(*a dry attic.*)

128 Water-ices and ice-creams— (*water I sees, and I screams.*)

129 When it is eye-water—(*high-water.*)

130 Because he can make a D canter—(*decanter.*)

131 Grow, sir !—(*Grocer.*)

132 It is a deck oration—(*decoration.*)

133 She is between the poles.

134 All his works are *wicked*, and all his *wicked* works are brought to *light.*

135 Because its capital is always Dublin (*Doubling.*)

136 It is Pekin (*Peeking.*)

137 It is founded on Mersey (*Mercy*)

138 S. X. (*Essex.*)

139 He is likely to reign (*Rain.*)

140 Did you ever see the l-e-g on a Turkey ? (*Leg.*)

141 I am XL. (*Excel.*)

142 Dutch S (*Dutchess.*)

143 It is the capital of England.

144 Both inn convenient.

145 He is ruffled.

146 They have lost their nap.

147 Heigh-hos (*high hose.*)

148 A Tanner.

149 They are always under lashes.

150 Regular, irregular, and defective.

151 One speaks without reflecting, the other reflects without speaking.

152 It has three feet.

153 Music.

154 A bee follows it.

155 It is not currant (*current.*)

156 Expediency (*X P D N C E.*)

157 Mendicants (*Mend I can't.*)

158 He gives a cent (*assent.*)

159 Dandelion (*dandy,—lion.*)

160 They carry firelocks.

161 A pillow.

162 It follows the sea (*C.*)

163 They would go after tea (*T.*)

164 It is the centre of light.

165 Hebrews drink there (*He brews.*)

166 Both study the profits (*prophets.*)

167 It furnishes dates.

168 He is Sir mounted (*Surmounted.*)

169 He is full of pains (*Panes.*)

170 I scream, thou screamest, he screams.

171 From a selfish motive (*Sell fish*)
172 XIX—XX.
173 The out-side.
174 It makes hot shot (*Hot s-hot.*)
175 L O O T.
176 It makes a mango (*Man go.*)
177 They are both notable (*not able*)
178 They are in sects (*insects.*)
179 It was a Pat riot (*Patriot.*)
180 He lives on the skirts of the town.
181 E G and C (*Ægean Sea.*)
182 It would be D-ceased (*De-ceased.*)
183 The cat'll eat it (*The cattle eat it.*)
184 There are more of them.
185 He has pictures (*Picked yours.*)

186 A hopeless lie and a faithless lie (*Hope Leslie, and Faith Leslie.*)
187 He is bald Tim Moore (*Baltimore.*)
188 They are always forgetting (*For getting.*)
189 Paradise is in it (*Pair o' dice.*)
190 Her suit is hairy (In botany the word *hirsute* means hairy.)
191 They are over sights (*over-sights.*)
192 It is privateering (*private earing.*)
193 Effigy (*F E G.*)
194 The Tees (*tease.*)
195 He is Pat-rolling (*Patroling.*)
196 He was born 29th February.

ENIGMAS.

1 The letter H.
2 Eve.
3 Spectacles.
4 In a looking-glass.
5 Justice—(*just-ice.*)
6 A bed.
7 Alphabet.
8 A pair of skaits.
9 Highway.
10 The moon.
11 The feet.
12 The moon.

13 A tree.
14 Letter M.
15 Letter G.
16 Brush.
17 Ace of Trumps.
18 Bar.
19 On-I-on, (*onion.*)
20 The animal sent was an ante-lope (*Aunt elope.*) The fruit returned was a cante-lope (*Can't elope.*)

REBUSSES.

1 TOBACCO.
5 C-L-ark; or C-lark, (Clark.)
3 C-him-ney, (Chimney.)
4 Pope.
5 Abbot.
6 Tree.
7 Browne.
8 Stephens.
9 Kean.

10 Foote.
11 Vestris.
12 Kelley.
13 Elliston.
14 Munden.
15 Macready.
16 Kemble.
17 Blanchard.
18 Cooper.

19 Farren.
20 Cooke.
21 Liston.
22 Yates.
23 Bland.
24 Bunn.
25 Bartley.
26 Cubitt.
27 Wrench.
28 Powell.
29 Glover.
30 Hallande.
31 Paton.
32 Reeve.
33 Chester.
34 Matthews.
35 West.
36 Pearman.
37 Graddon.
38 Terry.
39 Keetley.
40 Power.
41 Warde.
42 Russell.
43 Ellar.
44 Romer.
45 Bay; lay; day; gay; May; hay; jay; ray; say; nay; pay; Tay; way.
46 Anacreon; Pythagoras; Epaminondas; Lycurgus; Lysippus; Euripides; Sappho; Apelles.
47 Ill; bill; gill; hill; will; till; sill; pill; dill; fill; mill; jill; rill; kill; vill; quill.
48 Room; moor.
49 Cowper; Chaucer; Ossian; Watts; Pindar; Erasmus; Raphael.
50 X S : S X.
51 Pope; Ilissus; Nelson; Death; Addison; Rogers; Pindar.
52 Kite.
53 Swallow
54 Thrush.
55 OWL.
56 Partridge.
57 Parrot.
58 Wren.
59 Goose.
60 Crow.
61 Crane.
62 Magpie.
63 Wheatear.
64 Gull.
65 Turkey.
66 Marten.
67 Starling.
68 Bat.
69 Sparrow.
70 Snipe.
71 Fieldfare.
72 Duck.
73 Pigeon.
74 Grate; great.
75 Caper; cape; cap.

M

1 Potentates.
2 Lawyers.
3 Christianity.
4 Old England.
5 Telegraphs.
6 Radical reform.
7 Horatio Nelson.

ANAGRAMS.

8 Charades.
9 Charles James Stuart.
10 Napoleon Bonaparte.
11 Astronomers.
12 The opposition.
13 Parishioners
14 Catalogues.

15 Revolution.
16 Presbyterian.
17 Penitentiary.
18 La Revolution Francaise.
19 Democratical.
20 Misanthrope.
21 Funeral.
22 Enigmatical.
23 Festival.
24 Solemnity.
25 Sovereignty.
26 Pedagogues.

27 James Stuart.
28 Disappointment.
29 Phaeton.
30 Monastically.
31 Patience.
32 Breath.
33 Wealth.
34 Arthur Wellesley.
35 Dissemination.
36 Miniature.
37 Parishioner.
38 Sweetheart.

LOGOGRIPHS.

1 Pillory : in which may be found pill ; ill ; lip ; roll ; Po ; pry ; poll ; rill ; ropy ; Polly ; lop ; lo ; lily ; rip ; oil ; oily ; or ; O. P.

2 Thread : in which may be found, death ; dear ; Até ; Terah ; the ; dearth ; tare ; hare ; hart ; rat ; art ; a ; date ; red ; era ; trade ; rated ; tar ; hat ; head ; heart ; tread ; hear ; heard ; re ; da ; at ; herd ; ah ; ha ; tear ; dare ; hate ; tea ; her ; eh ; hated ; dart ; hard ;

hater ; heat ; ear ; hatred ; eat.

3 Obscurity : in which may be found, sour ; city ; sty ; sot ; buoy ; tour ; story ; orb ; orbit ; rust ; rut ; sir ; or ; bust ; crust.

4 Amusement : in which may be found, Muse ; tea ; stream ; sun ; ant ; mate ; mast ; as ; man ; mete ; sum ; tease ; amuse ; meat ; mute ; ease ; aunt ; nut ; seat ; sea ; mane ; mames ; name ; seam ; east ; strum.

Thus ends our Key to the Riddler ; our young readers, we doubt not, have very frequently referred to it, in perusing the various questions and puzzles which precede it, in order to save themselves the trouble of tasking their ingenuity to discover the solutions. They ought not, however, to have recourse to the Answers, until they have made frequent attempts to solve the Riddles. Some persons cannot, without considerable difficulty, find the proper answer to an Enigma or a Rebus ; while others, of no greater general acuteness, do so with ease. It is no proof, therefore, of inferiority, not to be able to reply to a quaint Conundrum, so quickly as another. Many young people have displayed much ingenuity in the construction of different sorts of Riddles in rhyme,—they are, in general, the most happy in solving those of others. The admirers of these frequently amusing trifles, consider opposition in their component parts, or curious combinations, to be most essential in the construction of good Riddles.

THE ANGLER.

Embower'd upon the pleasant banks of Thames;
Or, by the silver stream of Isis, Cam,
Or yellow Avon, roaming, the Angler,
Joyous, pursues from morn till eve his sport.

ANGLING has long held a high rank among the sports of the people of
England; poets have written in its praise, and philosophers have delighted
in its practice; it is not confined to particular places, ages, or grades of society; wherever the brook wanders "through hazy shaw or broomy glen,"
—wherever the willow-branch laves in the streamlet,—wherever the Trout
leaps at the May-fly, or the Pike lurks in the bulrushes, or the Salmon springs
up the waterfall,—there also are Anglers. To enjoy this fine pastime,
the mountaineer descends to the valley-stream, the Magister Artium quits his
learned halls and collegiate ease for the banks of the deeps, the weirs, and the
tumbling bays of Cam; the citizen his shop and beloved leger for a hickory
rod and a creek in the Roding; and the courtier his rich Turkey carpet,
ottoman and lustre, for "nature's grassy foot-cloth," the rough bark of a
felled river-side tree, and the sparkling surface of a rippled stream. The
boy, who was but "breeched a Wednesday," often spends his holyday
hour on the bank of a brook, with a crooked pin for his hook, a needleful of
thread for his line, and an alder switch for his rod; and the gray-headed
statesman,—nay, even Royalty itself,—occasionally relaxes from the grave

duties attendant on such superior station, from weighing the balance of power, and determining the fate of nations, "to wield the rod, and cast the mimic fly."

RODS.

The first care of the Angler should be to procure good rods, lines, hooks, and floats. A great variety of rods may be had at the shops, of bamboo, vine, hazel, and hickory : for general fishing, those made of bamboo, having several tops of various strengths, are best ; but cane rods are much superior for fine fishing. The rod should be perfectly straight when put together, and gradually taper from the butt to the top. If you be desirous of making the rods yourself, the following directions must be observed :—The stocks should be cut in the winter ; hazel and yew switches are the best for tops, and crab-tree for stocks. Do not use them till fully seasoned, which will be in about sixteen months after they are cut ; but the longer they are kept the better. The rod should consist of five or six pieces, fitted so nicely, that the whole rod may appear as if it consisted of one piece only. The best rods are those that are brass ferruled ; but if they are bound together, it must be with thread, strongly waxed, the pieces being cut with a slope or slant, that they may join with the greater exactness. Six or eight inches must be taken from the top, and in its place a smooth round taper piece of whalebone substituted, on which a strong loop of horse-hair must be previously whipt. Fly-rods are made more taper than others. Rods for trolling must be furnished with brass rings, whipt all the way up, about ten or twelve inches distance, for the trolling lines to go through ; the tops for trolls must be strong, and have rings whipt on, with pieces of quill, to prevent the lines being cut. The tops of rods for Carp, Tench, Dace and Roach fishing, should be finer, and more elastic.

The rod must neither be kept too dry, nor too moist ; for the one will make it brittle, the other rotten. In very warm weather, always wet the joints, to make them adhere better ; if, however, by being too wet, they should stick, so that you cannot easily get them asunder, never use force, lest you should strain your rod, but rather wait till it be dry, or turn the ferrule of the joint which is fast, a few times over the flame of a candle, and it will separate.

LINES.

For the line, horse-hair is to be preferred ; it should be round, twisted even, and of equal thickness. The best colors are white and gray for clear waters, and sorrel for muddy rivers. The most easy method of making lines, is by a little machine, which may be bought at most of the shops, where also, you purchase your lines, if you think fit.

HOOKS.

Hooks are numbered, and made suitable in size to the fish they are intended to take. For Barbel-fishing, Nos. 5, 6, 7, 8, and 9, are used; for Gudgeons, Nos. 10 and 11; for Roach, Dace, and Bleak, Nos. 10, 11, or 12; for Tench, Carp, and Perch, Nos. 7, 8, and 9; for Trout, No. 6; for Chub, Nos. 8 or 9; for Eels, No. 8; for Grayling, No. 10; for Ruff, No. 9; for Minnows, &c. No. 13, &c. The above sizes are such as the best Anglers of the present day prefer, and are much smaller than those used formerly; but he who expects success at this sport must adopt the modern tackle, or he will be disappointed. For arming the hook, use fine, small, strong silk, well waxed, and lay the hair on the inside of the hook, otherwise the silk will fret and cut it asunder.

FLOATS.

Floats made of Muscovy-duck quills, are best for slow waters; sound cork, without flaws or holes, bored through with a hot iron, into which is put a quill of fit proportion, is preferable for strong streams : the cork should be pared to a pyramidical form, ground small with a pumice-stone, and colored according to fancy. Floats must be so poised with shot, when on the line, as to make them stand perpendicularly in the water, that the least nibble may be apparent.

BAITS.

The lob-worm, garden-worm, and dew-worm, or trechet, are found in gardens and church-yards at night; those with red heads, broad tails, and streaked down the back, are the best. These worms are excellent bait for Barbel, or Eels, and are found towards the latter end of the summer.

Gilt-tails, brandlings, and red worms are found in old dung-hills, hog's dung, cow's dung, and tanner's bark. The brandling and gilt-tail are excellent bait for Perch, Tench, Bream and Gudgeon. The red worms, well scoured, are taken by Tench, Perch, and Bream, in muddy waters.

The meadow, or marsh-worm, is of a lightish blue color, and a good bait for Perch; it is found in marshy ground, or in the banks of rivers in the months of August and September.

The tag-tail is found in meadows, or chalky ground after rain, in March and April; and esteemed a good bait for Trout, in cloudy weather.

The palmer-worm, woolbed, or canker, is found on herbs, plants, and trees; and takes the name of woolbed, from its rough and woolly coat. This is an excellent bait for Trout, Chub, Grayling, Roach, or Dace.

The oak-worm, caterpillar, cabbage-worm, crab-tree-worm colewort-worm or grub, may be gathered on the leaves of colewort and cabbage, or on the hawthorn, oak, or crab-tree ; and may be long preserved with the leaves of those trees or plants, in boxes bored with holes to admit the air. They are good baits for Chub, Dace, Roach, or Trout.

The bark-worm, or ash-grub, is found under the bark of a felled oak, ash, elder, or beach, or in the hollow of those trees where rotten. This bait may be used all the year for Grayling, Dace, Roach, or Chub. They are kept well in wheat-bran.

The cod-bait, caddis-worm, or case-worm, of which there are three sorts, is found in pits, ponds, or ditches; they are excellent baits for Bream, Tench, Bleaks, Chub, Trout, Grayling, and Dace.

Gentles, or maggots, are easily bred by putrefaction; they may be kept with flesh, and scoured with wheat-bran. They are good baits for Tench, Bream, Barbel, Dace, Gudgeon, Chub, Bleak, and Carp.

Cow-dung-bob is found under cow-dung, and somewhat resembles a gentle. It is best kept in earth; and is a good bait for Trout, Chub, Carp, Tench, Bream, Dace, and Roach.

The white-grub, or white-bait, is much larger than a maggot; it is found in sandy and mellow ground; and is an excellent bait from the middle of April till November, for Tench, Roach, Bream, Trout, Chub, Dace, and Carp. These baits should be kept in an earthen vessel, with the earth about them, and covered very close.

Flag or dock-worms are found among the small fibres of flag-roots, and in old pits or ponds. They may be kept in bran; and are good baits for Bream, Tench, Roach, Carp, Bleak, Dace, and Perch.

Boiled salmon-spawn is a very good bait for Chub, and in some rivers, for Trout.

Dace, minnows, roach, smelt, gudgeon, bleak, and miller's-thumb, are proper bait for Pike.

Grasshoppers, in June, July, and August, their legs and wings taken off, are good for Roach, Chub, Trout, and Grayling.

Cheese, or oat-cake, is reckoned killing for Chub, Barbel, Roach, and Dace; the cheese you may moisten with honey and water.

The water-cricket, water-louse or creeper, which is found in stony rivers, will often take Trout in March, April, and May.

White snails are good bait for Chub, early in the morning, and for Trout and Eels on night hooks.

House-crickets are also good, to dib with, for Chub.

TROUT.

In angling for Trout at the bottom, in the early part of the morning, and late at night, also during the day, if the water be much colored, use a strong rod, running tackle, and No. 6 hook. Angle with a float, putting sufficient shot on the line, placed about nine inches above the hook, to sink the bait, which should be one large lob-worm, or two marsh or dew-worms, well scoured, and very lively. Let your bait drag the bottom; do not strike the first time you feel a tug, but rather slacken your line, and when you feel two or three sharp pulls, strike smartly; if a heavy fish, give him line, and land him at leisure, as a Trout is very strong, and struggles most violently, leaping out of the water, and flying in all directions, as soon as he feels the hook.

The Minnow is a good killing bait for Trout. In fishing with a Minnow, hook it by the lips, or beneath the back fin; use a small cork float, No. 6 hook, and let your bait swim below mid-water in deep dark holes, which are free from eddies. Trout begin to feed in March, and continue in season till June. The first two or three months are best for bottom-fishing, they are then found in shallows; in summer time, the large Trout lie in deep holes, or eddies. As they seldom feed in the day, unless in dark weather, you must fish for Trout betimes in the morning, and late in the evening, or you will not be likely to be successful in your sport.

PERCH.

The perch generally takes a bait immediately it is offered. Perch angling continues from April to October. Strong tackle must be used in angling for them, a cork float, gut line, or a twisted hair, and hook No. 7. Bait with two red worms, well scoured, or a live Minnow hooked by the lips or back fin, shrimps, or large gray maggots taken from potato or turnip plants; give them a few minutes to pouch the bait; use running tackle or you will certainly lose your fish. During the hot months, Perch feed very little; dark, windy weather, if not too cold, is best; they lie about bridges, mill-pools, near locks in rivers and canals, in deep, dark, still holes and eddies, ponds about flood gates, on the gravel or sandy parts, and near rushes. If there be any Perch about, and they are inclined to feed, they will soon take the bait, so that you need not delay long in one place.

EELS.

Eels are taken with the rod and line, night lines, dead lines, and by bobbing and sniggling. When fishing with a rod, use gut, or twisted hair lines, with a float, and No. 8 hook; bait with a worm, fish at the bottom, and let the float remain a moment under water before you strike. The dead line should be made of whipcord; on which you may put five or six hooks, about nine inches apart. The night line must be strong, and baited with small fish, or lob-worms. Bobbing is practised from a boat; you must procure a large quantity of worms for this, pass a needle through them, from head to tail, and string them on worsted, until you have as many strung as will form a bunch as large as a good-sized turnip: then fasten them on the line, so that all the ends may hang level. Place a piece of lead of a conical form in the middle, cast the baits into the water, sink them to the bottom, raise them a few inches, and then drop them again until you have a bite; be as expert and steady in raising your lines as possible, so that your fish may drop off into the boat.   Immense numbers may be taken by this method.

NATURAL FLY-FISHING.

For Natural Fly-fishing, the rods should be long and slender, the lines fine, but not so long as those used for Artificial Fly-fishing ; the tackle running ; and the hooks short in their shanks, and well proportioned in size to the baits.   By fishing with the wind at one's back, the line is wafted through the air just above the surface of the water.   In streams, begin by fishing just under the banks or near the shore, and proceed by degrees, until at length you may throw your line the whole breadth of the water.   In rivers, which, during the summer months, produce an abundance of weeds, you should fish between those places where the current is strongest, taking care so to manage your line as not to get it entangled.   When fishing with natural flies, all the other haunts of the different fish which we have elsewhere mentioned should be frequented.   Let the fly just reach the surface of the water, and go gently down the stream ; the top of your rod should be a little raised, and the bait kept in motion upon the surface, by gently raising, lowering, and drawing it to and fro.   When a fish takes your bait, after a moment strike smartly ; and, if he be not so large as to break your tackle, lift him out immediately ; for by playing with him you may, probably, scare away others.   There is an immense variety of Natural Fly-fishing baits ; we shall describe those only which are in most general use.

NATURAL BAITS.

Hornets, wasps, and humble-bees, are good baits for Roach, Dace, Eels, Flounders, Bream and Chub ; some boil them, but it is best to dry them in an oven, or over a fire ; and, if not over done, they will keep a long time. The stone-fly is found at the sides of rivers, under hollow stones ; it is of a curious brown color, the body is pretty thick, and streaked with yellow on the back and belly.

The green drake is taken from May to July ; it is a long, slender fly, with wings like those of a butterfly ; its body is yellow, ribbed with green ; it turns its tail on its back.   These are good baits for Roach, Dace, Perch, Bleak, and Flounders.   The gray drake, in size and shape, resembles the green drake, but has black shining wings, and its body is a pale yellow, striped with black and green.   The time for taking this fly immediately succeeds that of taking the green drake, and it is used for the same fish.

Ant-flies are found in their hills from June till September ; two or three of them fixed on a small hook are certain baits for Roach, Dace, and Chub, if you do not angle above six inches from the bottom.   They may be kept in glass bottles, with some of the earth, from which they have been taken, about them. The fern-fly, or fern bob, is found among fern, from May to the end of August. It has a short, thick body, and two pair of wings, the uppermost reddish and hard, which may be taken off. The Chub never refuses it, and the Trout will take it very freely at the latter end of May.

The hawthorn-fly is found on hawthorn-trees, when the leaves are just shooting; it is of a black color, and is used to dib in a river for Trout.

The great moth is to be found, in the summer evenings, in gardens, trees, or plants; it is used as a bait in dibbing for Roach; it has a very large head and whitish wings.

The bonnet-fly is an excellent bait for Dace, Chub, &c.; it is to be found in the summer months, among standing grass.

The ash-fly, woodcock-fly, or oak-fly, is usually found, from May till September, in the body of an oak or ash-tree, with its head downward, toward the root; it is of a brownish color. This fly is a good bait for Trout. The red copper-colored beetle is a good bait for Trout, if the hard wings be clipped off, and the fly hung with its feet toward the water.

The best mode of keeping natural flies is as follows: Procure a horn bottle made in the shape of a cone, with a wooden bottom, in which several holes must be pierced; these should be sufficiently numerous to afford the flies air, but none of them large enough to suffer your smallest bait to escape; a cork must be obtained to fit the upper or smaller end, so that you may take your baits out, one by one, without losing any. If the flies be kept in a common box, there is a great chance of half a dozen flying out every time you lift the cover.

ARTIFICIAL FLY-FISHING.

The most elegant, clean, gentlemanly, and pleasant mode of fishing is, unquestionably, with the Artificial Fly. It has many advantages over bottom-fishing;—the Artificial fly-fisher is never under the necessity of making ground-bait, digging clay, &c.—he has not even the trouble of baiting his hook; he may ramble along the banks of a pleasant stream, with no burden (excepting a little book of flies and a light rod) but the fish which he may have the good fortune to take;—enjoying his sport, and luxuriating in gentle exercise, without scarcely soiling his fingers.

But though Artificial Fly-fishing possesses these advantages, it must be confessed that, in some points, the superiority is to be given to bottom-fishing. There are many fishes that will never rise at a fly; while all the "tenants of the stream" may be taken, at some time or other, by a bottom bait; and during the cold or wet weather, when the Fly-fisher cannot follow his sport, the staunch Angler, who uses bottom-baits, may still resort to the "grassy margin of the stream," and indulge in his piscatory pastime; for there are few days in the year when fish will not take a proper bait.

Artificial fly-fishing is, by far, the most difficult part of Angling; much time and practice are required to make the tyro an adept in it; by theory it can never be attained; a few months' instruction, under an experienced person, will be more beneficial toward its acquirement than the perusal of all the works extant on the subject. With the preliminary part, or rudiments of the science, (for so it may with propriety be called,) the young Angler may, however, make himself acquainted, by reading the following pages; and if he will carefully attend to the hints and instructions hereinafter given on the subject, he may, with good practice, even attain considerable proficiercy in Artificial Fly-fishing; but it cannot be learned so soon, or so well, from any book as from an experienced instructer.

CASTING THE LINES, &c.

Your rod for fly-fishing must be light and flexible, and of a length proportioned to your power of casting; when you have properly fixed the winch, and brought your line from it through the links, fix your fly on, and let out your line about the length of the rod, or something less; take the rod in your right hand, and the line, near the fly, in your left; when you move the rod backward to cast the line, let the latter go from your left hand. Practice several throws at this length, and increase it occasionally, as you improve, until you are able to throw almost any moderate length, with ease, to within an inch of any spot you desire. Draw the fly lightly toward the shore, and look sharply at it, so as to be able to strike instantly if a fish should rise at it; if you do not, you will most probably lose him, for he quickly discovers the nature of your bait. In raising your line for the second and subsequent throws, wave your rod round your head, instead of bringing it directly backward. You should not return the line before it has gone its full length behind you, lest you whip off your fly. In order to show your flies naturally to the fish, when you have thrown, raise your hand by degrees, with a slight quivering motion; and, as you thus draw the bait toward you, let it go down the stream, (for you must never bring your fly against it,) and before it comes too near you, prepare to cast again. If you see a fish rise at a natural fly, throw your line a little above him, so that the bait may come gently and naturally down toward him; fish every yard of water likely to afford sport, and never despair of success; for, sometimes it so happens, that, after many fruitless hours spent without a fish ever rising at your fly, you will fill your bag or basket during the last hour. The lighter your fly descends on the water, the greater chance you have of a bite; the way to throw with the requisite perfection in this respect, is only to be acquired by practice and love for the art. Use only one hook at a time, till you can throw to any given distance with certainty. You may acquire such a mastery, by dint of observation and practice, as to be able to cast your fly under banks, into holes, among bushes, &c., where the best fish are frequently found. Endeavour to keep the wind at your back, and when fishing in a small stream, where the middle is shallow, and the water ripples, cast your bait to the opposite side, slowly draw it to the rippling, and let it float down some distance. You must recollect to keep yourself out of sight, and your fly in motion, that it may appear to the fish as if alive. If you do not find the fish rise toward the top, sink your fly, by degrees, even to middle water. Before flies are naturally in season, the fish very rarely rise at them; therefore, in order that you may not be mistaken in your baiting, observe what flies are about the water, or on the bushes or trees near the ponds or rivers; and that fly which swarms there most, being chiefly in season, is to be used.

If the wind be pretty high, the fish will rise in the plain deep; but when little wind is stirring, it is best to angle in the stream. We need scarcely remind you of the propriety of taking your basket, landing-net, book of flies, and, if you are able to construct an artificial fly yourself, a few materials for fly-making; so that, if the fish, which are often whimsical, will not take any of the baits with which you are provided, and you observe them rising at natural flies, (and they will sometimes feed on such insignificant ones as, at other times, they will scarcely look at,) catch one of such flies, and make one for your bait as nearly like it as possible. This, certainly, is a great advantage, and every Angler ought, therefore, perhaps, to acquire sufficient knowledge in fly-making to be able to produce such a tolerable imitation, that the fish may not easily detect the difference between the natural and the artificial fly.

GENERAL RULES FOR ALL ANGLERS.

In bottom-fishing, plumb the depth truly, and with as little disturbance as may be; let your line, with the plummet to it, remain in the water while you cast in the ground-bait, by which time the line will be softened and stretched; keep as far from the water as you can. Use fine tackle, and you will the sooner become skilful: if you break your tackle, do not lose your temper, but sit down, and diligently repair it. If hail fall, or the day be cold, and the wind blow strong, the Angler must not expect much sport. In soft rain, or foggy, close weather, most fish will bite. Never drink water out of rivers or ponds while in a perspiration; keep your feet dry, by wearing strong boots and shoes. It is supposed that the best winds for Angling are the south, west, and south east. In hot weather, the cooler the wind blows the better; but in the early part of the season, and also in autumn, a warm wind is more advantageous. When the wind comes from a cold quarter, such places as are most protected from its influence should be resorted to. A cloudy day, with light showers, after a bright night, in general proves most favorable to the Angler, who may also expect good sport even on those days when heavy rains descend during the intervals between the showers. When a calm bright morning is succeeded by a gloomy day with a brisk wind, without any fall of rain, the fish,—at least, the larger sorts,—are almost sure to feed. Weather-wisdom is of the greatest benefit to the

Angler :—our young friends should therefore pay attention to, and remember the state of the wind, the clouds, &c., on those days when they find the fish bite, and when they refuse to take a bait.   They may thus not only be enabled to say when there is a prospect of sport, but also save themselves much trouble and disappointment, by staying at home to improve their tackle, or amusing themselves in some other manner, instead of following "the devious windings of the stream," when the weather is unpromising. When the wind blows right across the water, fish with your back toward it ; not merely because you can throw your line with more facility, but because the fish will certainly be on that side, watching for the flies, &c. that may be blown from the bank into the water.   Throw as near the bank on which you stand as the wind, if it be high, will suffer you.   In the summer time, when the sun is out in all his splendor, and there is scarcely a breath of wind stirring, you may often see the fish basking in clear low water, with their fins and a part of their backs above the surface.   On these occasions, they will rise greedily at a hackle, if your foot length be fine, and you fish at a sufficient distance to be unperceived, under banks or straight down the sides of streams.   Your line, for this purpose, must be long ; and if, when you hook a fish, the others should become alarmed and shoot off, retire for a short time and in all probability they will return again ; if not, you must try elsewhere.   Artificial Bait, and Apparatus for all kinds of Angling, may be had at Bradlee's near the Old South Church, in Boston.

RABBITS.

See where a motley litter sports around
The captive doe, whose native symmetry
Has so improved 'neath man's dominion,
That her grandsire's progeny, sporting wide
O'er hill and dale, in their plain russet coats,
Seem of no kin to her.

RABBIT-KEEPING was never, perhaps, so much practised in England as
it is at the present day. Not only do a multitude of young persons keep
common rabbits for their amusement, and poulterers and others for the
table, but of late, many gentlemen have become rabbit-breeders to a considerable extent; and though the varieties are so much less numerous, it
promises to become, ere long, as popular a fancy as that in pigeons. A
writer on this subject states, that there are, or were, two great feeders in
the counties of Oxford and Bucks, the former of whom kept a sufficient
number to produce three dozen rabbits for the market per week; the latter,
it is said, kept white rabbits only, on account of the superior value of their
skins for the purpose of trimming. These persons, however, must be considered rabbit feeders rather than fanciers.

Fancy rabbits are rarely to be met with in the hands of the common dealers, good ones being of too high a price to come within their means.

There are, however, several private individuals of great respectability in
the city, from whom excellent specimens may be obtained, by those who
wish to lay the foundation for a fancy stock. A rabbit, of whatever color
it may be, is certainly a beautiful little animal; but the common breed are

s

very inferior in beauty of appearance to the fine lop-eared creatures. We feel convinced that any person who sees a well-ordered rabbitry, containing some good specimens of fancy rabbits, will be so struck with their superior beauty of appearance, that he will not think of keeping merely common rabbits. The first is the only extra expense; for the fine lopped-eared animals do not require more or superior food than what ought to be afforded to the common ones. They are, we confess, rather more delicate in constitution; but their fine appearance will certainly compensate their keeper for the care he may take in keeping them in order; there is also a greater pleasure in breeding valuable animals, than rabbits, that, at best, will never be worth, when reared, above half a dozen shillings. And here let us impress upon our young readers the propriety of feeding their rabbits regularly. Poor creatures! they are caged, confined, and wholly dependent upon us—it would be the extreme of barbarity to neglect them. If we keep any living creature in a confined state, we enjoin a duty on ourselves of providing for their wants. Depend upon it, that the boy will rue the day, unless he have decidedly a bad heart, who sits down to a comfortable meal, while his rabbit or his bird—heretofore his idol and his toy, but now, in caprice, neglected—pines, in its prison, for his appearance with its usual daily food. If he be tired of that, which, when it was a novelty, he took so much delight in, he had better sell, give, or even humanely kill it, than suffer it to languish its solitary hours away in hunger and in thirst. It is a creature dependent on his care,—it is helpless and imprisoned—is he not cruel in the extreme if he omit to furnish it with its daily pittance?

THE WILD RABBIT.

Wild rabbits are considerably less than those which are kept in a domestic state; they are, for the most part, of a gray color; but a few black, black and white, and even fawn-colored rabbits are to be seen in some warrens. The flesh of wild rabbits is, in general, preferred to that of tame ones; but the latter may be much improved in flavor by judicious feeding, and affording the animals good air and sufficient room to exercise themselves.

It is said that the wild rabbit will breed eleven times a year, and bring forth, generally, eight young ones each time; at this rate, in four years, a couple of rabbits would produce a progeny of almost a million and a half.

THE COMMON DOMESTIC RABBIT.

One of the chief objects in keeping common rabbits is, for the purpose of occasionally furnishing a dish for the table; and, therefore, those persons, by whom they are kept, attend as particularly to the sort of rabbits whose flesh is said to be the best, as to their colors or shape.

The short-legged stout rabbits are generally supposed to be the most healthy, and also the best breeders. The large hare-colored variety is much esteemed by some people; but the white, or white mottled with black or yellow, are more delicate in flesh. The gray and some of the blacks, approach nearer to the flavour of the wild rabbit than any others.

LOP-EARED, OR FANCY RABBITS.

Formerly, a fine rabbit of any two colors, however short its ears, was accounted a fancy animal: it is now very different. In the eye of a fancier of the present day, the long lopped ear is an indispensable requisite. The first things that are looked at are the length and fall of the ears; the dewlap, if the animal be in its prime, is next noticed; the colors and markings are then inspected; and, lastly, the shape and general appearance. Rabbits, whose ears do not extend to fourteen inches from tip to tip, measured across the skull, would be reluctantly admitted into a fancier's stock, if they fell ever so finely; or, in case they exceeded that length, (and they sometimes are sixteen inches, and even upward,) if they did not lop or fall downward, in what is deemed a graceful and becoming manner. The dewlap, which is only seen in fancy rabbits, sometime after they have attained their full growth, adds materially to the beauty of their appearance: it commences immediately under the jaw, goes down the throat, and between the fore-legs: it is so broad, that when the head reposes upon it, it projects beneath the chin, and on each side beyond the jaws; it is usually parted in the centre in front, and is equal in size to a couple of good-sized eggs: when the fur on it is of a beautiful color, it produces a very fine effect.

The annexed cut is a portrait of WOWSKI, a first-rate fancy lop rabbit, in the possession of the writer. At the time of making the drawing for this

cut, Wowski was just ten weeks old; her ears matching perfectly with each other, and measuring, from tip to tip, nearly thirteen inches. The difference in the back, and general appearance, to say nothing of the ears, between the fancy and the common rabbit, cannot fail to strike the reader who will take the trouble of comparing the annexed engraving with the cut of the common domestic rabbit, inserted on page 273.

Fancy rabbits fetch high prices compared with those of the common ones; five, ten, and even as much as twenty guineas, have been given for a first-rate doe. Very good fancy rabbits may, however, be bought for less sums than these; the foundation of a fancy stock, provided young rabbits only be bought, may be made for even much less. We know a youth who began to keep fancy rabbits but two years ago, and has now a very brilliant little stock. He purchased three rabbits, each about two months old, of excellent breed; but being all deficient, in some respect, with regard to properties, they cost him between twenty and thirty shillings only. These three rabbits, being of the true fancy strain, have occasionally thrown very excellent specimens, which he has selected and reared: the first he has disposed of again, and his hutches did not, at the time we saw them, which was about three months since, contain an animal that would not pass muster in the rabbitry of a first-rate fancier.

THE RABBITRY AND HUTCHES.

The rabbit house should be dry and well ventilated; too much humidity, whether externally or internally, will cause the rabbits to rot. Where considerable numbers are kept, fresh air is absolutely necessary to preserve them in a state of health; still they should not be exposed to draughts, which, on many occasions, have brought on a disease called the snuffles—a dangerous, and frequently fatal malady. If economy be an object, or the young fancier be desirous of employing his mechanical abilities, he may construct hutches sufficiently good for common purposes himself. A tolerably good doe's hutch may be made out of an old egg-chest, and places for bucks and weaned rabbits, of tea-chests; the former are to be bought at a cheesemonger's, the latter at a grocer's shop. If our reader should become his own carpenter in this case, we recommend him to follow, as much as his abilities will admit, the directions which are given for making hutches in the following page. Young persons should begin by keeping common rabbits, for which common hutches, such as they can construct themselves, if so inclined, will be quite good enough. When they have acquired experience in the management of the Rabbitry, and not before, they may, by degrees, introduce superior animals to their stock, and dispose of the common ones. They should then also obtain superior hutches; for a fine lop-eared rabbit loses half the beauty of its appearance in a clumsy and ill-fashioned hutch.

The hutch for does should have a partition with a hole in it, to let them pass from one part to the other, and a slide to close this hole when necessary. For weaned rabbits, a hutch without this partition is preferable, and it is unnecessary to make any partition in the bucks' hutches. The breeding hutches should be about three feet long, two feet and a half in depth, and eighteen inches high; the breeding place may be from nine to twelve inches in breadth; it should have a door to fit the whole front of it, fastened by a separate latch or buckle to that used for the door of the feeding place. The latter door should extend the whole distance from the partition to the opposite part of the hutch, and in depth from the top to within two or three inches of the bottom; it must be made of a frame of wood tinned on the inside, with stout wire or slender iron rods nailed or driven into the top and bottom parts of the frame, from three quarters to an inch apart. Hang it on a pair of small hinges to that side of the hutch which is opposite the partition, and fasten it by a latch or buckle. Under this door, a drawer for food, well tinned round the edges, is to run in; it should be fastened by a buckle fixed to the lower part of the large door, or it may be so contrived that the door will keep it close without any fastening. Nail tin round the hole in the partition, (which ought to be circular,) and, in fact, to every other part of the interior of the hutch which the rabbits can take hold of with their teeth; as they are very destructive animals, and would actually gnaw themselves out of a mere wooden hutch. The bottom must be planed quite smooth, and a slip be taken off the lower part of the back of the hutch to let the urine run off: for this purpose, hutches should also be set a little on the slant backward.

The buck's hutch is made different in every respect from the breeding hutch; instead of being square, it is almost semicircular; the back and sides being gradually rounded off from the front. The wires are placed wider apart, and are thicker and stronger than those used for doe's hutches: it has no partition, and the drawer, instead of running the whole breadth of the cage, as there is never more than one rabbit at a time to feed out of it, is placed in the centre, to a cross piece which goes from side to side, as the front piece of the drawer in other hutches. There must be an aperture at the back close to the floor, for the purpose we have before mentioned, and the door, which, excepting the drawer, constitutes the entire front of the cage, should be well hinged and fastened with a stout button. The buck's hutch should not be less than twenty inches high, two feet and a half broad, and twenty inches at its deepest part.

The hutches may be stacked one above another, or set in a row, as choice or convenience may direct. They should, however, never be placed upon the ground, but elevated on wooden stools, or horses, a foot or two above it; neither ought the back parts of them to be put close against the wall, but sufficient room should be left for the dung to have a passage from the apertures made in the lower part of the back to the floor.

FEEDING.

This is a most important subject. On his skill, as a feeder, mainly depends the young Fancier's chance of prosperity with his stock. If too much food be given at once, the animals will get disgusted with and refuse it, so that a rabbit may be nearly starved by affording it too great a quantity of food. Most persons feed their rabbits twice, but, for our own part, we feed ours thrice a day. To a full-grown doe, without a litter, in the morning, we give a little hay, or dry clover, and a few of such vegetables as are in season; in the afternoon, we put two handfuls of good corn into her trough; and, at night, we give her a boiled potato or two, more vegetables, and if her hutch be clear of what we gave her in the morning, but by no means otherwise, a little more hay or clover.   If you give rabbits more hay than they can eat in a few hours, except it be to a doe just about to litter, they will tread it under foot, and waste it; if you give them but a moderate quantity at a time, they will eat and enjoy it.   Generally speaking, rabbits prefer green or moist food to corn: but it is necessary to make them eat a sufficient proportion of solid food to keep them in health; occasionally, instead of corn, we give our rabbits a few split or whole gray peas.   When a doe has a litter by her side, and also for rabbits recently weaned, we soak the peas for a few hours previously to putting them in the trough.   If a rabbit will not eat a proper quantity of corn, we mix a small quantity of squeezed tea-leaves with her portion, and stint her proportionately in green meat. Barley-meal, dry as well as scalded, we occasionally use, to fatten for the table, or to bring a poor rabbit into good condition; and in winter, when greens are scarce, but not otherwise, we feed with fresh grains mixed with oats, peas, meal, or pollard.   Tea-leaves, in small quantities, well squeezed, may at all times be given, by way of a treat; but it is highly improper to make them a daily substitute for green meat.

Almost all the vegetables and roots used for the table may be given to rabbits; in preference to all others, we choose celery, parsley and the roots and tops of carrots; and in this choice the animals themselves heartily agree with us; lettuce, the leaves, and, what are much better, the stumps of cabbages and cauliflowers, they eat with avidity, but they must be given to them with a sparing hand; turnips, parsneps and even potatoes in a raw state we occasionally afford our stock, on an emergency, when better roots or good greens are scarce.   In the spring time no soft meat is better for them than tares, so that they be not wet : in fact, no green ought to be given to rabbits when there is much moisture on its surface.   We have heard of some country persons feeding their rabbits on marshmallows, but we never did so ourselves.   Dandelions, milk thistles, we know, by long experience, they take in preference to all other food, except celery, parsley, and carrots; and nothing, we are convinced, as green meat, can be better for them.

It must be remembered that a doe will eat nearly twice as much when suckling as at other times; and, when her litter begin to eat, the allowance of food must be gradually increased.   In our own Rabbitry we never admit chaff, and grains only, in a dearth of green food.   If we can obtain neither greens, roots, nor grains, at feeding time, we make it a practice to moisten the corn with water, milk, or, as we before stated, with tea-leaves.   Though a rabbit must be restricted from rioting in green or soft meat according to its own appetite, for its own sake, yet it is cruel to afford it only such food as will increase rather than appease its thirst; for this reason, in such a case as we have mentioned, we moisten the grain; and some rabbits will even do well with an occasional table-spoonful of water, beer, or milk; but it is a dangerous experiment to try the effect of a liquid on their stomachs.

BREEDING.

The doe will breed at the age of six months; her period of gestation is thirty-days. The rabbits are not to be left together above ten minutes. Some days before kindling, hay is to be given to the doe, with which, and the flue which nature has instructed her to tear from her body, she will make her nest. Biting the hay into short pieces, and carrying it about in her mouth, are almost certain signs of her being with young. The number produced varies from three to eleven. Destroy the weak and sickly ones, as soon as their defects can be perceived, until the litter is reduced to five or six. If you leave more to be suckled, some will, perhaps, die, others be sickly, and none of them fine. The old rabbits are not to be put together till the expiration of six weeks: the young may be separated from the doe and weaned a fortnight after. If more than five or six litters are obtained in a year, the doe will be soon worn out, and the young ones not worth much. The doe should not be disturbed by any other rabbit, while with young. Should she be weak after kindling, give her a malt mash, scalded fine pollard, or barley-meal, in which may be mixed a small quantity of cordial horse-ball. In this case, and, in fact, whenever a doe is weak, bread—soaked in milk, and squeezed rather dry again, if she will take it, will considerably strengthen her.

If well fed, and kept warm, does will breed all the year; but most fanciers are contented with five litters a year, and let them rest during the winter. Mowbray states, that the produce of rabbits is so multitudinous, that one might be well satisfied with this practice; for that even four litters in the year would be equal to two thousand young rabbits annually, from a stock of one hundred does. If does devour their young, or do not breed for any considerable time, rabbit fanciers dispose of them as useless incumbrances to their stock. It is advisable so to manage, that two or three does should kindle about the same time; you may then take from the doe that has the greatest number, and put the excess under her that has the least; taking care not to leave more than six young ones to each. It is advisable to obtain rabbits for breeding from a litter of two, three, or four only, as they are generally stronger and finer than those which come from a more numerous one. It is a disadvantage, rather than otherwise, to have above six produced in a litter, as the young rabbits, when that is the case, are almost invariably weak and puny; and even if they be reduced to a moderate quantity, by removing some of them to another doe, or otherwise, they rarely become remarkable for their size or beauty.

DISEASES.

Diseases may, in a great measure, be prevented, by regularity in feeding, good food, and cleanliness. The refuse of vegetables should always be scrupulously rejected. For the liver complaint, to which rabbits are subject, there is no cure : when they are attacked by it, fatten them, if possible, for the table.

The snuffles are occasioned by damp or cold. If there be any cure for this disorder, it must be dryness in their hutches and food.

Squeezed tea-leaves generally restore a doe to health, if weak, or otherwise affected after kindling, if the food which we have directed to be given at that time, under the head of Breeding, should fail. When old rabbits are attacked by a looseness, dry food will, in general, restore them ; but do what you will, it is very difficult, and, in most cases, impossible, to save young ones from sinking under it ; dry food for them, as well as for the old ones, is the only remedy.

GENERAL OBSERVATIONS.

Be careful to keep your rabbit-hutches particularly clean ; a short hoe, or a trowel, and a hand-brush, will be necessary for this purpose. Do not handle your rabbits, particularly the young ones, too much ; when you lift them, take them with one hand by the ears, and place the other under the lower part of their backs. Never slacken in attention ; a neglect of a day will do your stock much injury ; while by constant care you may breed to great perfection. Those who are fanciful in colors should not only look at those of the rabbits they buy for breeding, but also ascertain, if possible, the colors of the does they come from ; for rabbits frequently throw litters, in which not a single young one of their own color can be found. If there happen, for instance, to have been a single cross of gray in your stock for three or four generations back, it will frequently appear in stock, although every breeding rabbit in your hutches be of a different color. Gray is the most difficult of all colors to eradicate ; but even gray rabbits do not always have young ones of their own color.

The more you vary the food, the fatter your rabbits will be ; but observe, that when they are once *full fat*, (to use a term of breeders,) they frequently fall off and pine away to bad condition. It is impossible to lay down rules for the precise quantity of each sort of food to be allowed ; a little experience alone can teach the youthful fancier this secret.

GUINEA PIGS.

"A rat without a tail."
MACBETH.

THESE little animals were originally natives of Brazil, but they have long been introduced to this and other European countries. They propagate in temperate, and even cold climates; and would be exceedingly numerous, had they not, like most other animals whose produce is abundant, a great number of enemies. The males frequently devour their own offspring, which also suffer much from cats, &c. It is said, however, that rats will carefully avoid them; and under this idea, they are frequently bred by rabbit-fanciers, for a protection to their young stock against those destructive vermin. In a rabbit-house they are by no means troublesome, as they may be suffered to run loose under the lower tier of hutches, and will feed on the waste food, which is spilled about the floor. If kept up, through choice or necessity, they will do best in hutches similar to those made for rabbits; they need not, of course, be of such large dimensions. They will eat bread, grain, and, in fact, whatever is commonly given to rabbits; tea-leaves, however, they seem to prefer to all other food, but they ought not to be kept constantly on them.

They breed, according to some naturalists, at two months old, and, it is said, have from four to twelve young ones at a time: for our own part, we have frequently known them to have two, and never more than six, in a litter. In size they are considerably less than a rabbit; the upper lip is only half divided; they have two cutting teeth in each jaw, and their ears are broad and erect. They are of varied colors, white, black, and fawn; the tortoise-shell, (*i. e.*) a mixture of the three colors, is generally preferred. Some of the white ones have red eyes, similar to ferrets and white rabbits. Their flesh is eatable, but by no means good; in this country they are never used for the table, and have been tasted only, it is presumed, from motives of curiosity. They are perfectly harmless, and, unless it be true that they keep rats away from rabbit-hutches, altogether useless. They may be bought at the shops of the rabbit or pigeon dealers, at from sixpence upward, according to their age, shape, and color.

Nature, which has so abundantly provided the Cape of Good Hope sheep with tails, that the farmers, it is said, are frequently obliged to provide small wagons to support them, has left the little Guinea pig totally destitute of this usual ornament to the hind quarters of animals. Were it not for their color, they might, indeed, be properly compared to "A rat without a tail."

PIGEONS.

Aloft in air the rapid pigeon soars,
The messenger, by turns, of joy and wo;
But heedless ever of her high envoy,
Even while cleaving yonder distant cloud,
Her heart is fixed on home, and her loved young;
Thus does brute instinct in man's hand become
A mighty engine.

THE life of this beautiful and useful bird is said to extend to about eight years; but it is useless for the purpose of breeding after it has attained half that age, and ought then to be destroyed, or it will molest those which are in their prime. The pigeon lays two white eggs, and sits fifteen days after the second egg is laid. The female keeps to the nest from four or five o'clock in the evening until nine the next morning; she then goes off to feed, and the cock takes her place during the day. If the hen delay, the cock leaves the nest at the usual time, seeks her out, and drives her to her duty; the hen does the same in case of negligence in this respect on the part of the cock.

The young ones are usually of different sexes. For the first three days after they are hatched, the female seldom leaves them ; after that time, the cock and hen attend to feed them indiscriminately. The way in which the old supply the young with food is singular : the parent birds collect a quantity of grain and water in their crops, which are very capacious, and after it has lain there until soft and macerated, they cast it up into the throats of the young ones. As the young birds acquire strength, the old ones give the food less preparation, and at last drive them out to provide in part for themselves ; but they are often seen feeding their young ones even when the latter are able to fly, and they themselves are going to nest again. The young ones, while fed by the cock and hen, are called squabs, under six months old squeakers, and after that age they are denominated pigeons, being in a fit state to mate and breed.

THE DOVE-COTE, OR PIGEON-HOUSE.

As many young people will take a pleasure in breeding a little flock of birds from a common box, fitted up against a wall or elsewhere, we shall give

them a few words of advice on the subject. The form of the box is immaterial ; the triangular is, perhaps, the best, because it allows the wet to run off quickest ; it may be made with any number of holes, which should be sufficiently large for the pigeons to turn round in them with ease. Shelves and partitions of six or eight inches deep should run along the front, to keep the couples apart, and afford them good resting-places. It will be an advantage, if you can allow two holes between each partition for each couple of birds. The box may also be made square ; or in fact, according to the convenience or fancy of the individual fitting it up. It should be fixed where it will be secure from rats and cats, and ought always to face a warm quarter ; cold winds being very pernicious to the birds.

PIGEON LOFTS.

We shall now proceed to give the young Fancier proper instructions for building pigeon lofts, which are used for breeding and keeping the more curious sort of birds, or what are commonly denominated Fancy pigeons.

Many persons convert the spaces between the garrets and the roofs of their houses into lofts, by making an aperture in the tiling, which opens on a platform, fixed on the outside. It is necessary in this, as in all other cases, to erect proper fences to keep out the cats. If possible, for the sake of warmth, your loft should face the south or southwest; but, as it rarely happens that convenience will allow of a room being occupied entirely by pigeons, it is seldom that the birds are indulged with this advantage. Any place, in fact, that is dry, light, airy, and sufficiently commodious, may be converted into a good loft.

The shelves for the breeding place should be fourteen inches, or a little more, in breadth; and if you breed Pouters, there ought to be twenty inches between the upper and lower shelves, or otherwise the pigeons will acquire a trick of stooping, which will spoil their deportment. Partitions should be made in these shelves, about three feet apart, and a slip of board run along the front of the lower shelves about four inches high, to keep in the nests. This slip should run in a groove, or be otherwise managed so that it may be easily removed, in order to clean out the nests when expedient. A similar slip must also be fixed in the middle of each three feet division, which is thus adapted for a double nest, in one of which, the old hen may lay in quietness without being disturbed by her young ones in the other, as she often leaves them when about three weeks old to the care of the cock, and goes to nest again. Some Fanciers darken the nest by setting up a board a few inches within the edge of the shelves, having an entrance hole cut through it; thus dividing the partition into an outer shelf or landing place, and an inner room or nest: in this case, of course, the slip is unnecessary. A good contrivance to keep the birds private when setting is, perhaps, worth attention, as they are sometimes shy, and set uneasy, or even fly off their eggs, in alarm, on any person's entering the loft. Some tame pigeons will not make their nests; to such it will be right to afford a little hay. Straw buckets and pans of earthen-ware are used by many Fanciers for nests. When the latter are adopted, it is usual to place a brick between them (there being two pans in every partition) for the convenience of the birds, as well as more effectually to divide and support the nest. The pans should vary in size according to the pigeons for which they are intended. The straw baskets are in general preferred, as the egg is liable to be broken in the pan, unless it be strowed with hay, straw, or frail, of which the latter, for many reasons, is the best for the purpose.

FEEDING, MATING, &c.

Gravel should be strowed on the shelves and floor, the birds being fond of picking it; besides, it gives the loft a much cleaner appearance. Cleanliness is indispensable; if you suffer the loft to be filthy, the dirt will produce effects which will be equally annoying to yourself and your birds. Do not handle your squabs or young birds too much, lest you bring an illness on them which may prove fatal.

The common pigeon will, during a great part of the year, seek the principal part of its own food, and live upon almost any grain; the fancy birds require delicate food and much attention. Of all grain, old tares prove to be the best suited to the nature of these birds; new tares should be given very sparingly, especially to young pigeons, as they are very liable to do them much injury. Horse beans are esteemed the next best food to tares; the smallest of these are preferred, especially small ticks. Wheat, barley, oats, and peas, ought only to be given now and then for a change of diet, as they sometimes hurt them. Rape, canary, and hemp-seed, pigeons are immoderately fond of; but these must not by any means be made a constant diet.

Mating or coupling of pigeons is often attended with much difficulty. In order to effect it, let two coops be built close together with a partition of lath between them, so that the birds may see each other, and they should feed out of the same vessels; by supplying them well with hemp-seed, you may soon make them fit for mating, and when you perceive the hen to sweep her tail, you may remove her to the cock's pen, and they will soon agree. When this convenience is wanting, and you are compelled to put them both into the coop at first, put the cock in three or four days before the hen, that he may get master of the coop, particularly if the hen be a termagant, or else they will quarrel so much, that their bickerings will end in an irreconcilable hatred. When the pigeons are matched, you can give them the run of the loft to choose a nest for themselves, or fix them to one, by inclosing them within it, by a lath railing, giving them food and water in plenty for eight or nine days.

DISEASES AND REMEDIES.

For the wet roup, give them three or four pepper-corns once in three or four days, and steep a handful of green rue in their water, which you may let all the pigeons drink of. The dry roup is known by a dry husky cough, it proceeds from a cold; to cure it, give them three or four cloves of garlic every day.

The canker arises from the cocks pecking each other: for this, rub the affected part every day with burnt alum and honey. When the flesh round the eyes is torn or pecked, bathe it with salt water for several days; if this do not prove successful, wash the aggrieved part with two drachms of alum dissolved in an ounce and a half of water

When pigeons are infested with insects, smoke their feathers well with tobacco.

Pigeons are apt to gorge themselves when they have fasted rather longer than usual. When this happens, put the bird into a tight stocking with its feet downward, smoothing up the crop, that the over-loaded bag of meat may not hang down; then hitch up the stocking on a nail, and keep it in this posture, supplying it with a little water now and then, till the food is digested. When taken out of the stocking, put the bird in an open coop or basket, and feed it but very moderately for some time.

The megrims is a disease, in which the pigeon flutters about at random, with its head reverted in such a manner that its beak rests upon its back. This malady is pronounced incurable.

When pigeons do not moult freely, put them into some warm place, and mix a good quantity of hemp-seed in their common food, and a little saffron in their water.

If they be lame, or the palls of their feet become swelled, either from cold, being cut with glass, or any other accident, spread some Venice turpentine on a piece of brown paper, and put it to the part affected.

FENCING.

Wouldst have thy son acquire a graceful port,
A manly bearing ;—make his eye acute
As that of the hawk, and his young limbs vie
With those of roe-bucks in agility ?—
The noble art of Fencing let him learn.

In those days, when a small sword was an indispensable ornament to the person of a gentleman, objections were sometimes raised to the cultivation of the art of Fencing, as tending to lead young persons into broils and duels ; but nothing can now be said against it on this score ; the wearing of swords, except among military men, has long ceased, and duels being invariably decided in this country by pistols. The art of Fencing is acquired, therefore, as the means of affording excellent exercise, elegant amusement, and imparting an easy deportment and graceful action, as well as extraordinary acuteness of eye, and agility of body. That it has these merits, there can be no doubt ; and it is, therefore, confidently recommended to youth, as being not only perfectly unexceptionable, but even superior, in most respects, to all other exercises.

FOILS, MASKS, &c.

The foils should be proportioned to the size of those who use them. Thirty-one inches is the medium for men ; it is advisable to use a glove on the right hand, padded on the back and the outsides of the fingers ; the masks must have wire fronts, stout enough to resist an accidental thrust at the face. An easy dress should be worn, and it is usual, in academies, to have a spot, or heart, on the left side of the breast of the waistcoat.

HOW TO HOLD THE FOIL.

The hilt must be flat in your hand ; so that the two edges are nearly horizontal when you throw yourself upon guard ; your thumb should be stretched along the upper flat part of the hilt, within half an inch of the shell, and the pommel should rest under your wrist.

T

COMMON GUARDS OF CARTE AND TIERCE.

Stand in the first position, which is similar to the first position in dancing, that is, your right foot forward, with the heel advanced; then throw yourself upon the common guard or carte, by advancing your right foot about half a yard from the left. The two heels should be in the same line. Turn your wrist so that the nails may appear upward. Let your hand be on a line with the lower part of your breast; the arm not stretched, but a little bent, and the elbow inclined a little to the outside. The point of your

foil should be about fifteen degrees elevated, and nearly fixed on a line with the upper part of your adversary's breast. The left arm (which is necessary to balance the body in its different movements) must be raised in a semi-circular manner, on a line with the forehead, the hand kept open in an easy manner, the thumb and first finger nearly meeting. Your body should be sideways, and your head turned toward the right, so as to keep sight of your point. Let the balance of your body rest upon the left leg, keep the left knee bent, and flexible, so that you may incline a little backward; the right knee should also be rather bent, and perpendicular to the point where your right heel rests.

The position of the guard in tierce is similar to that of carte, only the hand must be a little reversed, so that the nails may be half turned downward. The arm should be a little stretched outward, in order to secure or cover the outside, and the point should be as in carte.

ENGAGING AND DISENGAGING.

Engaging in carte, or in tierce, is opposing your adversary's blade, either inside or outside, when you first join or cross blades on guard. Disengaging is performed by dexterously shifting the point of your foil from one side of your adversary's blade to the other; that is, from carte to tierce, or *viceversa*.

THE ADVANCE AND RETREAT.

In order to advance, move the right foot easily forward to the distance of more than a foot, and let the left foot instantly follow to the same distance; these two movements must be performed in the same moment. Keep your body firm and steady while you repeat this five or six times; and let there be a short pause between every advance. After making five or six advances, observe if the distance and position of your guard be exactly the same as your distance and position were when you commenced. In the retreat, your left foot makes the first movement backward, and your right follows at the same moment.

THE SIMPLE PARADES OF CARTE AND TIERCE.

These are distinguished from all the others, on account of their securing the breast, as upper parades. To perform that of carte, place yourself on the common guard, and throw your hand toward the left, or inward, about six inches from guard, making a gradual turn upward with the wrist, in order to throw off your adversary's blade with the greater ease; at the same time draw your hand a little toward your body, that the opposition may be more powerful.

The simple parade of tierce is also performed from the common guard by throwing and stretching your arm obliquely downward to the right, (or outwardly,) the nails being reversed by the gradual turn of the wrist, in forming the parade. It parries the simple thrust of carte over the arm and seconde. The distance of the hand from the common guard should be six inches. The point of your foil, your body and legs, should not deviate from the line of direction in performing either of these parades.

THE PARADES OF OCTAVE AND SEMI-CIRCLE.

To perform the octave parade, raise the hand as high as your chin, the nails must not be turned up so much as in semi-circle; your arm should be well stretched and thrown outward, the distance of six inches; the wrist should be bent as much as possible, in order that the point may fall on a

line with your adversary's flank, making nearly the same angle from guard-point as semi-circle.

Semi-circle parade is useful against thrusts of low carte, seconde, and the disengage and thrust of carte over the arm. Let your body be steadily inclined upon the left side; drop your point, with the nails upward, so as to form an angle of nearly forty-five degrees with the guard-point. At the same time, stretch your arm well out, raise the hand as high as your mouth, and throw your arm inward, the distance of six inches, from the line of direction in your common guard, that your point may appear to the eye in looking to your arm. (*Vide cut.*)

THE SIMPLE PARADES OF SECONDE AND PRIME.

These two parades are not used so frequently as the preceding four. Seconde is very powerful against the simple thrusts of low carte and seconde.

To perform it from carte to tierce, the nails and wrist should be turned downward, the point be dropped, and the hand opposed outward, as in the parade of octave. The point's tract from guard is also nearly the same with the parade in octave, and the inclination of the blade should form the angle of forty-five degrees. (*Vide cut*)

Prime is performed with the nails turned downward, the hand raised higher than the mouth, and opposed inward, in the same manner as semi-circle. The arm should be drawn well in toward the body, and the wrist bent downward, that the point may fall more than in other low parade.

THE EXTENSION, LONGE, THRUSTS OF CARTE, CARTE OVER THE ARM, AND TIERCE.

Thrusts are, for the most part, executed with the longe, except thrusts of the wrist, and thrusts of the extension. They may be performed either

after disengaging the point or not. To perform the straight thrust of carte inside, your point must be directed to your adversary's breast, the arm well raised, and opposed inside, the nails upward, your body projecting forward, and an extension performed of the right arm and left leg. (*Vide cut*, which represents the position of extension.) Then push home the thrust in carte by longeing out to a distance proportionate with your height. Your left arm should be stretched down by the flank, at the distance of two or three inches, and always raised as you recover upon guard, by way of grace

and balance to your movements. Your body should incline a little forward; the head be raised upright, looking outward over the shoulders, so as to have a full view of the point. As you approach your adversary's breast, make a gradual resistance against his foil inward, by way of cover to your longe. Keep the right knee bent, and in a perpendicular posture with your heel; the left knee and ham stretched, with the foot firmly fixed to the ground.

To recover yourself with the requisite ease, lean with some degree of force on the heels of both feet; the greatest force is first upon the right, then it falls on the left; by bending the left knee at the same time, and inclining the body backward, you come to guard. The thrust of carte over the arm is performed in the same manner as carte inside, by disengaging to tierce, with this difference, that the head is raised upright on the inside, and the hand well opposed outward, in order to be well covered. The thrust of tierce differs only from carte over the arm, by reversing the wrist, the hand being well raised and opposed outward.

LOW CARTE, OCTAVE, SECONDE, AND PRIME THRUSTS.

Low carte, sometimes called semi-circle thrust, is delivered after forming the parade of semi-circle, in the same manner as simple carte thrust; only the hand and point must be fixed lower. It is an excellent thrust, if your adversary have frequent recourse to his high parades.

Octave thrust is delivered after the parade of octave, on the flank or belly; the arm being well opposed outward. If you parry your adversary's thrust by octave, your return will naturally be the thrust of octave, which may, at the same time, touch him with the extension only, without the longe.

The thrust in seconde is delivered after the parade of the tierce, or when engaged by tierce, by dropping your point under your adversary's wrist with the nails downward; longe and deliver the thrust on the flank.

Prime is the natural thrust in return, after having parried your adversary's force, when advanced considerably within his measure, and pressing vigorously upon you. It is only an extension of the arm from the opposition of the parade to your adversary's body, the nails being kept downward. The arm should be well raised, and opposed inward.

VARIATIONS AND LESSON ON ENGAGING AND DISENGAGING, ADVANCING AND RETREATING, SIMPLE PARADES, AND THRUSTS OF CARTE AND TIERCE.

Suppose you are engaged in carte with an adversary, he retreats, you advance, well covered in carte; he retreats again, you advance with a disengagement to tierce, and so forth, alternately; taking care that you are properly covered on each engagement; his retreat and your advance should be comprehended in the same moment of time; in the same manner, you may retreat while he advances. On the engagement of carte, your adversary delivers a thrust in carte; oppose it by forming your parade in carte, then return the straight thrust thereof. He again thrusts straight in the same manner; also throw it off by forming your parade in carte, deliver in return the thrust of carte over the arm, by disengaging to tierce. On the engagement in tierce, he disengages and thrusts carte inside; throw it off by your parade in carte, disengage, and thrust carte over the arm; he parries, and returns in tierce, which you parry by a parade in tierce, and longe home with a straight thrust in tierce.

LESSONS AND VARIATIONS IN SEMICIRCLE, LOW CARTE, AND OCTAVE.

On the engagement of carte, drop your point and deliver the thrust of low carte. On the same engagement, your adversary thrusts straight

home; throw it off by parade in carte, then deliver a return of the thrust in low carte. On the same engagement, disengage to tierce, and thrust carte over the arm; he opposes it with his parade, and returns a disengaged thrust in carte; which throw off with the parade of carte; then, with vivacity, drop your point, and deliver a thrust in low carte. On the engagement of tierce, your adversary, by disengaging, attempts to deliver a thrust in low carte; throw it off by performing the parade of octave (*Vide cut;*) then make a quick return of the thrust in octave.

On the engagement of carte, he thrusts low carte, parry it by octave;

instantly form your extension, fix your point well to his body, and you may almost make sure of touching him.   (*Vide cut.*)

On the engagement of carte, he disengages to tierce, and thrusts; throw it off by your parade of tierce; then reverse your nails upward, and return a thrust in octave.

On the same engagement, he thrusts low carte, oppose it by forming your parade in semi-circle; then deliver a thrust in octave, by disengaging over his arm, commonly called a counter disengagement.

LESSON AND VARIATIONS IN PRIME AND SECONDE.

On the engagement of tierce, your adversary advances within his measure, and delivers a thrust in tierce or carte over the arm; oppose his blade by the parade of prime, and return a thrust in prime.   (*Vide cut.*)

On the same engagement, he advances, disengages, and forcibly thrusts carte; drop your point, and parry it with prime; then disengage over his arm, and return a thrust in seconde.

On the engagement of carte, he disengages, and thrusts carte over the arm; parry it with simple tierce, and return a thrust in tierce; he advances, as you recover, within his measure, forcing upon your blade; form your parade in prime, and deliver a quick return of the thrust thereof. On the same engagement, he again disengages, and thrusts carte over the arm, which parry with tierce, and return the thrust thereof; he forces a thrust without advancing, parry it with prime, then disengage over the arm, and return your thrust in seconde.

THE SALUTE.

Place yourself on guard, engage your adversary's blade on the outside; by way of compliment, desire him to thrust first at you; then drop your point, by reversing the nails downward, with a circular motion; draw your right foot close behind the left, stretching both hams; raise your right arm, and, with your left hand, take off your hat gracefully; then make a circular motion with your wrist, with the nails upward, while you advance your right foot forward, forming your proper extension. Your adversary makes the same motions, keeping equal time with you; but, instead of forming the extension, he makes a full longe, as if going to thrust carte inside, in order to take his measure, presenting his point at a little distance from your body, while you remain uncovered on the extension. (*Vide cut.*)

When your adversary recovers his position, after having taken his measure, you also recover by drawing the right foot or heel close to the heel of the left; the right hand well stretched and raised, the nails upward, and the point dropped; the left hand raised in a semi-circular form, as if on guard, your hat held therein with ease and gracefulness; the head upright.

and the hams stretched. In this attitude, salute first in carte, by forming that parade; then, salute in tierce, by forming the parade of tierce; lastly, make a circular motion with the wrist, by dropping your point in tierce, at that moment putting on your hat, and throwing yourself upon the guard of carte.

When it is your turn to push, the salute only differs in one particular from the above; that is, instead of forming the extension, and uncovering the body, you make a full longe from the first position of the right foot behind the left in carte; then, recover to the second position, by placing the right foot or heel close to the heel of the left; and conclude with the other movements. All these motions should be performed with ease, grace, and without precipitation. After performing the salute, and being engaged in carte, your adversary, agreeably to the compliment offered, pushes at your breast by disengaging nimbly to tierce, and thrusting carte over the arm. Observe, that the wrist is never reversed when he disengages; oppose it by performing the parade of tierce, then drop the point, by way of accustoming yourself to make the return in seconde, which may be termed the grace on the parade of tierce. Remain on this grace till your adversary recovers to guard; then join his blade in tierce; he disengages, by thrusting carte inside; throw it off by forming the parade of carte.

The grace or ornament to be used after forming this parade, while your adversary is upon the longe, is by allowing the foil to remain flexible in your hand, with the point downward, keeping your hand in the same direction as if covered upon the parade.

Your adversary, after pushing tierce and carte alternately, commences the salute; and while he is on the extension, you take the measure by longeing in carte. Having joined blades in carte, disengage, and thrust carte over the arm. Again, he joins your blade in tierce, disengage nimbly, and thrust carte inside. (*Vide cut.*)

He opposes in carte; then let the blade and point fly loosely over the hand, having hold of your foil between the thumb and two first fingers, by which you will have a view of your adversary through the angle made thereby. This is the grace upon the longe of carte inside.

THE COUNTER, OR ROUND PARADES, IN CARTE AND TIERCE.

The counter-parade in carte, is esteemed one of the most essential, as it baffles a variety of thrusts, throws off the disengagements over the arm, &c. In order to perform it when your adversary disengages, follow his blade closely, with a small circle, entirely from the motion of the wrist, by which you join his blade always in carte. If he make a thrust with the disengagement, oppose it, by gradually covering yourself with the parade of carte, after having followed his blade round.

The counter, or round parade in tierce, is performed in a similar manner to the counter-parade of carte, only that the course of the point is reversed. For example; your adversary disengages to carte, with a view to thrust carte inside; follow his blade closely, with a small circle, made by the motion of the wrist reversed in tierce, stretching your arm, and giving his blade a smart and abrupt throw-off, as you overtake or meet it in tierce. The course of the point in forming the counter in carte is inward, from left to right; and in the counter-parade of tierce, the contrary.

COUNTER DISENGAGEMENTS IN OCTAVE AND SEMI-CIRCLE.

The counter-disengagement in octave may be performed after your adversary has thrust in seconde, and you have parried by semi-circle; as he recovers, counter-disengage, and thrust in octave. (*Vide cut.*)

To give a further exemplification of the counter-disengagement in octave : it is also performed by first making a feint, as if you intended to thrust octave ; he naturally opposes it, by forming his parade in octave ; then nimbly disengage over his arm to carte inside, and deliver either that thrust, or the thrust of low carte.

The counter-disengagement in semi-circle is performed on the engagement of carte, when your adversary accustoms himself to take the parade of semi-circle, by first making a feint, as if you meant to thrust low carte, which he attempts to parry with semi-circle, then nimbly disengaging over his arm, and delivering your thrust in octave.

THE COUNTER-DISENGAGEMENTS IN PRIME AND SECONDE.

The counter-disengagement in prime is seldom used in attacks ; but being so nearly related to prime parade and thrust, we shall here describe it. It is performed from the engagement of tierce, by forcing on your adversary's blade, if he betake himself to the parade of prime, then nimbly disengaging over his arm, and delivering your thrust in seconde.

The counter-disengagement of seconde may be more frequently used ; it is performed from the engagement of carte, by dropping your point, or making a feint, as if you intended to thrust prime ; your adversary opposes it, by performing the parade of seconde ; then disengage over his arm, and deliver your thrust by longeing in prime.

LESSONS AND VARIATIONS ON THE COUNTER-PARADES IN CARTE AND TIERCE, AND THE COUNTER DISENGAGEMENTS IN OCTAVE, &c.

On the engagement of carte, disengage and thrust carte over the arm ; your adversary opposes it, by forming the counter-parade of carte. Upon recovering, he, in return, disengages and thrusts carte over the arm ; oppose it by counter-parade in carte, &c.; disengaging and parrying alternately, always making complete longes with the thrusts, and moving well to guard, while forming the counter-parades. Make your movements very slow and exact in the beginning, and gradually quicken them. Exercise on the engagement of tierce in the same manner : first, by disengaging and thrusting carte inside, which he opposes, by forming the counter-parade in tierce ; in return, he disengages and thrusts carte inside, which parry with the counter-parade in tierce, &c. : thrusting and parrying as above, until you quicken your movements with all possible exactness.

On the engagement of tierce, if your adversary thrust octave in low carte, you may parry it with octave ; then counter-disengage, and deliver a thrust in low carte. On the same engagement, he counter-disengages, and thrusts low carte, which oppose by your counter-parade in octave, and return the thrust thereof. On the same engagement, he again counter-disengages, and thrusts low carte, which you may baffle by first forming the parade of octave, then forming the parade of semi-circle quickly after the other; and, as he recovers, counter-disengage, and thrust octave.

On the engagement of tierce, advance within measure, forcing upon your adversary's blade; he betakes himself to the simple parade of prime; counter-disengage, and thrust seconde. On the same engagement, he advances, forces, and counter disengages as above; but baffle his thrust in seconde, by the counter-parade in prime, and return the thrust thereof. On the same engagement, he counter-disengages; follow his blade by the counter-parade in prime; if he attempt to double or disengage again, stop him, by forming your simple parade of seconde.

On the engagement of carte, counter-disengage, when your adversary drops in seconde, and thrusts prime. On the same engagement, he counter-disengages, when you drop to seconde; oppose it, by your parade of seconde; then return a straight thrust in seconde. Or if, on the same engagement, he make a straight thrust in seconde, you may parry it with semi-circle, and return low carte thrust. On the same engagement, he counter-disengages, answer his movements by forming the simple parades of seconde and prime; then counter-disengage as he recovers, and deliver a thrust in seconde.

FEINTS.

Feints are used to oblige your adversary to give you openings. The simple feint, une, deux, (or one, two,) is performed by two separate disengagements, either on the engagement of carte or tierce, when your adversary throws his simple parades. If engaged in carte, disengage closely to tierce, then quickly disengage back to carte, and deliver the thrust thereof On the engagement of tierce, disengage first to carte, then disengage back to tierce, delivering the thrust of carte over the arm.

Feint seconde, carte over the arm, is performed when engaged in tierce, by dropping your point, and reversing the nails, as if you meant to thrust seconde; then quickly turn them upward, and deliver the thrust of carte over the arm. On the same engagement, you may mark feint seconde, and thrust carte inside, if there be an opening.

Feints une, deux, trois, (or one, two, three,) are performed by three separate disengagements, either from the engagement of carte or tierce. On the engagement of carte, mark feint, one, two, as above; if your adversary form his simple parade of carte, nimbly mark your third disengagement, by thrusting carte over the arm. On the engagement of tierce, disengage three times, and deliver your thrust in carte inside.

CUT OVER THE POINT.

This is performed when you perceive your adversary hold his hand low, and his point is raised upon guard. To perform it from carte to tierce, raise your point quickly, with the upward motion of your wrist, fairly over your adversary's point, without moving your arm from the line of direction, at the same time forming your extension, and deliver your thrust of carte over the arm.

In the same manner you may execute cuts over the point, from the engagement of tierce, when your adversary holds his point high.

THRUST OF THE WRIST.

This is performed when you perceive your adversary slow in making a return, after you have longed with a thrust; as on the engagement of carte, suppose you thrust carte over the arm, which your adversary naturally parries with simple tierce, lean with some degree of force upon his blade, and, as you recover to guard, deliver him a thrust with the wrist in seconde.

RETURN ON THE EXTENSION.

This is performed after your adversary makes a full longe with a thrust, which you may parry so powerfully, as to throw his arm out of the line of direction; then, with all possible quickness, extend your arm, and deliver him a straight thrust in return, before he has time to recover. If the extension of the arm be not within reach, from your complete extension of the leg and arm.

APPELS, BEATS ON THE BLADE, AND GLIZADES.

Appels, beats, and glizades, tend to plant you firm upon your guard, to embarrass your adversary, and cause him to give you openings; they may be performed previously to simple thrust, feints, or counter-disengagements, &c. An appel, or beat with the foot is performed either on the engagement of carte or tierce, by suddenly raising and letting fall the right foot, with a beat on the same spot; taking care to balance the body, and keep a good position on guard.

The beat on the blade, is abruptly touching your adversary's blade, so as to startle him, and get openings to thrust. If he resist the beat, instantaneously disengage, and thrust home. If he use a simple parade, mark feint one, two; or, if he use a counter-parade, counter-disengage, or double.

Glizades are slightly gliding your blade along your adversary's, at the same time forming the extension, of the arm, or the complete extension, managing and restraining your body, so as to be aware of his thrust, and to make sure of your own. If you be engaged in carte, out of measure, a quick advance, with a glizade, must infallibly give you some openings, either to mark feints or otherwise.

THE TIME-THRUST.

This thrust is performed when your adversary is dilatory. On attempting to deliver this thrust, cover yourself well, by forming a gradual and strong opposition to your adversary's blade; you can be in no danger of exposing yourself to an interchanged thrust, that is, a thrust at the same moment.

LESSONS AND VARIATIONS TO FEINTS, APPELS, &c.

On the engagement of carte, mark feint one, two, and thrust carte inside. On the engagement of tierce, feint one, two, and thrust carte over the arm. On the engagement of carte, mark a feint over the arm, and thrust low carte. On the same engagement, mark feint over the arm, reverse the wrist, and thrust seconde.

On the engagement of tierce, mark feint seconde, reverse the wrist, and thrust carte over the arm. On the same engagement, mark feint seconde, and thrust carte inside. On the engagement of carte, in attempting the feints one, two, if he baffle it by his counter-parade in carte, counter-disengage, and deliver the thrust of carte over the arm.

On the engagement of carte, suppose your adversary hold his guard low, and his point high, make a cut over the point, forming your extension, and thrust carte over the arm. On the engagement of carte, cut over the point; if he use a simple parade, disengage, and thrust carte inside. On the engagement of tierce, if your adversary hold his hand low, and point high, make a cut over the point, and thrust carte inside. On the same engagement, cut over the point twice, and deliver the thrust of carte over the arm. On the same engagement, cut over the point twice, then disengage, and thrust carte inside. On the same engagement, cut over the point, then mark feints one, two, and thrust carte inside.

On the engagement of carte, disengage to tierce, and thrust carte over the arm; if your adversary form his simple parade in tierce, and be slow in making a return, deliver him a thrust with the wrist in seconde, as you recover. On the engagement of tierce, disengage and thrust carte inside, or low carte; if he parry it with octave, disengage over his arm as you recover, and deliver him a thrust in low carte. On the engagement of carte, disengage and thrust seconde; if he parry it with seconde, counter disengage as you recover, and thrust prime. On the engagement of tierce, force upon his blade, disengage and thrust low carte: he parries it with prime, and if slow in making a return, deliver the thrust in seconde with the wrist, as you recover.

On the engagement of carte, give him some openings; if he mark the feints one, two, and thrust, form your counter parade in carte; then deliver him a quick return with the wrist in low carte, by forming the complete extension. On the engagement of tierce, in like manner, give him some openings: if he mark feints one, two, and thrust, form your counter parade in tierce; and, on the extension, deliver him a thrust in seconde. On the engagement of carte, if he execute low feints and thrusts, use the circle parade, and return a straight thrust on the extension, before he recovers.

On the engagement of carte, make an appel, or beat with the right foot, at the same time beating abruptly on your adversary's blade, which will give you an opening to thrust carte straight home. On the same engagement, make an appel, beat his blade, then disengage, and thrust carte over the arm. On the engagement of tierce, make an appel, beat his blade, and thrust tierce or carte over the arm. On the same engagement, make an appel, beat his blade, then disengage, and deliver a thrust in carte inside. On the engagement of tierce, make your appel, disengage to carte, by beating his blade, and thrust carte inside.

On the engagement of tierce, perform a glizade along his blade, with the extension; if he do not cover himself, deliver a straight thrust in carte over the arm. On the engagement of carte, make a glizade, drop your point, and deliver a thrust in low carte. On the engagement of tierce, perform a glizade, drop your point under his wrist, and deliver a thrust in octave.

On the engagement of tierce, he disengages to carte, then disengage contrarily, and thrust home carte over the arm. On the engagement of carte, when you find that your adversary holds his hand too low upon guard, and deviates from the guard rules, seize the opening, by pushing carte straight home. On the engagement of tierce, having the like opportunity, deliver the thrust of carte over the arm, straight home.

On the engagement of carte, your adversary disengages to tierce; that instant disengage contrarily, (that is, to carte,) and push home. (*Vide cut.*)

All these lessons should be performed repeatedly, and the pupil should often exercise with another who has had equal practice, executing all thrusts, feints, counter-disengagements, &c. while the other remains upon guard, making use of the necessary parades, &c.; he should then, in turn, perform the practical movements, in order that both may make mutual progress in the art.

THE SALUTE PREVIOUS TO ASSAULTS.

On the engagement of tierce, make two quick appels, or beats, with the right foot; bring it close behind the left, near the shoe-tie, raising and stretching your right arm with the nails upward, and the point of your foil dropped; at the same time, take off your hat gracefully, and hold it in your left hand, stretched down near the flank; then, with a circular motion of the wrist, as if forming the counter in tierce, throw your left foot backwards, to the distance of your common guard, and raising your left hand, make two other appels; bring your left foot forward to the former position, that is, before the right, near the shoe-tie; at the same time, stretching your arm, with the nails upward as before, and in that position, form gracefully the parades of carte and tierce; make a circular motion with the wrist, and advance your right foot, with vivacity, to your original guard, at the same time covering your head. All the movements in this salute should be performed in a more lively manner than those described in the salute previously to thrusting carte and tierce: observe, also, that these movements should keep exactly the same time with those of your adversary.

DISARMING.

After parrying your adversary's thrust by simple carte, or the counter in carte, without quitting his blade, lean abruptly thereon, and binding it with yours, reverse your wrist, with the nails downward, as if in seconde, and with the motion thereof, give his blade an abrupt twirl. (*Vide cut.*)

If this do not disarm him, it will throw his hand and blade out of the line of direction, so that you may effectually fix your point, and deliver him a thrust in seconde.

Also, after parrying by simple tierce, cross his blade before he recovers; make a strong and abrupt circular movement with your wrist in seconde without quitting his blade, and it will either disarm, or give you an opening to deliver him a thrust.

PRACTICAL OBSERVATIONS.

Assume a bold air and steady position; fix your eyes firmly on those of your adversary, so that he may not penetrate into your designs; and keep your proper distance and measure. It is a most essential point in assaults, exactly to know these: for this purpose, observe the height of your adversary, the length of his foil, &c., and make the necessary allowances accordingly. If he make frequent practice of disengaging, beating your blade, and otherwise embarrassing you, with a view to get openings, you may seize the occasion to deliver a time-thrust, taking care to cover yourself well, by forming a good opposition against his blade. When on the engagement of carte, by way of snare, hold your point higher than usual; if he attempt to make a cut over the point, that instant disengage contrarily, and thrust carte inside; or you may, in preference to this, deliver a straight thrust in carte over the arm. (*Vide cut.*)

Be not too eager in making your thrusts in return; as, by an over eagerness, learners contract a habit of returning their thrust by crooking the arm which is quite erroneous. Form your parades justly, and accustom yourself, at first, to make straight returns without disengaging. If you intend to return a thrust by disengaging, you should perform it the moment your adversary is recovering; it must proceed from the motion of the wrist, and not by crooking the arm. The distance of your guard should be moderate, two feet is the distance for men: by a wide guard, you keep your adversary at too great a distance, and have not that necessary command of throwing your body back far enough, when he advances and makes a full longe; neither can you retreat, or make returns with the necessary quickness; the lower part of the body is also more exposed than it would be on a proper medium guard.

Never extend yourself too far on the longe, as it impedes your recovering to guard with the necessary quickness. Always endeavour to recover quickly, and with as much ease as possible, fixing your point to your adversary's body, and forming the most natural parade, in case he should make a quick return. If engaged with an adversary of a shorter stature, attack him on the engagement of tierce, as being more advantageous for a number of feints and thrusts than the engagement of carte, particularly for feint seconde over the arm, &c.

If your adversary advance within his measure, and force in a straight thrust, carte over the arm, or in tierce, then raise and bend your arm, forming the parade of prime, and quickly return a straight thrust in prime, before he recovers; or, if you have not opening sufficient, disengage over his arm, and deliver a thrust in seconde.

When you first enter upon the assault, you may engage your adversary's blade out of measure in carte, as being easier than the other engagements for executing your different movements. (*Vide cut.*)

When you engage your adversary's blade, act on the defensive for some time, in order to discover what feints or thrusts he prefers. Vary your parades as much as possible so that he may not, in turn, ascertain your own favorites; for, if a good fencer be found to use one parade in preference to another, he may be deceived with much less difficulty than might be imagined, and, eventually, be touched, by a person far less skilful than himself. A learner, therefore, should practice all the parades, and change them continually, or, at least, as often as opportunities occur. He should endeavour to go from the high to the low parades, and from the latter to the former, with the utmost possible agility, until, by practice, he is enabled to parry almost every thrust.

If you engage the blade in carte, cover your inside a little, and if in tierce, cover your outside, to present straight thrusts on those engagements. When attacking, it is well to disengage dexterously, outside and inside, forming your extension as if you intended to thrust; if this plan do not afford you some openings, it will, at least, in all probability, be the means of discovering your adversary's choice parades. If he use simple parades only, you may easily deceive him by making feints one, two, or one, two, three. If, on the contrary, he be a skilful fencer, and use various counter-parades, you must endeavour to embarrass him, by appels, beats on the blade, extensions, glizades, counter-disengagements, &c.

INDEX.

OTHER APPLEWOOD TITLES
YOU WILL ENJOY

❧

The Girl's Own Book
LYDIA MARIA CHILD

Published in 1833, this book of entertainments for young
girls is filled with marvelous activities to help young girls
build character and have fun.

$4^{1}/_{2}$ x $5^{1}/_{2}$, 288 pp., $12.95

❧

The Education of a Daughter
ARCHBISHOP FENELON

Written in 1687, and first published in America in 1847, this
book is filled with sound wisdom on the ample subject of
rearing both daughters and sons. The Archbishop's writing is
sprinkled with proverbs, hints, and maxims, and his insights
into the psychology of a young mind as well as his outline
for the principles of education are invaluable.

5 x $7^{1}/_{4}$, 160 pp., $9.95

❧

The Mother's Book
LYDIA MARIA CHILD

Originally published in 1831, these instructions for mothers
on raising children are still applicable to today's parents.

5 x $8^{1}/_{4}$, 169 pp., $9.95

APPLEWOOD BOOKS, P.O. Box 365, Bedford, MA 01730